9/01

Natalia Ginzburg

Now in her seventies, Natalia Ginzburg is still writing and shows no sign of any decline in her ability to create perceptive and stimulating novels and plays about human relationships. Responsive and sympathetic to the problems of both sexes, Ginzburg is necessarily more immediately receptive to the difficulties encountered by women in their attempts to survive and find fulfilment in what is still, especially in Italy, very much a man's world, and her work provides revealing insights into the struggles which are an inevitable part of this process. At the same time she is aware that women can sometimes contribute significantly to their own misfortune through naivety or stupidity and can thus be their own worst enemies in a social context which is already to their disadvantage. The author discusses these various elements of Natalia Ginzburg's writing and examines the development of her humorously pessimistic view of the human condition from the early short stories, through the novels, plays and essays of her middle years, to her most recent work focusing on the older generation.

Alan Bullock is Senior Lecturer in Italian, University of Leeds.

Berg Women's Series

Natalia Ginzburg

Human Relationships in a Changing World

Alan Bullock

BERG *New York/Oxford*
Distributed exclusively in the USA and Canada by
St Martin's Press, New York

First published in 1991 by
Berg Publishers Limited
Editorial Offices:
150 Cowley Road, Oxford OX4 1JJ, UK
165 Taber Avenue, Providence, RI 02906, USA

British Library Cataloguing in Publication Data
Bullock, Alan, *1938–*
  Natalia Ginzburg: human relationships in a changing world.
  – (Berg's women series)
  I. Title
  853.912
  ISBN 0–85496–178–X

Library of Congress Cataloging-in-Publication Data
Bullock, Alan. 1938–
  Natalia Ginzburg: human relationships in a changing world / Alan
  Bullock.
     p. cm. — (Berg women's series)
  Includes bibliographical references and index.
  ISBN 0–85496–178–X
  1. Ginzburg, Natalia—Criticism and interpretation. 2. Women in
literature. 3. Alienation (Social psychology) in literature.
4. Sex role in literature. I. Title. II. Series.
PQ4817.I5Z57 1990
853'.912—dc20   90–39079
                                                              CIP

Printed in Great Britain by
Billing & Sons Ltd, Worcester

Contents

Acknowledgements

I wish to extend my thanks to the following publishers for their kind permission to quote from their translations of certain of Natalia Ginzburg's works: to Carcanet for extracts from *The Little Virtues* (Manchester, 1985, trans. Dick Davis) and *All Our Yesterdays* (Manchester, 1985, trans. Angus Davidson); to Michael Joseph for extracts from *Never Must You Ask Me* (London, 1973, trans. Isabel Quigley); and to Peter Owen for extracts from *Dear Michael* (London, 1975, trans. Sheila Cudahy). The photograph of Natalia Ginzburg is by Jerry Bauer.

I have wherever possible quoted from published translations of Ginzburg's work, only occasionally departing from these texts and indicating my reasons in a footnote; where no translation exists I have undertaken my own, while leaving the title of the work in the original Italian, thereby indicating to the reader that no English version is available. Quotations from critical works in Italian or French are likewise given in my own translation, with the titles of books or articles in the original language. Works by Ginzburg are listed in chronological order in the Bibliography along with English titles where appropriate, together with an alphabetical list of critical writings under their respective authors.

I am grateful to my colleague Judy Rawson, Senior Lecturer and Head of the Department of Italian in the University of Warwick, for suggesting this book, to Dr Marion Berghahn for commissioning it, and to my wife, Gabriella Palange, to whom it is dedicated, for her assistance and patience during its production.

Introduction

Aptly described by Enzo Siciliano as 'a writer one either loves or hates'[1] Natalia Ginzburg has for many years been a figure whose work has provoked critical debate among the Italian establishment, while her books have likewise been both eagerly sought out and dismissively rejected by the general public. Born in 1916 in Palermo, where her father Giuseppe Levi was Professor of Anatomy at the University, her move to the other end of the country three years later following Levi's appointment to a Chair in Turin is typical of the radical changes that have characterised her existence in a period and a context where the social and political pressures determining how Europeans should live their lives have been especially rigorous. The youngest of five children, and thus doubly vulnerable through her sex and her age, Natalia was kept at home until the age of eleven as a precaution against contagious diseases, a procedure guaranteed to encourage morbid introspection, especially when exercised by a father who could be termed a benevolent despot, in many ways a typical Victorian paterfamilias, and a timorous submissive mother whose undoubted affection could not compensate for her daughter's increasingly strong feelings of alienation, further compounded by the fact that as the product of a mixed marriage and brought up as neither Catholic nor Jewish she instinctively felt confused and deprived. A sensitive child, unable to find fulfilment in this cloistered atmosphere, Natalia inevitably sought relief in fantasy, soon transferring her flights of fancy from her imagination to the pages of an exercise book and in due course graduating from these childish scribblings to a more adult examination of the world around her, both inside and outside the family circle, in writings which reveal an increasingly acute perception of the complex and contradictory nature of human behaviour. Highly sensitive to the rhythms of family life, and deeply conscious of the difficulties facing women in what is even now an essentially masculine society, Ginzburg exposes and analyses problems inherent in emotional relationships which transcend their immediate context and become instantly and universally recognisable, exposing the ambiguous feelings which motivate our actions and which frequently ensure that individuals are at greatest risk, in their instinctive search for happiness, from those

1

closest to them and most anxious they should achieve it. The irony implicit in this paradox is further manifest in Ginzburg's perception that the concept of male superiority, especially prevalent in Latin society, is in reality a myth, dependent for its survival on women's willingness to accept traditionally subordinate roles, while also appreciating that in these circumstances men are ultimately just as vulnerable as the so-called weaker sex and thus equally deserving of sympathy, a disinterested view of sexual politics that has inevitably alienated both male chauvinists and militant feminists.

Mussolini's rise to power and his establishment as Fascist dictator in 1922 inevitably sharpened the political sensibility of the Levi family, all essentially socialist in spirit and now prepared to engage in subversive activity such as harbouring a left-wing activist on the run or distributing anti-government propaganda, something which led to her father's temporary arrest in 1934. Though not directly involved herself in such activities Natalia, now a young adult, could not be unaware of the hostility surrounding her family and friends in a climate which thus strengthened the bonds between them and doubtless played its part in fostering her relationship with Leone Ginzburg, a Jewish Marxist who had been instrumental in getting her first short story published and whom she married in 1938, the same year that Mussolini's government proclaimed a series of Racial Laws actively discriminating against Jews and thereby effectively declaring Natalia and her husband second-class citizens.[2] When two years later Italy declared war on Great Britain and France all known left-wing activists were immediately arrested and deported to isolated areas of the country where they could be kept under close surveillance, and in Ginzburg's case this meant removal to Pizzoli, a primitive village in the depressed south where Natalia and their two children soon joined him. This sudden shift from what was still a relatively comfortable middle-class urban environment to a rudimentary rural community lacking all but the basic necessities of life, inevitably traumatic in personal terms, eventually proved beneficial on the artistic level, providing unexpected stimulus for a new burst of creative writing in which a wider experience of life and a greater maturity of spirit are clearly apparent.

If this first disturbing upheaval was thus ultimately something positive far worse was to follow shortly after Natalia's new flowering of original talent in a sudden and unexpected change in the political climate, raising hopes and enthusiasms which all too soon proved illusory. On 25 July 1943 Mussolini was deposed and the Fascist regime collapsed, thus liberating political exiles in a climate of freedom destined to prove short-lived. Less than two months later, on 8 September, the Italian government proclaimed an armistice with the Allied powers and withdrew from the war, creating a vacuum which the nation's former ally, Germany, filled by ruthlessly occupying the country and taking over all administrative power. Leone Ginzburg, who by this time had moved to Rome and recommenced political activity, went into hiding, and Natalia, who had remained in Pizzoli following the birth of their third child, decided to leave the village, now swarming with German troops, in order to avoid being herself identified, and rejoin him in the capital. Thanks to a declaration from some villagers that she was a relative from Naples who had lost her identification papers in an air-raid she was taken on board a German military lorry leaving Pizzoli for Rome, and, after a hazardous journey, which, ironically, she thus undertook under the wing of her worst enemies, reached her destination. But her reunion with her husband was only momentary; three weeks after her arrival Leone, now the editor of an underground newspaper, was arrested and tortured, eventually dying in a prison hospital while friends were making arrangements for him to escape. His death left Natalia and their three children in truly appalling circumstances, and she was fortunate in having friends able to take the family into hiding, moving them from one safe house to another under assumed non-Jewish names and eventually succeeding in sending them north to Florence, where Natalia's mother was living and where there was less danger of discovery. She returned to the capital after its liberation by Allied troops in June 1944, obtaining work with the publishing house of Einaudi, who had brought out her first full-length novel two years previously and with whom she therefore had useful contacts, and the following year succeeded in moving to their head office in Turin; here the Levis re-established themselves following the return of Natalia's father from Belgium where he had gone to escape anti-Semitic persecution, only to find himself further threatened when that country was also occupied by the Germans in 1940.

As normality gradually reasserted itself Ginzburg, now a free woman and no longer destitute, could once more contemplate something as exotic as creative writing, and her next novel, a grim study of an unhappy marriage very different from her own, clearly represents the anguish and frustration she had experienced during the war. Though obviously less distressing than in those dark years her life since 1945 has not been without incident, and it is plain she has continued to attract more than her fair share of stress and suffering. Her marriage to the distinguished academic Gabriele Baldini five years later, though fruitful on both the emotional and the artistic plane, was abruptly terminated in 1969 when her husband contracted hepatitis following a blood transfusion in hospital and died within hours of receiving contaminated plasma; in the interim she had twice more been obliged to uproot herself and settle in a new and initially alien environment: in 1952 in Rome, following Baldini's appointment to the Chair of English at the University, and, seven years later, in London, where the couple remained until 1961 during his term of office as Director of the Italian Cultural Institute. In the artistic sphere she has frequently suffered from writer's block and fears of creative sterility, while the political turmoils of 1968 throughout Europe (at a time when she was already in her fifties) have encouraged her to develop and indeed to indulge a latent pessimism always present in her writing and which has increased substantially as she has grown older. Her election to the Italian Parliament as an independent left-winger in 1983 has provided an additional outlet for her hopes and fears in a context where her pronouncements are perhaps more likely to receive attention than in the relatively limited world inhabited by lovers of literature, and in this context she seems indefatigable in her desire to draw attention to the abuses and the failings of Italian social life, whose more disturbing aspects she has also examined in a variety of short articles commissioned by various newspapers. Her last novel appeared in 1984 and rumour has it that she is now working on another; certainly she has at no time announced her intention to give up writing.

Though not exactly a household name in Italy Natalia Ginzburg is thus more widely known and acknowledged than one might expect of an elderly author whose main claim to fame remains her contribution to creative writing in the twentieth century. As someone who has lived through one of the most violent and destructive periods of European history, during which traditional norms governing emotional relationships of all kinds have altered beyond recognition, she has been able to reflect these changes in her work while at the same time creating characters and situations rooted in a basic humanity which is timeless and universal. Deeply aware both through her own experience and through observation that life's problems are a source of much tension and suffering Ginzburg also possesses an equally sharp consciousness, possibly through her Jewish heritage, that life also has a deeply humorous aspect in that much human activity is quite simply absurd, comic and tragic

4

elements being frequently intermingled and indeed inseparable; receptive readers of Ginzburg's work are invariably both touched and at the same time amused by the plight of her characters. Such a complex package has proved too disturbing for some professional critics, who, heedless of Pirandello's important distinction between the awareness of incongruity and its understanding,[3] have been unable to accept that something as traditionally frivolous as humour can have a place in creative writing, while being likewise uneasy at Ginzburg's attack on traditional values; in addition she has ensured a negative response from those unwilling to concede that it is possible to write both intelligently and simply in a style totally removed from the ornate traditions of Italian literary composition, a style reminiscent of English and American authors, with whom she has sometimes been pejoratively compared, and which conversely makes her especially attractive to those reluctant to tackle other contemporary writers who make more immediate demands on their audience.

In writing this book I have throughout tried to bear in mind that many readers will not have access to the original Italian, while those who are fluent in the language may none the less have difficulty in tracing the many articles Ginzburg has published in newspapers and which have not been reprinted in any of the three anthologies published between 1962 and 1974. I have thus drawn on such material only when it seems especially appropriate in connection with points relating to the author's fiction, most of which is available in translation, and have likewise quoted from the published anthologies only in so far as their themes and treatment throw light on those at issue in her creative work. There is thus no discussion of Ginzburg's political commitments or her resignation from post-war membership of the Italian Communist Party and subsequent election to parliament, as these have little direct relevance to her fictional writing;[4] in the same way it contains no significant treatment of Jewish themes, despite the fact that this connection has played a major part in her life, from her first experiences as the child of a mixed marriage, through the persecution and death of her first husband and the threat to her own survival during the German occupation, to her recent criticism of the state of Israel and support for the Palestinian refugees,[5] and this area of experience is thus examined solely in relation to *Family Sayings*, an autobiographical evocation of the author's life from early childhood to the time of her second marriage. Ginzburg's activities as a translator and her occasional ventures into literary criticism (such as her essay on

Proust and her introductions to creative work by other authors) are
clearly of secondary importance to her fiction, and thus outside the
scope of this volume.

Alan Bullock
Leeds
October, 1989

Notes

1. E. Siciliano, 'Natalia Ginzburg: il caso, la poesia', *Paragone*, XXII,
    no. 252 (1971), p. 124.
2. Under these new laws it became illegal for Jews to marry non-Jews, to
    hire non-Jewish domestic servants, to serve in the armed forces, to teach
    in universities or non-Jewish schools, to publish books, to be listed in
    the telephone directory, or to own a radio; other restrictions are too
    numerous to be listed here, but for a comprehensive listing see *Il Ponte*,
    XXXIV, nos 11–12 (1978), pp. 1510–32, which also gives the *Ma-
    nifesto della Razza* dated 26 July XVI (= 1938), pp. 1507–9, reproduced
    from *La difesa della razza*, 1, no. 1 (5 Aug. 1938), p. 2. Leone Ginzburg,
    at one time Professor of Russian at the University of Turin, had already
    been dismissed some years earlier for refusing to swear an oath of
    allegiance to the Fascist Party.
3. See Felicity Firth's Introduction to L. Pirandello, *Three Plays* (Man-
    chester University Press, Manchester, 1969), pp. xxiv–xxv, where she
    reproduces the well-known passage from Pirandello's essay *L'umorismo*
    in which he describes his reactions on seeing an elderly lady plastered
    with make-up and dressed in a youthful style quite inappropriate to her
    age; initial laughter deriving from his *awareness* of the incongruity of
    such a spectacle is succeeded by his realisation that the lady's grotesque
    appearance represents a pathetic attempt on her part to retain the
    affections of a much younger husband, an *understanding* which immedi-
    ately puts an end to superficial amusement while maintaining the
    humorous nature of the experience. Firth's comment on p. xxv that
    'The humorist as understood by Pirandello must be compassionate;
    humour is almost pity' applies equally well to Ginzburg.
4. There is an obvious parallel with the character of Raffaella in *Voices in
    the Evening*, whose resignation from the Party after 1945 mirrors Ginz-
    burg's realisation that the complexity of post-war politics no longer
    made it the automatic refuge for left-wing survivors of the Fascist
    regime; but this is no more than a passing reference in the novel.
5. The persecution of Jews figures in *All Our Yesterdays* as part and parcel of
    the horrors of war without emerging from the general background of
    progressive devastation, and is similarly employed as a means to an end

rather than an end in itself in the character of Franz in this novel; the few references elsewhere are minimal and have no bearing on plot or characterisation. Ginzburg's 1972 essay *Gli ebrei* (reprinted in *Vita immaginaria*, pp. 174–81), in which she discusses her conflicting feelings in relation to Israel and Jewishness, has no echo in her fictional writing.

1 Writing as a Vocation: Life and Work

> Writing is the only thing that gives me pleasure. Apart from my emotional ties I have nothing else to fall back on.[1]

> When I write I feel I'm doing the only thing in life which gives me great satisfaction.[2]

Now in her seventies Natalia Ginzburg has been writing since she was a child and shows no sign of stopping, her last novel having appeared in 1984 and her first efforts at composition going back to her infancy.[3] Her aim in writing is twofold: her essays, on a wide variety of subjects, focus on specific themes and are precise, sometimes impassioned, expressions of her ideas and principles; her novels, short stories, and plays are, in contrast, on one level, fictional creations with no particular purpose, no basic plan, and produced for reasons which their author is unable to identify,[4] all of which suggests an essential shallowness that has led some critics to define her work as trivial.[5] Ginzburg has at times appeared to confirm this view by emphasising her lack of formal education and her acceptance of artistic mediocrity in others;[6] however, there is also a further dimension to her fiction, as is apparent in other statements which suggest the need for a more accurate if less immediately obvious judgement of her aims and achievements: thus in an interview with Dacia Maraini in 1973 we find her defining literature as 'a way of concerning oneself with the things of this world through the written word',[7] while elsewhere she states that one of her main aims in writing is to achieve clarity of expression[8] and ensure protection against 'immobility', which she defines as 'ceasing to search for signs of life in the world around us'.[9]

The apparent contradiction between these two attitudes becomes easier to appreciate on discovering that, despite being prolific, Ginzburg has frequently found creative composition a hard and thankless task. The instinctive facility which led her to compose several novels during childhood was gradually replaced in adolescence by an increasing lack of confidence till she eventually found it impossible to go beyond the opening paragraphs of the many short stories which sprang from her pen only to dry up almost immediately. Insecurity concerning one's talents is, of course, an inherent part of growing up and thus perhaps an inevitable part of any budding author's development; in Ginzburg's case, however, it was accentuated by her obsessive need to compare everything she wrote with the work of Anton Chekhov and other authors of distinction whose work no-one in their teens could be expected to emulate, especially since, as she herself states with no little wit: 'I sucked at these books like a child sucking at the breast in my desire to absorb and penetrate the secrets of their prose style.'[10]

Ginzburg's first conscious awareness of her talents dates from 1926, when at ten years old she decided her vocation was to be a writer in preference to three other possibilities until then kept under review: painting, conquering new lands on horseback, and engineering.[11] Her sensitivity to things artistic is evident from the fact that the first medium to attract her and encourage her to put pen to paper was the most rarified form of literary expression – poetry, and that two years after having begun to compose verse of her own, which she later described as 'awkward . . . but quite amusing'[12] and which we may deduce was reasonably buoyant in tone and content, she produced a five-line poem drenched in gloom and inspired by the realisation that she no longer loved her holiday playmate Lucio and could not look forward to marrying him.[13] Her discovery of the muse of melancholy crystallised Ginzburg's aspirations to creative writing, till then unstructured,[14] opening up an area of human experience she was to make very much her own and which in later years was to dominate all other feelings, recreating the intensity of her childhood awareness in a broader and more mature form. Fired by this new sensation Ginzburg began to write with increasing freedom, eventually producing a poem a day, any slackening of inspiration being immediately cured by contact with the printed page; 'I realized', she states in *My Vocation*, 'that if I didn't want to write it was enough for me to read some poems by Pascoli or Gozzano or Corazzini and then I immediately wanted to.'[15] This technique had its limitations, as work composed in these circumstances was inevitably second-rate imitation of her masters, though it was some time before she became aware of the fact, and an initial euphoria during which Ginzburg was unable to see any difference between her own production and the published work of recognised authors gradually gave way to a disturbing awareness that 'not one of my poems was really and truly my own work, and that they were

9

all copied from someone else's writing',[16] something which filled their author with acute anguish, acquainting her for the first time with the unpleasantness of writer's block, and this at a period when her energies were supposed to be devoted to her school work.

Convinced in her naive enthusiasm that writing was what mattered most, and should thus take precedence over all other commitments, Ginzburg anticipated the freedom she would enjoy only later in life by dedicating most of her time to composing verse, writing it up in fair copy in an exercise book, drawing a pretty picture for the cover, and compiling her own index, her school books untouched and her homework ignored. Plans to recapture some of this lost time by getting up at five to study were never realised, and her backlog of work increased daily, while the guilt she experienced as a result, amply compensated initially by the thought that creative writing justified total failure elsewhere, became unbearable when doubts concerning the quality of her work, increasingly persistent, turned her days into long frustrating hours of inactivity during which she searched in vain for appropriate rhymes, stimulating subjects: in a word, something to say. This early contact with one of the most frightening and most common artistic experiences is, with the benefit of hindsight, a clear confirmation of her calling, further corroborated by the fact that even in moments of acute depression 'It never entered my head that I had mistaken my vocation – I wanted to write as much as ever, it was just that I could not understand why my days had suddenly become so barren and empty of words.'[17]

Ginzburg's attempts to penetrate the mysteries of prose composition seem to have developed along the same lines, though ultimately leading to a different and more satisfactory conclusion, doubtless because even while producing her poems with ease and simplicity her overall aim had been to become a writer of novels. Her ideal novel she imagined as 'an enormous book which would contain the whole of my life day by day, together with the lives of the people around me',[18] an impossible task which inevitably remained in the realms of wishful thinking, though it is clear in the light of this statement that *Family Sayings*, published when Ginzburg was in her late forties, represents a more mature version of this childhood dream.[19] Meanwhile she wrote adventure stories peopled by heroes and villains and involving kidnapped children, romantic lovers, and all the paraphernalia of youthful imagination, here too becoming gradually aware that second-hand inspiration cannot provide total satisfaction, especially when themes and characters from nineteenth-century French authors were combined with dramatic confrontations of the kind found in contemporary crime fiction. If all this is clearly undistinguished, and indeed typical of many an errant child too undisciplined and too lazy to let work take precedence over play, two things set Ginzburg apart from this cliché: the intensity of her creative drive and her fierce desire to produce work of high quality, her block being the result of an increasing difficulty in ensuring that both these incentives remained complementary.

Ginzburg's eventual inability to recapture and isolate the creative spark coincided with the inevitable result of long neglect of her studies: three failures in her examinations at seventeen, thus plunging her into a crisis which marks the first turning-point in her artistic career. Feelings of intense despair accompanied by tears and lamentations somehow created a context in which she unwittingly acquired a new maturity of spirit that brought forth what she later called her 'first real story',[20] written at a single sitting on a summer evening, and, when finished, releasing within her a degree of happiness never before experienced, together with a spiritual uplift making her aware that now 'I could write millions of stories'.[21] Possessed by a boundless energy, while also terrified of being unable to maintain her inspiration to the point where she could finish, Ginzburg realised she had written something that could fairly be described as '"adult"'[22] in form and content, a perfect creation with every part fitting exactly into the general whole; particularly striking, both as a general indication of her new maturity and as a pointer to one of her most characteristic attitudes as an author, is her awareness that the protagonists of this tale are 'neither good nor evil, but funny and a little sad and it seemed to me that I had discovered how people in books should be – funny and at the same time sad'.[23]

Having thus discovered her vocation, or, more accurately, realised how to pursue it more effectively, Ginzburg entered a new phase of intense activity, writing regularly but more slowly than in her unstructured childhood and producing a short story every one or two months. She soon discovered that despite now feeling capable of adult work her ability to write creatively was still limited, literary composition being an activity requiring considerable effort and concentration alongside emotional participation and involvement. When this happens spontaneously the writer becomes totally immersed in his or her work, forgetting all other considerations, whether sad or happy, and emerging drained from the experience; if on the other hand concentration is imposed by an effort of will rather than by a willing surrender of one's faculties the result is inferior writing, dictated solely by the intellect: 'One must write and think with one's heart and one's whole body, not with one's head and one's mind'.[24] Ginzburg's adherence to this dictum throughout her work means that she has rarely produced writing which does not reflect a strong personal bias of some kind,[25] and if this ensures the presence of a genuine spirit of enquiry, a high degree of engagement with her subject, and an openness leaving no room for ambiguity in the expression of her feelings and ideas, it also accounts at least in part for what some see as an excessive preoccupation with her own interests as opposed to more universal themes potentially of greater relevance to her readers and the world they live in. The link between emotional participation and personal interest was not clearly established in her mind until several years later, after the publication of her first short novel *The Road to the City*, at which point she realised that 'It was essential I avoid dealing with anything outside my experience or leaving me indifferent, and that my characters should always be based on real people with whom I had close relationships';[26] her writing is thus, as has been succinctly stated by Rita Signorelli Pappas, 'subtly intertwined with the events of her personal life', and can be seen overall as 'a deepening self-study'.[27] If it is doubtless exaggerated to claim, as Domenico Porzio does, that 'every single subject she deals with is presented as something personal, offered wholeheartedly as an exclusive individual experience in her emotional or intellectual life'[28] it is also undeniable that, as she herself has stated, 'I cannot in any way invent things out of thin air. Even when I tell a story I have made up I feel the need to include in it a real character, someone who really exists.' Clearly the key concept in this statement is *invention*, which Ginzburg sees as the fictional representation of an aspect of reality, the ideal combination being one in which these two elements exist in a kind of equilibrium where 'When I invent something I end up by coming face to face with reality.'[29]

Whether or not one accepts that she achieves this will depend on one's reactions to Ginzburg's view of reality, which elsewhere she equates with truth. In an article published in 1975 she deals directly with critics' accusations of self-centredness, admitting that things which touch her directly may be of limited interest to others but also stressing her right to an individual style, which she defines as 'an attempt to confront truth as closely as possible, bearing in mind that truth is both single in kind and multi-faceted, limitless in its manifestations and its appearance';[30] those who seek it are thus unconcerned whether it is to be found in public or in private places, since what matters is not the dimension it inhabits but the writer's ability to grasp and expose it. In any case who is to decide, and with what authority, where private matters end and public ones begin, given that all questions of public importance contain within them an area of private experience in which they have their origin?[31] Those who seek to possess truth are constantly torn between fear that their attempts will reveal the paucity and indifference of their instruments and hope that their words will enrich humanity; constantly wavering between self-abnegation and self-confidence they are aware that nothing can be achieved without some degree of ambition, and that if the writer is to have any chance of succeeding in his aims he must be allowed a free rein at all times, 'whether he wishes to write about ocean liners or anthills'.[32] Above all he must be free from ideological pressures, which are particularly strong in post-war Italian society where political attitudes are frequently imposed on artistic and intellectual contexts to a degree quite unimaginable elsewhere. In another article Ginzburg stresses her belief in the objective nature of truth while admitting that it is often 'concealed from our eyes and difficult to uncover', maintaining that the writer's supreme duty is 'to provide something real for other people'. Problems arise when one attempts to explain exactly what is meant by 'something real' in that 'it is extremely difficult and perhaps indeed impossible to define reality';[33] trapped in this awkward situation the writer must disregard the beliefs and the advice of those around him, isolating himself from his fellows in order that he may reflect and create as he thinks fit, ignoring the fact that 'Nowadays novelists are required to have complicated, provocative, and highly-structured relationships with their characters . . . to focus on their social standing . . . to give them a historical and critical dimension' as opposed to simply 'understanding and loving [one's] character and presenting him in such a way that others may understand and love him in their turn . . . a simple aim which is now despised and seen as redundant.'[34] Here the key concept is *simplicity*, and the essential point grasped by Ginzburg and unperceived by many authors and critics is that truth does not necessarily have to be complex, the fruit of intense analysis or high intellectual endeavour, but can also reside in the faithful reproduction of a personality, something which at its best provides the reader with the shock of recognition and increased awareness of the human condition.[35]

Clearly a writer who wishes to communicate feelings and ideas must possess a degree of knowledge and experience ensuring that his *simplicity* remain something quite distinct from superficiality (which, as already indicated, it may resemble on first acquaintance) or self-indulgent fantasy; equally clearly such knowledge and such experience are necessarily limited during first youth and adolescence, and it is hardly surprising that if Ginzburg's emotional participation and personal interest in her subject matter were boundless in her new enthusiasm for adult writing her ability to draw on reality and represent truth was correspondingly restricted. If, therefore, during this period Ginzburg's principal concern was 'myself and my work',[36] so that years later she would say 'I'm astonished now when I recall how much time I spent thinking about my writing',[37] this near-obsessional involvement with her main interest was, inevitably, not merely the natural impulsiveness and single-mindedness of youth but also the need to compensate for a natural deficiency by cultivating a talent for observation, scrutiny, and awareness of human behaviour. Conscious that the quality of her adult story derived from its protagonists she began observing people in the street or on the tramcar and using their characteristics as a starting-point for imaginative writing, memorising aspects of attractive locations for future use, even noting down striking phrases or significant snatches of dialogue which flashed into her mind from time to time and would prove highly effective when used at key moments of her narrative. This activity consumed not only large sections of her free time but also much of her energy, since Ginzburg was by nature absent-minded and lacking in imagination;[38] in addition she rapidly discovered that material of this kind, though attractive and stimulating, could not easily be incorporated into her writing, her precious notebook becoming not, as intended, a source of inspiration, but 'a kind of museum of phrases that were crystallised and embalmed'.[39] It is clear with the benefit of hindsight that Ginzburg's work during this period, remarkable in someone not yet twenty years old, was none the less as limited, albeit in a different and more subtle way, as her childhood romances, and destined to lead in due course to another period of writer's block. Its main characteristic, as impressed upon her by a painter she greatly admired and whose judgement she respected, is its fortuitousness, a concept she elaborates on in the Preface to *Cinque romanzi brevi*:

> . . . he said that my short stories were not at all badly written, but that they were *fortuitous*, that is to say I knew nothing about reality, and used my imagination, living in an unreal world as do all adolescents; the objects I described and the events I narrated only had the semblance of reality and truth; I had come across them *fortuitously*, fishing haphazardly in a void. I was struck dumb by the truth of these words. I did indeed write *fortuitously*, spying on other people's lives without really understanding them and

without knowing anything about them, using my imagination and *pretending to understand.* (p. 9)[40]

This approach, inevitable in someone of Ginzburg's age, was intensified by a fierce desire to exclude from her writing anything remotely personal. Despite being in some ways 'a happy girl'[41] she hated life at this period, another characteristically adolescent feeling, being 'horrified and terrified by autobiographical material and feminine sentimentalism',[42] and her anxiety to avoid '"sloppy and sentimental"' writing and eliminate 'a strong tendency to . . . an odious feminine blemish'[43] is, of course, totally at variance with her subsequent awareness that one can only write effectively about what comes from within; it is thus clear that in her attempts to solve this problem she over-compensated by deliberately concentrating on sentiments at the other end of the spectrum, drawing on her instinctive melancholy to create characters and situations which are essentially pessimistic. The result is a series of impressive short stories in which, however, the accent is on 'grey, squalid people and things . . . a contemptible kind of reality lacking in glory . . . an avid, mean desire for little things',[44] and in which the author's emotional participation is conditioned by her own instinctive reactions to this material: contempt for her characters and 'a malign resentment against reality'[45] deriving from consciousness of her own naivety and the need to transcend it. Her ability to produce tales in which irony and malice create a near-perfect reflection of emotional disorder or pin-point exactly the more abject aspects of human behaviour reached its peak in 1937 with *Casa al mare*, a story in which her coldness and detachment were so marked as to make her feel it was both an admirable piece of work, and at the same time, somehow, repugnant, and she gradually realised that while it might indeed be appropriate to create characters that were 'funny and at the same time sad',[46] to concentrate solely on the negative qualities of her protagonists meant treating them like puppets on a string, totally credible within their own terms of reference, but, ultimately, lacking in humanity. As she became more adept at this kind of writing, turning out 'dry, clear stories . . . that came to a convincing conclusion',[47] she became increasingly aware that her interest in doing so was correspondingly declining; meanwhile her attempts to eliminate fortuitousness in her writing were largely unsuccessful, since, as she soon discovered, constant checking on the relationship between her subjects and her experience meant she never put pen to paper at all. She was once more in crisis:

The faces of the people in the street no longer said anything interesting to me . . . I was fed up with looking at things and people and describing them to myself. The world became silent for me. I could no longer find words to describe it, I no longer had any words capable of giving me pleasure.[48]

Ginzburg's deliberate exclusion of the personal element from her work at this time she now sees as a form of avarice characterised by a strong determination 'to ignore [my] own thoughts, or to transform them into something noble, lovable and flattering', an attitude based on 'fear of revealing my bare, uncultivated, foggy world'.[49] Her escape from this new prison was, as before, triggered by an outside event which changed her life completely, this time in a more complex and contradictory way than her failure to pass school examinations at seventeen. Her marriage one year after writing *Casa al mare* to the Jewish Slavist Leone Ginzburg, a Marxist whose race and politics made him a natural target for the attentions of the Fascist police, brought her face to face with a state of political conflict she had previously observed from the sidelines in the bosom of the family and which now became – quite literally overnight – part of her daily routine. This radical change in her personal circumstances would in itself have been sufficient to turn her attention away from creative composition, and any chance of resolving these problems was further postponed by two successive pregnancies which made it impossible for her to devote any time or energy to something other than the daily care of her offspring. When in 1940 Italy's declaration of war led to her husband being exiled to the village of Pizzoli in the depressed south she lost little time in following him, together with their children, and starting a new life in a primitive environment in which the family was required to live on a shoestring with no knowledge of when their situation might improve.

It is clear in retrospect that Ginzburg used the precariousness of her new life and the claims of her maternal responsibilities as an excuse to put off the painful investigation of her talents as a prose writer. Ironically it was the absence of distractions and of direct political harassment in her lonely village which provided the stimulus for a new period of creativity, inevitably very different from what had gone before. An initial rejection of artistic commitment, total and unqualified, to the point where, as we read in *My Vocation*, Ginzburg felt only contempt for her work,[50] gradually gave way to feelings of acute nostalgia for the joys of writing, memories which, she tells us, often brought her to the verge of tears. Little by little she established a less obsessive relationship with her children, allowed

16

her imagination to have free access to dimensions outside the domestic sphere, and, in due course, put pen to paper once more. Her new environment was one she both loved and hated, a beautiful village surrounded by lovely countryside, which, however, she had not chosen to inhabit and which was thus at the same time a source of resentment, peopled by simple country folk who were kind and helpful but with whom she and her husband had nothing in common, urban intellectuals surrounded by primitive peasants. The protagonist of *Mio marito*, which she wrote in the spring of 1941, is a woman who, despite being 'as different as possible from myself and my circumstances',[51] none the less has much more in common with Ginzburg than any of her previous literary creations: a woman who moves from a provincial city to the country following her marriage to a rural doctor and whose life thereafter is conditioned by his responsibilities to the village community and his sexual obsession with a local peasant girl. If the plot of this tale and its tragic conclusion are indeed very different from the author's life the background is clearly identical, the minor characters based directly on inhabitants of the area,[52] and, most significantly, the doctor whose destructive passion is at the centre of the story the exact physical replica of the man who treated Ginzburg's children during the three years she spent in Pizzoli. Her discovery of this fact was both a shock and a revelation, opening her eyes to the knowledge that literary creation was not something she could plan in advance, but, at least in part, the result of a subconscious assimilation of impressions which came to fruition in their own good time and could contribute to far more effective results overall than a cold deterministic desire to create good literature. Four months after completing *Mio marito* Ginzburg began her first novel, *The Road to the City*, a work whose title perfectly expresses the contrast between rural and urban environments, and, as such, her state of mind, in which the beauty and attraction of her surroundings together with her love–hate relationship with the village were combined with strong feelings of nostalgia for her past life and an intense homesickness for Turin, its wide avenues and tall buildings, taken for granted while she had lived and moved within them and now seen as a great loss. Still anxious to avoid sentimentality and self-indulgence Ginzburg was now aware that she could draw on people and things around her with a freedom of approach which allowed her to include in a new package memories of relatives and friends alongside aspects of life as lived around her and before her eyes. This process, an amalgam of memory and invention,[53] partly deliberate and partly unconscious,

17

meant she was no longer writing fortuitously:

> My characters were the inhabitants of the village ... some of
> them I recognised immediately, others only after I had finished
> writing. But at the same time they also included – in no way
> deliberately – my friends and my closest relatives ... the road
> which cut the village in two and led through fields and hills to the
> city of Aquila had also found its way into my narrative ... the city
> was both Aquila and Turin. The village was the one I'd been
> living in for over a year, which I both loved and hated and now
> knew like the back of my hand. The girl who acts as narrator was
> a girl I always met in the village streets. The house was her house
> and the mother her mother. But at the same time she was partly
> an old school-friend whom I hadn't seen for years, and in ad-
> dition, in some tortuous and unclear way, she was myself. And
> from that moment on whenever I wrote a narrative in the first
> person I realised my own personality would infiltrate my writing,
> unconsciously, undeliberately ... I must no longer write about
> things which were indifferent to me ... my characters must
> always be modelled on real people with whom I had close
> relationships ... and I realised this meant I would not be writing
> *fortuitously* ... relying exclusively on observation and invention
> alone, things which exist outside us, choosing at random among
> people, places, and things which leave us cold. To write other
> than *fortuitously* was to write about things we love. Memory is
> motivated by love and is never *fortuitous*; its roots stretch deep into
> our very lives and what it brings forth is thus never *fortuitous* but
> always impassioned and irresistible.[54]

If there were further problems awaiting Ginzburg in future years
it is clear that at this point in her life she had achieved a break-
through and was beginning to produce work in which 'imagination
goes hand in hand with reliance on reality'.[55] Her second crisis over,
she was once more ecstatic in the fulfilment of her vocation, conscious that, as she would state years later, 'when a writer becomes
an adult writing is something as natural as living or breathing',[56]
and now aware that while short stories need to be carried in one's
head in their entirety producing a long narrative is like unravelling a
ball of wool, so that a novel 'virtually *writes itself*'.[57] She had spent
some considerable time on the opening pages of *The Road to the City*,
consciously trying to achieve a precision of style, after which she had
written the remainder at full gallop, as if frightened she might grind
to a halt before reaching the end, and if one bears in mind the nature
of the creative process as described above it becomes easier to accept
what lies behind her apparent inability to explain her fiction and to

understand more accurately her claim that 'When I write I am quite empty. I have no schemes, no ideas, no plans . . .', especially when she qualifies this statement by adding 'all I am anxious to do is to isolate some human manifestation, to discover the truth about how things happen',[58] in other words, as already indicated, to isolate truth and describe reality. She is thus in no sense a didactic writer as one normally understands the term, openly admitting that she has never 'despatched messages in the true sense of the word', her aim being something more subtle: to provide 'information and communication about myself . . . in the constant hope that someone might stumble upon it and experience a sense of recognition'.[59] As Michele Rago has concisely stated: 'Her fiction is based on the desire to focus on sincerity',[60] and it is up to the reader to reflect on its implications and draw appropriate conclusions. In this context it is interesting to note that Ginzburg's essay *My Vocation*, written all of eight years later in 1949, after traumas and difficulties she had no inkling of at the end of *The Road to the City*, ends by listing the elements which nourish her calling and which are a clear expression of the range of incentives typical of any major writer: 'The days of our life and the experiences we undergo, other people's lives and their experiences we are able to witness, the books we read, the things we see, the thoughts we have, the things we say';[61] in addition she makes it clear in this same essay that for someone like herself writing is never a pastime or a form of therapy but a tyrannical force driving its victims mercilessly through blood and tears while at other times becoming a source of strength, a bulwark against folly and despair, a further indication that Ginzburg shares with other less controversial authors the attitudes and characteristics associated with great artists.

Ginzburg's discovery of the relationship between memory and imagination convinced her she was now in a position to approach her subjects with a greater degree of humanity, and it is clear that in this first novel she has created a story with a universality of theme not apparent in her earlier work. If *Un'assenza*, *Casa al mare*, and *Mio marito* are totally convincing in their presentation of specific problems it is no coincidence that all three stories have at their centre a character who is the victim of emotional disorder and whose behaviour is incompatible with any conventional understanding of normality, while the plots of two other tales published during Ginzburg's first youth likewise focus on emotional crises which, however brilliantly described, do not relate to common experience.[62] In *The Road to the City*, by contrast, the protagonist's ingenuousness and general apathy are equally destructive but in no sense pathological or circumscribed by specific events; rather, they are extreme examples of an attitude not restricted to peasant communities but common to large sections of humanity. This refinement in Ginzburg's narrative technique, though illuminating a new vein of inspiration, did not immediately herald a new crop of novels or short stories; indeed she tells us that for several years thereafter she forgot what she had just learned and continued to write 'stories . . . in which I toyed with people and things that only aroused in me an indifferent curiosity',[63] and the apparent illogicality of this is perhaps explained by her subsequent realisation that, despite having discovered an important truth about literary creation through her exile to Pizzoli and the pressures this had created, she was still writing in a context that was both privileged and deprived: that of a healthy happy woman whose emotional needs were fully satisfied within her new family and whose material hardships were not so great as to affect her state of mind, a condition clearly quite naive in someone living in a country at war and whose political convictions were at variance with those of the authorities. Untouched by human suffering in any extreme sense Ginzburg could draw on her reserves of melancholy and exploit her imaginative talents, now fertilised by memory; what she still lacked in her ignorance of life's hardships as experienced within herself was the sentiment of compassion for her characters, a participation which would no longer be merely the result of a blending of various gifts she possessed but would also spring from identification with their misfortunes. As Ginzburg herself states, with rare perception, a writer lacking in compassion creates characters dispassionately, coolly and objectively, exposing their faults and weaknesses from a superior standpoint, and while this is in one sense a sound basis for effective characterisation, allowing the author to polish and refine his work, to make full use of his talent for irony, and to pass judgement unhindered by any doubts or hesitations, the absence of what she calls 'any tender, intimate sympathy with our characters and with things we write about'[64] makes for a certain sterility of composition in which the depiction of anguish and the darker side of human experience is necessarily based on conjecture and the proficient deployment of imaginative talent. Having discovered the importance of memory as source material Ginzburg now needed to increase its scope to include aspects of reality she had until then been fortunate enough to avoid.

This gap in her artistic arsenal was soon filled to overflowing. Italy's surrender in September 1943 and her subsequent occupation by her former ally, Germany, created a situation in which Ginzburg and her family found themselves deeply involved. Hopes raised by the fall of the Fascist regime two months previously and the all-too-brief flowering of political activity in the interim were quickly dashed and replaced by the harshness of martial law and anti-Semitic persecution. Her husband's arrest in Rome, where he had moved in July and where she had soon joined him, her virtual destitution following his death in prison under torture, and her need to go into hiding to escape arrest and deportation in her turn, all ensured that she had more than her fair share of fear and suffering, rapidly achieving a maturity of spirit in a relatively short space of time in a manner recalling Pirandello's description in *The Late Mattia Pascal* of fruiterers who mature unripe pears by beating them with blunt instruments. Her return to the capital after its liberation by Allied troops in June 1944 and her employment with the publishing house of Einaudi, first in Rome and a year later in their head office in Turin, while signalling the beginning of a return to normality proved only the beginning of a long and laborious process of readjustment among the hardships investing every aspect of daily life in a country torn apart by war and civil strife and in which poverty and squalor were the norm. 'Totally defenceless and miserable'[65] as she then was it is hardly surprising that Ginzburg's first attempts at narrative fiction in peacetime should result in a novel – *The Dry Heart* – whose protagonist is the epitome of naive innocence brutalised by misfortune, a young woman whose inability to defend herself against the blows of life leads her first to murder and then to suicide. When seen in context it is clear that this novel is the mirror image of *The Road to the City*: a work in which the author has drawn too freely and too deeply on the anguish of past memories to create a character with whom she has a rapport corresponding perfectly to the description she provides in *My Vocation*:

> When we are happy our imagination is stronger; when we are unhappy our memory works with greater vitality. Suffering makes the imagination weak and lazy . . . it is difficult for us to turn our eyes away from our own life and our own state, from the thirst and restlessness that pervades us. And so memories of our own past constantly crop up in the things we write, our own voice constantly echoes there and we are unable to silence it. A particular sympathy grows up between us and the characters we invent . . . a sympathy that is tender and almost maternal, warm and damp with tears, intimately physical and stifling . . . then we risk foundering on a dark lake of stagnant, dead water, and dragging our

mind's creations down with us, so that they are left to perish . . .
in a dark, warm whirlpool.[66]

Clearly in the two years that elapsed between the completion of
The Dry Heart and the composition of this essay Ginzburg was able
to transcend the shocks she had so recently undergone and begin to
adapt to a new life in which some degree of emotional and spiritual
stability could be achieved alongside a gradual improvement in her
material circumstances. Having known the extremes of joy and
sorrow and, in due course, come to terms with them, she was now
fully aware of the degree to which a writer's personal acquaintance
with the facts of life and the range of human experience should
influence the process of creative composition. Her naive faith in the
stability of social structures and her instinctive assumption that
happiness, or at least satisfaction, is a recognisable norm in human
existence had been swept away by the war and replaced by an
intense awareness of the potential for unhappiness that exists in the
human make-up, an awareness which, harking back to the intuitive
feeling enabling her to focus on distress in her earliest characters,
now allowed her to distinguish consciously and creatively between
feelings of victimisation which may dominate an individual in a
specific context and an intellectual realisation that suffering is a
fundamental part of the human condition.[67]

If Ginzburg's state of mind in 1947 was such – understandably –
as to bring forth a work in which self-indulgence is combined with
elements of her old fortuitousness of approach[68] it is clear that a new
perception and a new mastery were already in existence when she
composed her short story *La madre* just over eighteen months later.
Here too the protagonist is an unhappy young woman and the
conclusion no less tragic, but the narrative technique is far more
controlled and perfectly balanced between objective description and
personal involvement, well in keeping with the author's definition of
successful writing as an amalgam of 'ruthlessness, pride, irony,
physical tenderness . . . imagination and memory . . . clarity and
obscurity'.[69] We may see this improvement as indicative of a new
lease of life, made manifest two years later by her marriage to
Gabriele Baldini, later appointed to the Chair of English in Rome,
where she subsequently took up residence (and still lives). This
radical change in her personal circumstances in no way inhibited
her creative activity, as is apparent from her production of three
novels in the next few years: *Valentino* in 1951, *All Our Yesterdays* the
year after, and *Sagittarius* in 1957, but already while writing the

second of these Ginzburg was aware of a new problem which was to lead eventually to a recurrence of writer's block: an increasing inability to deal with direct speech between her characters. There is little dialogue in *Valentino* but no sense of artificiality, as the greater part of the story is an account by the protagonist's sister Caterina of his progress – or decay – from adolescence through early manhood and an unsuccessful marriage to middle age, an account in which the accent is on narrative, and direct speech is largely reserved for moments of confrontation or extended conversations of particular significance. One year later, however, as Ginzburg herself states unambiguously: 'my characters had lost the knack of speaking to each other',[70] a fact expressed with even greater clarity in an interview in 1963 in which she states bluntly: 'I was no longer able to write dialogue',[71] and if this is clearly an exaggeration, in that there is *some* direct speech in *All Our Yesterdays*, it is equally clear Ginzburg found it far easier to have her characters communicate indirectly through the impersonal narrator in a fast-flowing sequence which allowed her to provide useful information on personality and temperament alongside the veiled transcript of their exchanges. In the five years that followed, during which she published nothing, she appears not only to have lost touch completely with direct speech but also to have encountered basic difficulties in constructing a narrative and bringing it to a satisfactory conclusion; *Sagittarius* contains not a single line of dialogue and is the only one of Ginzburg's works with a relatively conventional plot based on the successful working of a confidence trick, and it seems clear that this reliance on what can be seen as a standard model indicates a certain flagging of inspiration. She was again in difficulty and in need of something to break the mould.

Once again it was outside events which intervened to change things for the better. Two years after finishing *Sagittarius* Ginzburg's life took a radically different direction when she moved from Rome to London following her husband's appointment there as the Director of the Italian Institute, and found herself in a new world where her inevitable isolation from an Italian environment created new spiritual hardships in a form of exile which, though obviously more sophisticated than her youthful experiences in Pizzoli, was equally productive in literary terms. Just as in 1941 her feelings of homesickness for Turin had provided the incentive for a new kind of writing so now in London she suffered similar feelings of nostalgia for the familiar surroundings of both her childhood and her married life in the Italian capital, something she encouraged by what might at first appear a self-indulgent waste of useful time: long hours devoted to leafing through back numbers of newspapers in the Institute's library 'looking for . . . the names of streets in Turin and Rome where things were happening and crimes were being committed'.[72] In the event this proved a powerful mechanism for reawakening in Ginzburg the desire to put pen to paper,[73] a desire which bore fruit when combined with two further pressures on her at this time: a lively awareness of the countless differences between everyday life in London and in Rome, particularly striking in the period preceding the so-called swinging sixties, and her discovery of the novels of Ivy Compton-Burnett. The conventional surprise and diffidence of the average Latin at large in the London scene at this time were experienced no less by Ginzburg, and became a stimulant; her essay *England: Eulogy and Lament*, written in the spring of 1961, touches on a number of disparate themes which are a clear indication of an alert and inquisitive spirit and a high degree of receptiveness which acquired a precise direction when she first picked up a novel by Compton-Burnett and immediately fell under the spell of that writer's unique narrative style.[74]

The intensity of the impression created in Ginzburg by this contact with an author previously unknown to her is apparent in her claim to have felt 'caught in a trap . . . pinned to the ground',[75] and this despite the fact that her knowledge of English was limited and her reading thus only accomplished with extreme hardship. Such an extreme reaction becomes more easily understandable when seen in the context of Ginzburg's awareness, at this precise moment in her life, that the appalling events described by Compton-Burnett in her novels are communicated not through descriptions of people and places but, almost exclusively, through the use of direct speech, in 'words that seemed like snake bites',[76] exchanges 'full of stubbornness and malice'.[77] The result was a sudden feeling of liberation, an awareness that she too could, after all, be capable of writing direct speech: '. . . it was a long time since I had written anything myself, and suddenly I felt something that had been lifeless quicken in me. Those dry, precise sounds suddenly and imperiously led me back on to a path I had lost'.[78] Still in the grip of diffidence and uncertain about how to externalise this feeling Ginzburg began work 'on a short story of two or three pages',[79] only to discover almost immediately that she had enough creative energy at her disposal to produce a whole novel. The curious combination of nostalgia for her past life and a positive euphoria at the thought of once more creating dialogue burst forth in *Voices in the Evening*, one of her best-known works, in which places and people from her childhood are presented with only the thinnest of fictional disguises and characters have no inhibitions about using direct speech in a succession of short paragraphs in complete contrast to the long explanatory narration of *Sagittarius*. The desire to maintain such a close relationship with her characters recalls Ginzburg's near-obsessive rapport with the narrator of *The Dry Heart* fourteen years earlier, but this time there is a vital difference: the influence of a writer of recognised genius able to pin-point evil and suffering through a masterly idiosyncratic use of a particular literary device, here reinterpreted within an equally personal context in a novel emphasising a different kind of victimisation, one caused by insensitivity or incompetence and existing in a different dimension. The result is a deceptively simple book in which the temptation to self-indulgence is kept in check by an artistic influence that prevented Ginzburg ever losing sight of the different levels on which she was working, ensuring a near-perfect combination of memory and imagination, strong personal involvement and lucid objectivity of thought, essentially pessimistic and yet shot through with humour, all conceived in a language whose essential simplicity contributes more than is immediately obvious to the creation of character.

If this novel thus represents something positive both in itself and in its significance for its author, once more reconciled to her vocation, its reception among critics was not without reservations; indeed the simplicity always characteristic of Ginzburg's writing, here more apparent than in anything produced previously, was so different from the broad tradition of Italian prose writing as to make some degree of opposition inevitable, and her adaptation of a device peculiar to an author as quintessentially Anglo-Saxon as Ivy Compton-Burnett led to predictable reactions from the Italian establishment. Thus alongside praise for its 'compact and fast-flowing' content Paolo Milano also mentions the 'mannered simplicity' of Ginzburg's dialogue, 'full of understatements and jerkiness';[80] Giorgio Pullini similarly speaks of 'this leit-motif of "he said" and "she said", whose constant repetition engenders boredom';[81] while Walter Mauro notes the author's ability to communicate 'aspects of the human condition that pinpoint the reality of squalor' but is disturbed by what he sees as 'a dryness which often becomes impoverishment when applied to dialogue . . . giving rise to the suspicion that what we have here is a deliberate striving for effect, something which is no longer spontaneous but mannered and insincere'.[82] More surprising perhaps is the reaction of some British critics,

25

possibly influenced by having read the book in translation; thus Brigid Brophy sees it as 'an academic frieze in very low relief';[83] Gillian Freeman speaks of 'skeletal writing' and ends her review by saying 'Simplicity is a virtue, but this is over-simplification';[84] while Jocelyn Brooke, admitting to 'only a smattering of Italian' and unable to approach the original text, speaks disparagingly of 'a curiously blunt *terre-à-terre* quality' where 'this happens, and then that happens, she says this, he says that (and often twice over, for emphasis)', even going so far as to compare Ginzburg's writing to that of Beatrix Potter.[85] In contrast there were those such as Franco Antonicelli, who notes the existence of 'a string of "He said" and "She said" which may appear an unimaginative mechanical device' but which, when applied to a wide range of characters, introduces an equally wide range of emotional states of mind,[86] and Giancarlo Vigorelli, who has no hesitation in describing the book as 'a small masterpiece that is dry but in no way arid', written in a style he defines as 'antilyrical, concrete, and solid', and recounting a story which is 'cruel and translucent, like truth'.[87]

This concept of translucence is indeed central to all of Ginzburg's writing, which has always been simple, unrhetorical, and immediately accessible to the general reader, thus also, incidentally, making it somewhat easier for those whose knowledge of Italian is limited to grasp the content of her output without feeling impeded by its form. It is significant that alongside Chekhov and Proust, undisputed masters of the art of communicating states of mind, Ginzburg also greatly admires Italo Svevo, a writer whose links with the city of Trieste, 'an isolated environment . . . with few connections with the basic trends of Italian literary tradition',[88] place him in the unique position of being also largely foreign in temperament while writing in a language having an astringency and clarity more usually associated with English. There is still a strong belief within the Italian establishment in a basic difference between the spoken language of everyday life, necessarily simple and practical in its role as a functional instrument for immediate communication, and what appears in print, where cultural considerations and a belief in the superior status of the writer ensure the survival of a dense and frequently convoluted style in which long sentences involving abstract concepts and subtle metaphors are a clear indication of intellectual prowess and seriousness of intent, in short the very opposite of translucence.[89] While aware that it is indeed possible for some authors to write effectively through a skilful use of colourful and rhetorical language[90] Ginzburg herself has never sought to do this, conscious that in her case it would be counter-productive; particularly revealing in this context are the views expressed in an interview in 1971 with Delia Lennie in which she states that 'clarity implies an awareness of one's own limitations',[91] stressing that she sees this as essential if she is to capture and retain the attention and the interest of her readers.[92] Her conviction dates from the earliest days of her writing, when she realised that a spontaneous outpouring of one's innermost thoughts is not necessarily the best way of expressing what one has to say, and that discipline is necessary to achieve maximum effect:

> I remember that when I started writing I would write at great length and then put it all on one side and write it again. I would always make two or three drafts, trying to get everything down with as few words as possible. Now of course I don't need to go over things to the same extent, but when I first started I sometimes wrote my opening paragraphs eighteen or twenty times until they were really very concise indeed.[93]

If we know this did not apply to her first '"adult"' story, which exists in a class of its own, it seems clear that this attitude will have been uppermost in her mind both during the period betwen *Un'assenza* and *The Road to the City*, in her anxiety to avoid writing that was '"sloppy and sentimental"',[94] and in the composition of her first novel, during which 'I wrote the first pages over and over again, trying to be as dry and as concise as possible. I wanted each phrase to be like a blow from a whip or a slap in the face.'[95] Her desire to achieve such a sparseness of style in the interests of clarity derives from her conviction that although creative composition is a source of personal fulfilment it does not exist in a void, but, ultimately, reflects one's relationship with fellow human beings in that 'We do not write for ourselves but for others', and that consequently 'one's choice of language is not something aesthetic but something moral'.[96] In this sense Ginzburg sees the persistence of traditional attitudes to literacy in education as something essentially negative since they perpetuate the idea that 'one needs to employ a complex linguistic code in order to demonstrate one's maturity and prove that one is cultured', when in reality 'people ought to be free to express themselves with the utmost simplicity'[97] and children encouraged to aspire to 'clarity, contempt for clichés, and a form of expression which is plain and simple and avoids anything else, these and these alone being a sign of maturity'.[98]

It is clear from these statements that Ginzburg's frequent and somewhat irritating claims to be lacking in 'culture' derive from her feelings of antipathy for the official interpretation of this term and a total incompatibility with what she calls 'the smell of mothballs' in prose composition,[99] aware that the effort required to create a style that taxes the patience of the average reader would be better employed in refining one's expression to the point where it can communicate complex concepts or pin-point intense emotions with a degree of immediacy ensuring that they are more willingly received and easily retained. It is thus no surprise to read that what she appreciates in the novels of Ennio Flaiano is 'everything which appears to have been written down spontaneously, as if in moments of idleness' while on the contrary she describes as 'less effective everything that is structured',[100] and that she likewise sees Alberto Moravia's novels as 'unattractive and misguided' when 'he writes by drawing on his intellect' and believes he has produced his best work 'by using not his intellect but exclusively his inner being, which is translucent, unpretentious, and responsible'.[101] If clarity of communication is thus the ideal to which a prose writer must aspire through a careful process in which the dross of cultural pretentiousness is discarded, the intricacy of intellectual activity refined, and the force of emotional stimulation disciplined, it follows that the end product must have a universality of tone making it accessible to readers of either sex, constituting 'a type of writing which, while springing from the personal experiences of a man or a woman, does not reveal the sex of its author, a style which is meaningful not to men or women but to human beings',[102] in which, ideally, the qualities of both sexes are combined.[103]

Ginzburg's awareness that writing is in some sense a duty towards her fellow human beings gives a further dimension to her anguish in those periods of her life when she has suffered from writer's block, and make it easier to understand how the fear of creative impotence has rarely, if ever, been totally absent from her thoughts. Her inspiration, her creative urge, is thus accompanied by a pressing need to realise what she has within her before it vanishes into thin air: ' . . . when I write I'm under great stress, I feel as though I'm possessed by the devil, and at the same time I'm frightened something may happen to prevent me from going on, so I work as fast as I can . . .'[104] In the same way she has never been entirely able to eliminate guilt feelings when not actively engaged in fulfilling her creative function; despite being aware that 'novelists enjoy being inactive, and indeed need to have periods of inactivity' she is also fully conscious that 'they are at the same time frightened of being too inactive and thus feeling bone idle' because 'when they've finished their writing and are taking a rest they don't know what to do with themselves or how to organise themselves',[105] and if she has partly come to terms with these feelings, so that in 1964 she could state 'Now I never feel guilty when I'm not writing, and I never try to write when I'm not in the mood', in contrast to her reactions as a young girl when 'even if I felt no desire to do anything . . . I would force myself to try to write',[106] this appears to have been an essentially transitory feeling of spiritual equilibrium, possibly as a result of having won a literary prize the previous summer. Thus in 1975 we find her telling Enzo Biagi that '"One stops writing as one gets older, which is something that distresses me"',[107] and six years later in another interview, this time with Lietta Tornabuoni, '"When I can't write I feel bad"',[108] and it is doubtless significant that both statements date from periods in which some time had elapsed since the publication of her last novel. When Ginzburg is able to realise her potential it correspondingly takes precedence over all other considerations, driving her from her bed in the middle of the night to her sofa, where she sits with a pad on her knees, writing with apparent casualness in a manner far removed from the traditional image of the author at his typewriter:

> I've never learned how to use a typewriter, and anyway I'd find it a nuisance to write in that way . . . I have a collection of biros and I do my writing between four and eight in the morning, as these are the hours during which I feel most intelligent and at my best. During the rest of the day I'm constantly being interrupted, and I feel less intelligent . . .[109]

The speed with which she works means that her books are completed in a very short space of time, particularly since when in the grip of what she calls 'the white heat of inspiration' Ginzburg's energy is boundless, causing her to begin her day even earlier and work unceasingly to the detriment of all else:

> I usually finish in twenty days, a month, two months by the time I've polished everything up. When it's done it's done. I polish very intensely, but it all happens during the white heat of inspiration and while that lasts I sit and write all day and part of the night. I wake up at three in the morning and start to write.[110]

The result of such a concentrated and exclusive attention, which, it appears, comes upon her suddenly, 'so that I start work in a state of emotional excitement',[111] is an intensely close relationship with her characters, who take on a life of their own to the extent that when the novel is completed she experiences withdrawal symptoms along-side feelings of relief at having completed her task: 'when I finish a book I'm pleased because it's finished, but the experience of breaking the links that bind me to my characters is something very strong, it's like leaving somewhere, going away, losing touch with one's loved ones. It's something which grieves me.'[112]

This feeling was particularly marked in relation to *Voices in the Evening*, doubtless in view of the particular circumstances in which the book was written and which have already been mentioned; so marked indeed that Ginzburg felt obliged to record the fact in a note which precedes the opening of the first chapter and in which, after having stated that the people and places figuring therein are fictional, she then adds 'I am sorry to say this, having loved them as though they were real' (p. 6).[113] If, as has been suggested, the influence of Ivy Compton-Burnett ensured that this novel is in no way self-indulgent despite the fact that during its composition 'memory was so strong and joyous within me that it effortlessly discarded everything extraneous to it',[114] it is clear that Ginzburg's reawakening of creative talent was, this time, cast in a specific mould and needing a new outlet for adequate realisation. Ever mindful of the dangers of over-identification with one's characters she once more skilfully avoided repeating the mistakes she had made in *The Dry Heart* by writing next what she herself describes as 'a novel of pure memory, naked, manifest, and unadorned':[115] *Family Sayings*. The process of composition was similar to that of *Voices in the Evening* in that she began by thinking she would produce 'five or six pages about the way they used to talk in my family . . . which then grew into a great mass of material; a book, in other words',[116] which in 1964 she defined as 'the only book I have written in a state of total freedom . . . if I am to write any more books I know I shall have to experience the same feelings of total and absolute freedom'.[117] *Family Sayings*, though usually referred to as a novel for purposes of convenience, is not really one in the accepted sense, having no plot, no conventional structure, and nothing in it which does not relate to Ginzburg's life, starting from her earliest childhood and ending after the war and her move to Rome following her second marriage; at the same time it is not a historical chronicle of that particularly violent period of Italian history but a selection of significant moments, characteristic pronouncements, and, in its wealth of detail, a rounded portrait of the Levi family, whose personalities emerge with the total clarity and perceptiveness we associate with the protagonist of a well-written novel whose author has the freedom to invent whatever best suits his purpose. The result is a curious hybrid in which Ginzburg's talent for observation and her ability to communicate the complexities of human personalities through an accumulation of particulars, sometimes disparate and frequently trivial if viewed in isolation, are here applied to a reality no longer reinterpreted through fiction but drawn from the very stuff of life itself, in a work which, while once again communicating truths about the human condition through the depiction of a specific environment, also recreates the distinctive flavour of an epoch still – at that time, less than twenty years after the end of the war – intensely vivid in the minds of many of her readers.

This curious combination and its successful outcome makes it clear that *Family Sayings* is something more than what one would expect from the average light autobiography, and explains how a book which may at first appear little more than a random collection of anecdotes and nostalgic jottings could win the Strega Prize in 1963. If, however, Ginzburg's talent is fundamental to the successful realisation of this work it is also clear, on reflection, that she had at her disposal a collection of individuals many of whom were distinctly eccentric and with whom direct contact over a long period had guaranteed the existence of an infinite range of memories on which to draw. The deliberate desire to choose from this boundless store those elements which seemed most appropriate[118] in relation to a gallery of characters who are interesting in themselves and whose comical aspects are emphasised throughout ensures that the reader's interest is constantly maintained, notwithstanding the apparent aimlessness of Ginzburg's narration, in a context in which her familiar simplicity of style is entirely suitable to the matter in hand; and it is perhaps the sense of joy she derived from the composition of this book which led her to undertake a similar experiment twenty years later with *The Manzoni Family*, a work which appeared all of six years after the publication of her last novel and which she tells us she undertook under the influence of her friend Dinda Gallo, who 'knew all about the Manzoni family, and I nothing' and whose conversations on the subject made her want to discover its history 'more intimately and thoroughly'.[119]

The similarity between the titles of these two works is, of course, consistent with Ginzburg's perennial interest in the family, and it is tempting, in the light of what we know about her progress as a writer, to deduce that in the period between 1977 and 1983 she had once more felt her inspiration dry up and was hoping to revive it by a variation on the original theme of *Family Sayings*. Be that as it may[120] the work involved in researching the lives and letters of individuals who are separated from us by over two hundred years (the book begins with the birth of Giulia Beccaria in 1762) is, of course, very different from that of recalling incidents and comments relating to people we have known and loved directly, while the instinctive feelings of respect one has for artists whose names are an integral part of popular culture means that one is unlikely to adopt a humorous approach in one's presentation, especially if the subjects themselves are not particularly amusing. In Ginzburg's case the combination of all these factors, together with a desire to be as complete as possible in the use of all the documentation at her disposal, has unfortunately led to the production of an unwieldy mass of factual information, much of which is of very limited interest to the general reader, while the deliberate absence of any interpretation of the events presented means that the book is also likely to be of equally restricted appeal to the historian. Ginzburg's explanation of her impersonal approach to her subject is touchingly naive: 'I did not want to make any comments, limiting myself to a bare and simple account of events. I wanted the events to speak for themselves. I wanted the letters . . . to speak for themselves. Nonetheless I found it impossible not to comment from time to time. These comments are rare and brief',[121] and its effect, very different from what she intended, is cruelly but accurately pin-pointed by Bernard Levin:

> I do not exaggerate when I say that I have rarely read a book so entirely devoid of the novelist's art . . . nowhere in it, even in the most unconsidered aside, is there so much as a sentence that presumes to enter the thoughts or the feelings of the characters without documentary evidence . . . the author has taken Othello's advice: nothing extenuate, nor set down aught in malice . . . all have their even measure of the author's attention, as she struggles to avoid drowning in the mass of material at her disposal.[122]

It is perhaps unfair to reproach Ginzburg for having been too assiduous in her efforts to bring to life the intimate details of a family group whose members all reflect to a greater or lesser degree the light that emanated from Alessandro Manzoni, a recognised genius among men of letters (albeit largely unknown to Anglo-Saxon readers despite having provided the inspiration for Verdi's *Requiem*). The fact remains, none the less, that the private life and domestic routine of this family is not, for the most part, particularly enthralling; and if it is also the case, as Levin admits, that 'The *mores* and customs of the society portrayed are delineated no less faithfully' on a background 'that provides the very finest detail',[123] here too the absence of any degree of selection over more than three hundred pages of text rapidly produces feelings of indifference which lead inexorably to intense boredom, though it is only right to indicate that despite this many critics' reactions were essentially favourable and that indeed the book won the Bagutta Prize in November 1983.[124] Thus Lucienne Portier speaks of 'a new and successful method' of composition[125] and stresses the value of 'a complete document . . . for which we thank the author and congratulate her' notwithstanding the existence of sections which are 'a little long and repetitive',[126] while Geno Pampaloni describes the work as 'fascinating' while admitting that it is difficult to explain what this fascination consists of without reading the book.[127] Clearly it is difficult for literate Italians to approach any work dealing with an author of this stature other than with instinctive reverence, grateful for any addition to the contents of his output regardless of how the information is conveyed.[128] This essentially submissive and unquestioning attitude is particularly apparent in the comments of Sergio Romagnoli, who ends his review of the book by describing it as an example of how culture can occasionally coincide with popular taste in a family saga 'which has none of the vulgarity of *Dallas* or *Dynasty*',[129] a crass remark confirming the quality of what might, with that same vulgarity, be defined as the knee-jerk school of literary criticism. It is ironic that one of Ginzburg's intentions in producing this book should have been to bring the great man down off his pedestal[130] when her efforts seem, if anything, to have consolidated his position.

The intense satisfaction Ginzburg experienced during the writing of *Family Sayings*, doubtless compounded by the applause with which the book was received, seems to have filled her with an unusually high degree of confidence, without which she might not have presumed, at this stage in her life, to try her hand in a medium she had previously ignored: the theatre. Her aversion to dramatic representation was long-standing and based in large measure on her belief that the Italian contribution to this art is of decidedly poor quality:

> There has never been much writing for the theatre in Italy, and what there is seems to me rather inadequate. As soon as anyone thinks of using this medium he is immediately stopped in his tracks by the thought of all those appalling plays written by Italian authors . . . Pirandello is not to our liking, nor is D'Annunzio . . . when we think of the theatre and try to imagine a

play set in present-day Italy, a play which deals with contemporary reality, all we can think of is a compendium of the most unsuccessful, dreary, lifeless plays that make up the Italian theatre.[131]

This rather drastic judgement becomes more acceptable when we realise that what Ginzburg objects to in traditional Italian theatre is not plot structure or characterisation but that most important and most immediate element of dramatic action: the language chosen by the author through which his protagonists are required to express themselves. The development of what is now the official Italian language has been a complex procedure influenced by historical and political considerations, while the language itself, hotly debated by professional linguisticians, who still debate points of grammar and syntax not only in learned journals but also, in some cases, in the pages of daily newspapers, is still seen by many Italians as a form of expression imposed from above whose function is to provide a common code understandable throughout the country in which regional differences and dialect forms are absorbed or eliminated. The overall advantages of such a code are obvious and need no elaboration; its disadvantages in a theatrical context, less immediately clear, become equally manifest when we consider the problems involved in the dramatic presentation of characters who in real life would express themselves in a manner appropriate to their region and their class but who in drama are required to use conventional Italian in order that what they say may be understood by a national audience. It is no coincidence that the two playwrights whom Ginzburg excepts from her general condemnation are Goldoni and De Filippo: the former, a recognised genius in the history of Western theatre, an author who wrote for the most part in the Venetian dialect, 'and even when he didn't the rich pulsating vein of his dialect runs through everything',[132] and the latter a contemporary writer whose favourite means of expression is Neapolitan.

If this problem of linguistic codes is clearly not something which relates exclusively to theatrical composition but inevitably also affects the novel and the short story, where the same difficulties may arise, it is undoubtedly true that it is at its most apparent on the stage and screen, where there is no narrator and thus no direct intervention through devices such as description or character analysis which can cushion an audience from direct contact with the spoken word. In recent years, however, with the increasing mobility of modern life and the all-pervasive influence of television, linguistic barriers are breaking down with increasing speed, and the gap between 'spontaneous' and 'official' parlance is rapidly diminishing, at least in urban areas, as Ginzburg herself expresses it:

> . . . before the war I felt I had to find a form of language which somehow incorporated all our dialects or at least was understandable throughout the country. But . . . I think we've now gone past that stage, it's no longer impossible for people from different regions to understand each other. That doesn't happen any longer, or, at least, it happens much less.[133]

Another result of the increasing speed of modern life is, Ginzburg believes, a similar reduction in the gap between the written and the spoken language. While one would hesitate to agree unreservedly with her claim that 'it no longer exists; we have learned to write as we speak'[134] it is undoubtedly true that, as she states a little more cautiously and in the same breath, 'or at least we are now able to do so'.[135] This, however, has its own share of difficulties, in that the spontaneity of real exchanges between people means that most conversation tends to be either about practical matters requiring immediate attention, or, whether consciously or unconsciously, pitched at a level of basic simplicity intended to ensure maximum accessibility and understanding; a writer who tries to reproduce this is in danger of creating work which, however authentic, will appear trivial and boring on the printed page or in direct contact with an audience. In addition the unstructured nature of most conversations is in total contrast to the theatre's need for a recognisable flow of speech without the truncations, the pauses, and the distractions of real communication, which are replaced by a process of selection in which the main points at issue are communicated in a condensed form which, while credible and convincing, is in fact quite artificial. If Ginzburg has found her own solution to this problem, as we shall shortly indicate, she seems to have been put off for some time by the difficulties involved in rendering the complexities of the human personality through a medium in which natural expression would of necessity appear largely superficial:

> When writing . . . something that wasn't a novel but a play I saw my fellow-creatures not as something impenetrable and mysterious but as a group of real live people, totally distinct from myself and full of hostility towards me, and my relationship with this group of real people, that is to say with the public, not as something deep and secret but as something obvious, superficial, lacking in depth, and that made me feel embarrassed, made me shy and at the same time revolted me.[136]

35

In short Ginzburg appears to have baulked at the idea of exposing her creative work – and through her work her own self, similarly laid bare – no longer through a printed text destined for a series of ideal readers each of whom would commune with it in isolation and in private, but, instead, through a text whose first impact would be via the spoken word in a public auditorium and whose content, necessarily more accessible, would inevitably be received on a more superficial level and judged accordingly. Thus while having no inhibitions about reproducing within the structure of a narrative phrases which in isolation would appear trivial[137] she had until then been quite unable to contemplate doing something similar in a theatrical context: 'I would very much like to write a play. But I couldn't possibly. Every time I've started by writing at the top of a page "Piero: Where's my hat?" I've been overcome by the most dreadful embarrassment and have had to stop because I felt quite revolted.'[138]

In 1965, three years after completing *Family Sayings*, Ginzburg felt able to overcome this impediment, beginning her first play, *Ti ho sposato per allegria*, with the precise phrase she had quoted in the extract above as being a source of such embarrassment and revulsion. There appears to have been no specific reason for this radical change, hence the suggestion that it may have been a reaction to the success of her last novel; she herself states that she began writing 'quite by chance', but also states in the same breath that 'evidently there was some deep need within me to move in this direction'. As on previous occasions she began work without any pre-defined ideas as to what precisely she was doing, seeing her writing as 'an experiment. I thought: it might work, it might not . . . I wasn't too hopeful.'[139]

Critical reaction to Ginzburg's theatrical work has been mixed, its characteristics being frequently interpreted in radically different ways by individual writers and reviewers. Its most obvious and striking trait is the total absence of anything dramatic as we normally understand the term, the emphasis being on the re-evocation of past events or the delineation of character through dialogue or soliloquy; as Elena Clementelli has perceptively stated:

> the most conspicuous characteristic of Ginzburg's theatre is precisely the absence of any kind of action . . . when there is something happening it is secondary, if not fortuitous; what matters is what is said, what matters above all is the selfish silence of the world outside, ready to swallow up and eliminate the voices of the speakers.[140]

This is of course incompatible with the traditional concept of theatre, which demands 'an *action*, around which everything unravels, develops, and takes place',[141] and it was perhaps inevitable that those unprepared for a different and more modern approach should make the obvious comment that Ginzburg is unable to differentiate between one medium and the other, while not necessarily drawing the same conclusions. Thus Marco Garzonio reproaches her for her 'inability to transcend narrative structures and rhythms', graciously adding that 'this is understandable in someone writing for the theatre for the first time' (in his analysis of *Ti ho sposato per allegria*,[142]) and the American Joseph Ricapito, in his review of *Paese di mare e altre commedie*, published eight years later, shows, by claiming that 'the literary substance here is much closer to the novella form than to a truly dramatic genre',[143] that old reactions die hard. On the other hand there are those who see in Ginzburg's reliance on the power of speech alone to hold and maintain the attention of her audience something which has a significance and a fascination of its own; thus Raul Radice believes she has done well to 'ignore much of what is happening in the contemporary theatre' and 'rely on her own ear for the dramatic transcript of a language within which resides the secret of her narrative powers and beneath which one senses the presence of something unsaid', suggesting that the structure of her apparently aimless dialogue is in reality carefully planned;[144] and Ettore Capriolo proclaims the text of her first play to be '"custom-made" . . . able to subsist without any concessions to normal theatrical conventions' in a language which remains 'fresh and elegant'.[145]

If the absence of a conventional plot structure, itself a disconcerting phenomenon by traditional standards, necessarily focuses an audience's attention even more closely on the texts of these plays, little reassurance is forthcoming, at least at first, from this sphere. Ginzburg's protagonists not only do very little; they appear to spend all their time either passing comments of the utmost banality or indulging themselves in extremely long speeches whose ostensible recipients are reduced to the level of passive listeners unable to contribute in any meaningful way to what passes for communication.[146] Closer attention to the text reveals, however, that while the exchanges between characters may well be trivial if viewed in isolation they are in no way an end in themselves, but are clearly chosen with care in order that, little by little, they should contribute to the emergence of distinctive personalities whose interaction creates a lively tension in no way inferior to the more obvious appeal provided by a sequence of events. The result is a delicate and subtle presentation of recognisable human types who are also individuals, caught up in relationships which they cannot control or do not fully understand but which are none the less crucial to their existence, faced with problems they struggle to resolve, usually unsuccessfully, and whose implications are no less striking for being expressed verbally rather than through physical confrontation or dramatic action.

This concentration on verbal exchange as a means for the communication of complex states of mind and emotional tension is a technique well suited to the exposure of truths normally kept hidden during contact with our fellows; just as an attentive listener can recognise feelings of hostility or affection beneath the bland surface of casual conversation in someone he has known well over a period of time so a skilful author can, likewise, reveal what lies behind 'daily chit-chat which betrays our true personalities, wretched and insignificant', exposing 'the neuroses, the frustrations, the anguish hidden behind a phrase like "Nice day, isn't it?"'.[147] In addition to this approach, occasionally interspersed with moments in which characters speak their mind in order to release their tension or to come to grips with their problems, Ginzburg also employs a device usually associated with classical drama and avoided by most modern playwrights: the soliloquy, in which characters describe at length their past experiences, their childhood, or the background to their present situation, once more inevitably straining the patience of the audience, and, apparently, holding up the development of the plot. Here, too, much critical reaction has been unfavourable, and for the same reasons, producing comments such as those of Paolo Lucchesini, who regrets that 'her characters are totally literary and live in their images reflected in long monologues instead of coming to the forefront of things through closely-knit and sparkling dialogue'.[148]

Such criticism, if understandable on first contact, is, in fact, simplistic, in that it either concentrates on form instead of content, thus losing sight of the fact that in this day and age there are no longer any rigid rules governing what happens in the theatre, or, worse, reveals beneath an apparent tolerance of what is unconventional a patronising attitude which is no less short-sighted. A more intelligent reaction is that of Martin Esslin, whose unreserved championing of Ginzburg's play *The Advertisement* contributed to its winning the Marzotto Prize in 1968, and whose defence of one of the longest speeches in the whole of her theatre deserves quoting in its entirety for its awareness of a fundamental truth about dramatic writing: that its object is to engage and maintain the attention of the listener at a high level, and any technique that achieves this is more than justified:

> this long speech . . . is indeed a short story, almost a short novel in itself . . . Yet the critics who were laboriously pointing out these very obvious facts nevertheless missed the point. To start a play with a speech lasting forty minutes or more is a highly unorthodox proceeding in drama . . . But a long speech of this kind is not in itself undramatic provided that the tension between the teller of the tale and the listener is palpably present; provided also that there is a tension between what is told and the manner of the telling . . . The audience in the theatre not only hears Teresa's tale, it also watches Elena's reaction . . . This in itself, is already of the essence of drama: The members of the audience are on their own; each has to make up his own mind whether to take Teresa's story as the objective truth or merely a distorted reflection of it in the mind of a kindly but inadequate person.[149]

Ginzburg is clearly aware that it is possible to build up an atmosphere of tension or unease not only by a skilful use of apparently aimless dialogue, which in reality exposes the hidden sentiments of her protagonists, but also by a process of refinement in which important information is communicated through a contact between two individuals which acts an emotional trip-wire, releasing feelings which are crucial for our understanding of a particular relationship or which reveal the limitations of a particular character, and that pour out with an intensity that brooks no interruption until their expression has run its course, these feelings also being dependent on the continued presence of the person who has provoked the outburst by arriving on the scene unexpectedly or by allowing himself to be used as an excuse for self-assertion by someone who has no other outlet for his feelings. The presence of the listener is no mere formality in that these 'virtual monologues' are precisely that: long speeches which are frequently interrupted, albeit briefly, by comments, suggestions, or requests for clarification ensuring that the speaker maintains the emotional drive behind his (or, usually, her) flow, so that, as David Wade has correctly indicated, 'the other party [is] silent, and at the same time incomparably eloquent'.[150] The process is refined even further in three of Ginzburg's later plays: *La segretaria*, written two years after *The Advertisement*, *La porta sbagliata*, from 1968, and *La parrucca*, dated 1971, in which the physical presence of the other party is replaced by the telephone, with the result that the audience hears only the main speaker, a process which sharpens the dramatic effect through a skilful use of the pregnant pause while allowing the listener's attention to focus exclusively on the protagonist. In *La parrucca*, a play in one act, this process is carried to its logical conclusion by having both objects of the protagonist's rambling discourse off stage the whole time: her husband in the bath adjacent to their hotel bedroom and her mother at the other end of the telephone, the only other character (apart from telephone operators) being a chamber-maid who brings in a boiled egg and exits immediately without saying a word. It is tempting, in the light of this process of technical attrition, to suggest a comparison with Samuel Beckett, a writer whose unique combination of humour and despair finds an echo in Ginzburg's theatre and who has likewise written in an increasingly sparse style with the passing of time, though Ginzburg's unfailing modesty might well lead her to deny any affinity with an author of such universally recognised stature.

Ginzburg's discovery in 1965 that she could, after all, write for the theatre, and her resultant awareness that there now existed a further dimension for her creative talent naturally encouraged her to exploit this new medium. Conscious that 'the things I had in mind were more easily expressed in plays than in novels'[151] she wrote her second a mere four months after finishing her first, producing a further half-dozen in the next six years, during which, as is now clear, she gradually completed a further cycle of artistic activity before once more reaching a kind of impasse. If her last play, *La parrucca*, written in 1971, shows no sign of exhaustion or flagging inspiration, its brevity – a mere nine pages of text in the original – takes on a new significance in the light of her comments in an essay written three months previously in which she makes it clear she had lost all faith in her ability to write anything worthwhile, overcoming her embarrassment through a narration in the third person very different from the forthright approach of *My Vocation* in 1949:

> Now that he is old he writes rather slowly. Ten times over he will stop to rewrite what he has written . . . Sometimes he feels he has nothing else to bring out, or else that he still has things which are very complicated, muddled and twisted . . . Now his future is merely a stretch of rough, broken, grassless road. He despises himself . . . he . . . would give away all he had: but sometimes he wonders if he has anything left to give . . . In the past, he did use parts of his own life but he mixed them and built inventions round them . . . His spirit cannot achieve a change like this now, or else it refuses to try.[152]

Unable yet again to fulfil the demands of her vocation Ginzburg published no literary works for all of two years, during which, as she tells us in the above essay, she experienced feelings of nostalgia for happier and more fruitful periods in the past. The background to this new attack of creative sterility is more complex than on previous occasions in that it clearly relates to a general feeling of pessimism no longer restricted to her function as an artist or to her personal circumstances but combined in addition with a strong awareness that the political turmoils of 1968 and their aftermath had assaulted the very fabric of Western society; they had radically altered not only the more superficial aspects of life such as the traditional dictates of fashion and the length of young people's hair, but, more importantly, basic concepts till then taken for granted such as the sanctity of the family and the power of the state, creating a climate in which insecurity and doubt flourished unchecked among the older generation, unable now to rely on the fixed points which had hitherto regulated their lives and unwilling to throw in their lot with the young rebels whose enthusiasm for a brave new world was, as later became clear, unaccompanied by any clear concept of how it might be achieved. This general rejection of traditional values appears to have been little short of traumatic for Ginzburg, whose essential modesty and simplicity of spirit reacted strongly to what she has called 'the absence of a strict adult judgement which can reveal to us all with total precision what sort of person we are';[153] thus was created within her a degree of uncertainty about the world around her and a sense of incompatibility with it which makes it easy to understand how her lack of confidence should extend beyond her own inadequacy to doubts about the continued existence of literature itself, or, more accurately, one of its main elements: the novel. In an essay entitled 'A Hundred Years of Solitude' published in La Stampa in 1969 she discusses the suggestion, particularly strong in some quarters at that time, that the novel was, if not already dead, then certainly in its death-throes, something inevitable in view of its supposedly total lack of contact with the reality of contemporary human existence. This view she identifies as quite misguided despite being depressingly seductive:

> The idea has spread that it is wrong to succumb to novels, that the novel means escape and consolation and we mustn't escape and be consoled but must stand firmly nailed to reality. We are oppressed by a sense of guilt in the face of reality. This sense of guilt makes us fear novels as something that can take us away from reality . . . If we try to write a novel today, we have a feeling

41

that we are doing something nobody wants any more, which is therefore aimed at no one, and this makes our hand weak and our imagination cold and weary . . . [in] *A Hundred Years of Solitude* [there is] no consolation, only a bitter, emphatic awareness of the truth . . . Real novels have the power to take us suddenly into the heart of truth.[154]

We have already mentioned Ginzburg's belief in the importance of truth and its close identification with the concept of reality, and it is clear that the direct expression of these views in 1972 and 1975 (see notes 29 and 30) is here being foreshadowed in a moment in which social and political pressures were threatening the continued existence of a medium she had employed so extensively in past years. If, however, the strength of her feelings and her determination to resist fashionable heresies of the day are clear from her vigorous assurance in this same essay that 'real novels have the gift of being able to restore to us the love of life and the concrete sense of what we want from life', so that despite having 'no visible reason for existence' and being thus 'totally useless' the novel is in fact 'necessary to life, like bread and water',[155] it is not surprising that she should none the less have been affected by the atmosphere of those times and felt profoundly discouraged about her own future as a creative artist,[156] withdrawing into her shell and emphasising the impossibility of dealing with anything other than what is strictly personal; thus in the summer of 1972 we find her stating in an interview that

Nowadays . . . an author can only write in the first person, but we have understood how limiting this is; each one of us is like a man contemplating the universe from a very small outcrop of rock, and all he can write about is what he can hold in his hands and see beneath his feet. He can have no certainty about anything else.[157]

However, at the very same time as she was making such profoundly discouraging statements[158] Ginzburg was preparing a new novel, her first for ten years and one very different from anything she had produced previously. This was to be a book in which the profound pessimism that had gradually enveloped her during the past few years in relation to things both social and artistic found eloquent expression, a work which, while maintaining the traditional format involving plot and impersonal narration, also allowed her to give free rein to her need to concentrate on the first person: an epistolary novel, a genre which flourished in the eighteenth and nineteenth centuries and which in her hands took on a new lease of life. If it is tempting to reproach her for avoiding any mention of this in the interview with Claudio Toscani to which we have just referred the reasons for her silence become more understandable when we read in another exchange, published shortly after the appearance of *Dear Michael* in the spring of 1973, that she felt 'uncomfortable' to start with and overcome by 'deep melancholy':

> I was under the impression that I was no longer able to write novels, and I was also of the opinion that this inability was something general . . . the creative process, which at one time was something fruitful and life-enhancing, now brings us face to face with our most painful losses; we no longer communicate with our fellows, we no longer see a future before us, there are no longer any moral values; in short it gives us the measure of our helplessness and solitude.[159]

Ginzburg is clearly to be congratulated on transforming such essentially negative sentiments into a kind of stimulus for once more putting pen to paper and thus again breaking a mould which this time had threatened to condemn her to permanent silence. Anxious perhaps to exorcise her feelings by expressing them in detail and in depth she describes in this book the gradual disintegration of the links which bind a young man – the Michael of the title – to his family and his environment through a complex interplay of emotional relationships; the structure of the novel provides ample evidence of Ginzburg's feelings in that of the forty-two chapters which make up the book only five consist of a conventional mixture of narration and dialogue, while a further three combine one or both of these with the reproduction of a letter whose content is at the centre of things. In contrast the remaining thirty-four chapters consist exclusively of written communications relating to Michael, a character who never appears in person but whose existence is of crucial importance to all the other protagonists, obliged, as a result of his absence, to communicate with him through a medium which eschews small talk and the trivia of everyday conversation to concentrate instead on what really matters in a relationship, thereby exposing and analysing the deepest and most intimate aspects of their personality; meanwhile Michael himself, in his replies to his various correspondents, reveals a naivety and a lack of foresight which, while touching in their implications, expose mercilessly the limitations and, ultimately, the insignificance of youthful idealism, powerless when confronted by the social and political realities of life in contemporary Western society.

This ability to expose and communicate the essence of personalities and relationships through a technique which combines the traditional omnipotence of the narrator with the capacity to identify directly with each protagonist is something of considerable importance to Ginzburg, anxious here to create a complex whole in which objective and subjective elements are closely intertwined. Her understanding of and sympathy with characters whose defects she ruthlessly exposes is a constant throughout her writing, ensuring that we recognise and understand even those we find pathetic or odious, responding to their basic humanity irrespective of whether or not we are familiar with their background. This reaches its peak in her last work, *The City and the House*, a novel consisting entirely of letters exchanged between a variety of characters whose emotional ties cannot adequately resolve a basic incompatibility, here skilfully symbolised by the distance between, on the one hand, urban and rural environments and, on the other, an even greater separation, both literally and metaphorically, between Europe and the United States. It is clear with the benefit of hindsight that in the ten years following the publication of *Dear Michael* Ginzburg had become increasingly aware of the power of the letter as a means of in-depth examination, an awareness doubtless confirmed in her work on the Manzoni papers, in which, as indicated, the deliberate absence of any degree of selection within the material at her disposal, together with the need to locate people and events in their historical context, resulted in a work over-endowed with factual information and an exaggerated respect for the frequently tedious expressions of a great man and his domestic ties. No longer restricted by a predetermined range of plot and characterisation, and no longer inhibited by excessive admiration for her subject, Ginzburg has this time used her freedom to create a wide range of well-defined individuals whose communications she has likewise structured in such a way as to reveal their inner essence in a masterly exposition of thoughts and feelings which has rightly been described as 'clipped, deadpan, clear, seemingly impulsive but in reality extremely controlled and sure of its effects';[160] one critic has indeed gone so far as to claim that *The Manzoni Family* is in reality a kind of trial run for *The City and the House*, defining Ginzburg's research in relation to the former as 'merely the workshop in which she has constructed this new book totally rooted in contemporary reality, in characters living here and now and involved in situations that reflect the present day'.[161] If this is perhaps ultimately too extreme a view it none the less finds an echo in an interview with Severino Cesari for *Il Manifesto* in 1984, during which Ginzburg was asked if there is any direct connection between the two works:

> Perhaps there is a connection. I had a strong desire to write in the first person but I also wanted to use the third; I wanted to have the best of both worlds. I wanted to use the first person while writing about someone else, a first person who would be many-sided, multifarious. That's how the letters are. There isn't just a single person describing himself and other people, but a lot of people using the first person and describing themselves ... I think this is the most difficult thing for a writer to accomplish at the present time. A third-person narration is indispensable, but at the same time it's something very difficult to achieve. In our day and age it's no longer possible; there's nothing one can rely on any more ... *The Manzoni Family* is an attempt to write in the third person.[162]

As in *Dear Michael* so too in *The City and the House* characters unable to contact each other directly, and who are thus forced to put pen to paper, find that the process induces a contemplative state of mind in which they can analyse their deepest sentiments, convey intimate truths about themselves, and lose all inhibition in what they feel able and willing to impart. Their lack of familiarity with this traditional means of communication in a social context where it has largely been replaced by the telephone paradoxically acts as a liberating factor as they discover that an essential prerequisite for composing a letter is concentration of the mind, in contrast to what happens on the phone, where, as Ginzburg herself puts it, 'people talk without thinking, without addressing each other with appropriate care or sensitivity'.[163] The result is an increasingly subtle exploration of a hitherto unknown dimension in which each writer finds he can analyse and clarify his behaviour, his experience, and his very nature not only to his correspondents but also, in the process, to himself, so that ultimately 'the characters do not so much correspond with each other as commune with their own isolation'.[164] Opinions differ as to whether Ginzburg has succeeded in establishing recognisable and contrasting personalities for each of these characters, especially since she is on record as stating that while wanting 'each person to speak in the first person and the facts described to leap off the page, each having his own precise individuality, I didn't want and wouldn't have been able to use a different style of expression for each one';[165] thus Dick Davis, while describing the book as 'an excellent novel', ends his review by drawing attention to 'a stylistic problem ... Though the characters ... write their letters in recognizably distinct styles many of them tend to write like their creator much of the time';[166] in contrast Maria Teresa Giuffré praises the ability with which Ginzburg has managed to distinguish between her protagonists through 'a style which never varies' but which conceals 'an individual approach to things, a distinct train of thought which springs from a careful study of human behaviour'.[167]

If this last offering by Ginzburg confirms beyond any doubt the essential pessimism of her declining years it has also given rise to statements and declarations which indicate equally clearly that she is once more reconciled with her vocation and at peace with the demands of her artistic talent. In her 1970 essay on creative writing her lack of confidence in her ability extends not only to doubts about her future as an author but also backwards to the tangible evidence of her past activities, here seen as essentially negative, so much so that she speaks of experiencing 'a slight shudder' at the sight of her books in print, adding that she hopes 'other people will like them';[168] now in the closing decades of the twentieth century she can, in complete contrast, express a genuine and unashamed satisfaction at hearing that her complete works are to be reprinted by Mondadori in a series devoted to great writers of all time, indicating that they will thus be 'protected' and, in their chronological sequence, 'provide evidence of how I have developed'.[169] In the same way her despairing lament concerning her inability to combine truth with fiction is now happily contradicted by a return to her familiar technique of 'combining things I've seen or experienced with things I've invented'[170] and an awareness that 'now more than ever I need to attach myself to things I've seen and people I've known', confirming that 'in this novel too the protagonists are fictional but contain characteristics of people I've met during my life'.[171] Our suggestion that Ginzburg's regeneration was the result of her capacity to derive a new kind of inspiration from the pessimism that enveloped her in the aftermath of 1968 would seem to be confirmed not merely by the content of *Dear Michael* but also by two short novels published in 1977, *Borghesia* and *Family*, both of which have as their main protagonist an individual already in middle age and involved in domestic or emotional relationships which are essentially negative or destructive. There is here a significant difference *vis-à-vis* Ginzburg's presentation of Michael's mother, whose separation from her son gradually leads her, through a process of self-analysis and a constructive evocation of her past life, to a kind of spiritual maturity that we deduce will help her survive the shock of

Michael's death; in contrast both protagonists of these later works, ground down by a succession of emotional shocks from which there is nothing to be learned other than a progressively deeper awareness that decay and disintegration are at the centre of human life, appropriately end their own existence while still in middle age after developing cancer, their deaths confirming the sense of futility that is the dominating characteristic of these tales. This grim pessimism is perhaps already discernible in the so-called 'mini-novel' *Lessico famigliare No. 2*, published in two instalments in *Corriere della sera* in 1975, where Ginzburg evokes memories of her childhood which, following an initial period of contentment in infancy, are largely unhappy; she emphasises her shyness, her hatred of school, her feelings of inferiority when confronted by other children, and, after an intermediate stage during which she succeeded in making friends and composing poetry, an awareness of the essentially bleak nature of human existence:

I suddenly stopped writing poetry. I also stopped being friends with Bianca. I was no longer in love with anyone. I no longer wept tears, I was no longer racked by melancholy, I no longer had any friends. I saw the whole universe as an enormous desert, bleak and parched, and I stood in this desert . . . waiting for something to happen, waiting for this bleak and unbearable coldness to vanish from my spirit.[172]

This progression through the different stages of childhood accompanied by an increasing realisation that life, while providing deeply contrasting emotions, is essentially dominated by melancholy, can be seen as a kind of *éducation sentimentale* apparent in much of Ginzburg's creative writing; but it is especially noticeable in *Borghesia* and *Family*, where the protagonists' gradual emotional and spiritual impoverishment leads them to a similar immobility, both literal and metaphorical, from which the only escape is death. It seems clear that in transferring her attention from her own experience to the creation of a fictional context Ginzburg found it easier to maintain the narrative method she had found appropriate in her second *Lessico*, extending and refining it to produce a complex whole incorporating descriptions of events, the reactions of the characters concerned, and a limited use of dialogue. The result is a strangely haunting style which defies analysis; as Isabel Quigly has perceptively stated: '[The characters] are not described very closely, yet the flat phrases used about them take on an extraordinary vividness: an anorak, a hairstyle, a way of walking, why are they memorable and seemingly familiar?'[173]

The intense gloom that characterises *Borghesia* and *Family* and which leads inexorably to the triumph of death leaves scant space for the exercise of Ginzburg's lively sense of humour, and if none the less it appears more than one would imagine possible or appropriate this is clearly because even in her blackest moments she has rarely lost sight of the discovery that her characters should always be 'funny and at the same time sad'.[174] The effective absence of this element from *The Manzoni Family* – something which contributes in no small way to the book's tediousness, as we have hinted – is perhaps an indication that Ginzburg's pessimism had gradually overshadowed all other sentiments in the interim, and that at this point in her life she would have been unable to create fictional characters who were other than symbols of utter despair. In the absence of any tangible evidence we can do no more than suggest that the preparation of this curious book, so radically different from anything she had produced before, served as a kind of emotional and spiritual therapy enabling her, through total immersion in a historical period other than her own and among characters whose personalities and whose very lives were already established, to regain some kind of equilibrium which in turn allowed her to resume her usual style of creative writing in *The City and the House*. Here too there is much unhappiness, there is death, there is estrangement, but no longer the oppressive atmosphere which dominates in *Borghesia* and *Family*, and no longer the feeling that the author's intention is to present characters who are doomed to failure in every aspect of their lives. Instead we have a collection of people whose attempts at self-realisation in a variety of spheres and through a wide range of actions, usually abortive, create a touchingly humorous picture of human weakness in which hope springs eternal[175] and the contradictory aspects of human nature appear in a context which is instantly recognisable whatever the circumstances and whether or not we are familiar with the various environments in which the events take place. At the end of the book the two ex-lovers have undergone several deeply painful experiences, but they have survived and are ready to face the future, in which their paths may cross once more; Lucrezia's last letter to Giuseppe, in which she recalls his appearance in terms which are both moving and comical, confirms the impression, apparent throughout the novel, that Ginzburg is once more in complete control of her talent, and encourages us to hope she may continue to be productive in her old age.

As will by now be clear Ginzburg's essays are often a source of useful information about her innermost feelings and a key to the understanding of what lies behind her creative writing, but they are not, of course, restricted to this one subject, covering a wide range of ideas and providing significant comments both on general principles for living, and, frequently, specific events which reflect on the times we live in, and, more particularly, the society she herself inhabits. In contrast to the pattern of her other work, where, as already indicated, periods of fruitfulness alternate with moments of discouragement and sterility, her activity in this area has shown a constant if irregular development of a skill enabling her to make her mark in journalism as well as in the more demanding field of artistic composition.

Her first essays, or, at least, the earliest ones available for consultation, show an intense personal involvement in her subject matter and are clearly the result of strong feelings which impelled her to put pen to paper. Thus *Winter in the Abruzzi* evokes the love–hate relationship which characterised her exile to the depressed south during the war and ends with an explicit reference to her husband's arrest and death, together with the moving statement that while throughout her time in Pizzoli 'I believed in a simple and happy future, rich with hopes that were fulfilled, with experiences and plans that were shared' she is now aware 'that was the best time of my life, and only now that it has gone from me forever – only now do I realize it';[176] *Worn-Out Shoes*, written a year later in 1945, describes the poverty of the immediate post-war period in the capital, this time contrasting the wretchedness of daily existence with hopes for her children's future in a more reflective and less anguished tone;[177] while *The Son of Man*, written in 1946, considers the implications of the painful maturity which the war and its upheavals have visited upon the younger generation, ever mindful of the fact that there is no such thing as absolute security, whether literally or metaphorically, in contrast to the reactions of older people, who are anxious to surrender themselves once more to the consoling myths of a more naive society whose fixed points of reference have disappeared for ever.[178] At this stage in her life Ginzburg appears to have had little or no conception of using the essay as a predetermined means of communication with her fellows, indeed proclaiming her inability to do so in *My Vocation*, written in 1949:

If I try to write a critical essay or an article that has been commissioned for a newspaper I don't do it very well. I have to search laboriously, as it were outside myself for what I am

49

writing ... And I always feel that I am cheating the reader with words that I have borrowed or filched from various places. I suffer and feel that I am in exile.[179]

and it is interesting to compare this statement with one made twenty-five years later, in which Ginzburg makes it clear that she had subsequently learned to reconcile her intuitive desire to express herself in writing with the demands of journalism; though still finding it difficult to write to order the pleasure she derives from doing so when stimulated now threatens to bring forth a never-ending stream of articles and essays:

> Sometimes the thought of having to write an article is something unbearable, sometimes it makes me wildly enthusiastic ... [sometimes] I've felt I'm drowning in a sea of paper; at other times I've polished off an article in a single morning ... what I enjoy doing ... is setting down everything which passes through my mind ... I may reach a point where everything that passes through my mind becomes the basis for an article, and I don't quite know what I can do to prevent this happening.[180]

Ginzburg began to write regularly for the arts pages of quality newspapers in the mid-1960s, partly because of a specific request to do so which she presumably felt unwilling to turn down, but, more importantly it seems, in view of 'a commitment I had taken on above all with myself', perhaps because 'I could not find any trace within me of a capacity to fulfil an obligation where writing was concerned',[181] in other words as a kind of attempt at self-discipline. The obstacle to her achieving this aim was similar to that preventing her from writing for the theatre: a reluctance to enter into direct contact with a public whose nature is essentially different from that of the solitary reflective reader attracted to the novel, a public eager instead to establish 'a rapport which is, so to speak, drenched in sunlight, because a newspaper article immediately becomes a target for agreement and dissent, unlike a book'.[182] The stimulus for undertaking this task and persevering with it was thus essentially moral as well as practical, as is clear from her detailed list of the various impulses recollected in tranquillity following the publication in 1974 of her third collection of essays under the title *Vita immaginaria*:

> The laborious satisfaction a novelist derives from writing literary articles for newspapers springs from his repugnance for the uncompromising openness of his relationship with his readers, his

fear of writing badly under pressure and in a state of agitation, his desire to bury pressure and agitation within the deepest recesses of his soul while annihilating within himself all desire for approval or anxiety at the possibility of rejection, and his need to write as he has always written, that is to say calmly and without undue haste, and to establish a mysterious and hidden rapport with his readers.[183]

In short Ginzburg wishes to engage in journalism with the same fluidity that characterises her literary work, and, despite the essential differences involved in both composition and reception, to achieve a form of communication which can combine a degree of immediacy appropriate to an essentially ephemeral medium with her usual appeal to the deeper and more fundamental interests of her readers. The most obvious of these differences is clearly the very nature of the essay, in which the writer expresses himself no longer through the veil of a fictional narrative but directly, something which necessarily places his own views at the centre of whatever subject he chooses to write on. If this is in one sense a restricting factor it also clearly makes for greater freedom of expression and greater concentration within this area; thus it comes as no surprise to find Ginzburg stating that while her fictional characters are a combination of memory and invention 'they never contain within them everything I carry in my mind', while in contrast 'When I write an essay nothing is invented and the real me is there for all to see.'[184]

This emphasis on the total exposure of the personality is, of course, consistent with Ginzburg's interest in the workings of the human mind and the analysis of the human personality so apparent in her creative writing. Together with the essential simplicity of language which characterises all her production it results in a straightforward and uncomplicated presentation of ideas and suggestions which have been received with mixed feelings by the critical establishment, more accustomed to a traditional complexity of style and a more impersonal approach to one's subject. Thus Olga Lombardi stresses how the regular use of the first person makes Ginzburg 'a collaborator rather than a judge' in relation to her subjects, and identifies what she sees as 'a feminine inability to . . . consider things objectively', something which makes the author 'incapable of analysing things strictly in a way which has any critical validity'.[185] In contrast these same characteristics are seen by other critics as a breath of fresh air, infusing life into a genre too long associated with dry scholarly pronouncements; thus Domenico Porzio

praises Ginzburg's 'lack of intellectual astuteness' and 'her innocence, which has nothing naive about it', drawing attention to 'the
confident clarity of her exposition' which he goes on to describe,
significantly, as 'a scandalous ability to make herself understood'.[186]

The exact number of articles appearing in print under Ginzburg's
name is difficult to establish, there being no comprehensive listing
available for consultation. The most easily accessible are of course
those reprinted, together with some new material, in her three
anthologies *The Little Virtues, Never Must You Ask Me*, and *Vita
immaginaria*, and which presumably represent a kind of microcosm of
her activity in this genre through which she is content to remain
identified. With the passing of time Ginzburg has widened her range
of subjects as a source of inspiration, and if her basic point of
departure is still invariably a personal one she has increasingly used
this as a starting point for considerations which relate to the ideas,
the feelings, and the experiences of her contemporaries in the world
around her; thus she writes on such varied themes as the education
of children, the difficulty of establishing fruitful human relationships, the Anglo-Saxon temperament, the nature of old age, the
existence of God, the female condition, the contradiction she feels
between an instinctive sympathy for things Jewish and antipathy for
the state of Israel, traffic problems in the Roman capital, and so
on.[187] In addition the last two collections also contain reflections on
the work of other writers and film directors such as Emily Dickinson,
Mario Soldati, Samuel Beckett, Elizabeth Smart, John Schlesinger,
Ingmar Bergman, and Federico Fellini.[188] If the increased pessimism we have indicated as characteristic of her development in
creative writing is also apparent here – most strikingly perhaps in
her affirmation in the essay entitled *Vita immaginaria* that 'as we grow
old a sense of inevitability comes to accompany us throughout our
daily lives'[189] – this if anything sharpens Ginzburg's ability to
communicate what has rightly been called 'a personal and private
discovery of the reasons behind our painful and distorted existence'[190] and to undertake 'an analysis of our time and its
misfortunes'.[191]

Notes

1. Natalia Ginzburg (hereafter NG) in an interview with Alda Gasparini published in *La fiera letteraria*, XLVIII, no. 40, 1 Oct. 1972, p. 9, entitled 'Incontro con NG. Ai concerti si addormenta'.
2. NG in an interview with Luciano Simonelli published in *Domenica del corriere*, 30 Jan. 1975, p. 51, entitled 'Intervista-confessione con la più polemica scrittrice italiana: "Oggi i bambini vivono soffocati dalle troppe paure dei genitori"'.
3. See the Preface to *Cinque romanzi brevi*, p. 5.
4. See her comment in an interview with Raffaello Baldini published in *Panorama*, 3 May 1973, p. 135, entitled 'Questo mondo non mi piace: Intervista con NG': 'The books I write have no particular purpose. If I had to explain why I write them I wouldn't know what to say . . . When I write novels I invent things and have no particular aim in mind.'
5. E.g. Irving Wardle, who in 'Unhappy Opening Night for new season', *The Times*, 25 Sept. 1968, p. 9, defined the staging of *The Advertisement* at the National Theatre as 'a disgrace', a judgement contrasting strongly with views expressed over twenty years later in the review of a Paris production in which the title of the play had been changed to *Teresa*: 'A solidly constructed play, it has plenty of astute observation . . . and . . . biting humour . . . shot through with withering one-liners'; see D. Hill, 'Bitter-sweet sensuality', *The Times*, 9 Feb. 1989, p. 20.
6. See her comment in Baldini, 'Questo mondo non mi piace', p. 132: 'I realised I would always be extremely ignorant . . . I have no cultural knowledge'; p. 134: 'Out of laziness I tend to make do with low-quality things: second-rate books, second-rate films . . .'.
7. D. Maraini, *E tu chi eri?* (Bompiani, Milan, 1973), p. 121.
8. See her comment in Baldini, 'Questo mondo non mi piace', p. 132: 'I have to express myself clearly and explain everything.'
9. Ibid., p. 131.
10. See the Preface to *Cinque romanzi brevi*, p. 5. The same phrase occurs in an interview with Silvia Del Pozzo published in *Panorama*, 24 Dec. 1984, p. 133, entitled 'Letteratura/Il caso Ginzburg: "Cari amici vi scrivo"'.
11. See *My Vocation* in *The Little Virtues*, p. 54; also her statement in *Family Sayings* in relation to a later period: 'I had not yet decided whether to spend my life studying beetles, chemistry and botany, or whether I would paint pictures or write novels', p. 50.
12. Dick Davis translates *goffe . . . ma abbastanza divertenti* as *clumsy . . . but . . . quite pleasant*; see *My Vocation* in *The Little Virtues*, p. 54.
13. See *Lessico famigliare no. 2: La luna pallidassi*, in *Corriere della sera*, 10 Aug. 1975, p. 8.
14. 'I had written other poems before this one, but they hadn't been sad', ibid.
15. *The Little Virtues*, p. 54.
16. *Lessico famigliare no. 2: Il cocchio d'oro*, in *Corriere della sera*, 17 Aug. 1975, p. 8.

17. *My Vocation* in *The Little Virtues*, p. 57.
18. Preface to *Cinque romanzi brevi*, p. 8.
19. See the Author's Preface to the novel, where she states 'ever since my childhood and adolescence I have always intended to write a book which would tell the story of the people who lived through those times with me. This is to some extent that book . . .', p. 7.
20. Preface to *Cinque romanzi brevi*, p. 5.
21. *My Vocation* in *The Little Virtues*, p. 58.
22. Preface to *Cinque romanzi brevi*, p. 6. The story is entitled *Un'assenza*.
23. *My Vocation* in *The Little Virtues*, p. 58. Two years after writing this essay Ginzburg stated in the Preface to *Cinque romanzi brevi* 'I don't remember if at the time I thought I'd written a good story', stressing instead her 'pride and amazement at having brought it to a conclusion', p. 6.
24. Preface to *Cinque romanzi brevi*, p. 16.
25. She mentions in ibid. that her dissatisfaction with one of her long short stories, *Sagittarius*, derives from the fact that she had to labour over it in order that it might be finished.
26. Ibid., p. 13.
27. R. Signorelli Pappas, Review of E. Clementelli, *Invito alla lettura di NG*, in *Forum Italicum*, vol. IX, nos. 2–3 (1975), p. 327.
28. D. Porzio, *Primi piani*, (Mondadori, Milan, 1976), p. 76.
29. See her comment in Gasparini, 'Incontro con NG'.
30. 'Raccontare i fatti propri', *Corriere della sera*, 10 May 1975, p. 3.
31. Ginzburg quotes as an example of this the opening of *Remembrance of Times Past*, pointing out with characteristic wit that if Proust had stopped to think that no one could possibly be interested in what time he went to bed in the evening he would not have written his masterpiece.
32. Ibid.
33. 'Chiarezza e oscurità', *Corriere della sera*, 22 Sept. 1974, p. 3.
34. 'Lo stile d'acqua', *Corriere della sera*, 20 July 1975, p. 3.
35. See the last paragraph of this article, where she speaks of 'a frail story-line in which everything has the moving quality of truth'; also her interview with Enzo Biagi published in *Corriere della sera*, 16 March 1975, p. 3, and entitled 'Incontro con le protagoniste italiane: la Ginzburg. Natalia, che cos'è il femminismo?', in which she claims the most important thing for an individual is '"The search for truth"'.
36. 'Dialogando con Landolfi', *Corriere della sera*, 21 June 1975, p. 3.
37. Preface to *Cinque romanzi brevi*, pp. 9–10.
38. See *Portrait of a Writer* in *Never Must You Ask Me*, p. 164.
39. *My Vocation* in *The Little Virtues*, p. 59. A similar procedure, though with positive results, is described by Barbara Pym on p. 386 of a radio talk entitled 'Finding a Voice', published in *Civil to Strangers and other writings* (Macmillan, London, 1987) pp. 381–8, in which she also mentions that 'I learned . . . how the novelist could even do "field-work" as the anthropologist did', p. 384.
40. See also *Portrait of a Writer* in *Never Must You Ask Me* where she describes how in youth she wrote with a clarity and sharpness that

was 'false' in that the world she saw before her was 'veiled in fog', p. 165. The painter is perhaps Carlo Levi; see 'Ricordo di Carlo Levi', *Corriere della sera*, 8 Jan. 1975, p. 3, where Ginzburg writes 'He was the only painter I had ever known well as a person, and I also saw him at his work' in her account of her contact with Levi, 'a friend of my brothers', when she was still a young girl.

41. *My Vocation* in *The Little Virtues*, p. 61.

42. NG in an interview with Ennio Cavalli published in *La fiera letteraria*, 30 March 1975, p. 11, entitled 'Intervista con NG: "Capisco solo la poesia"'.

43. Preface to *Cinque romanzi brevi*, p. 8.

44. *My Vocation*, in *The Little Virtues*, p. 60.

45. Ibid., p. 61.

46. Ibid., p. 58.

47. Ibid., pp. 61–2.

48. Ibid., p. 62; see also the opening paragraph of *Portrait of a Writer* in *Never Must You Ask Me*, where Ginzburg states that during her youth she experienced guilt feelings when writing because she felt she should be more cultivated and study 'in order to write more seriously', p. 162.

49. *Portrait of a Writer* in *Never Must You Ask Me*, pp. 164–5.

50. See *The Little Virtues*, p. 62.

51. Preface to *Cinque romanzi brevi*, p. 10.

52. See ibid., p. 11.

53. See her comment in *Portrait of a Writer* in *Never Must You Ask Me*, where she speaks of choosing aspects of real life and building inventions round them 'so that the few features of it . . . used became unrecognisable, not just to others but to [the author] himself', p. 167.

54. Preface to *Cinque romanzi brevi*, pp. 12–13.

55. Olga Lombardi, 'NG' in G. Grana (ed.), *Novecento: I contemporanei. Gli scrittori e la cultura letteraria nella società italiana* (10 vols, Marzorati, Milan, 1979), vol. 8, p. 7622; see also *My Vocation* in *The Little Virtues*: 'I put a few invented people into *The Road to the City* and a few real people from the countryside where we were living; and some of the words that came to me as I was writing were idioms and imprecations local to that area . . . and these new expressions were like a yeast that fermented and gave life to all the old words', p. 63.

56. NG in an interview with Claudio Toscani published in *Il raguaglio librario*, XXXIX, no. 6 (1972), p. 210, entitled 'Incontro con NG'; the statement echoes her affirmation in *Portrait of a Writer* in *Never Must You Ask Me* that for an author writing 'In the best moments . . . was and . . . is like living on this earth', p. 168.

57. Preface to *Cinque romanzi brevi*, p. 12.

58. NG in an interview with Delia Lennie published in *Posso presentarle?* (Longman, London, 1971) entitled 'Una scrittrice: NG', p. 68.

59. Toscani, 'Incontro con NG', p. 210.

60. M. Rago, 'Le "virtù" di NG', *L'Unità*, 19 Dec. 1962, p. 6.

61. Dick Davis translates differently on p. 68 of *The Little Virtues*.

62. *I bambini* and *Giulietta*, both published in 1934; see Chapters 2 and 5 respectively. In both cases the emphasis is on the degrading behaviour

of the character at the centre of things.

63. Preface to *Cinque romanzi brevi*, p. 14.
64. *My Vocation* in *The Little Virtues*, p. 65.
65. Preface to *Cinque romanzi brevi*, p. 14.
66. *The Little Virtues*, pp. 65–6.
67. See also her statement in the Preface to *Cinque romanzi brevi*: 'Unhappiness must not be something which fills us with tearful and anguished incomprehension but rather an awareness that is absolute, relentless, and basic', p. 15.
68. See also her statement in ibid.: 'I know to what extent this novel is well written and not *fortuitous*. But I also know how far it is *fortuitous* . . .', p. 14.
69. *My Vocation* in *The Little Virtues*, p. 66.
70. Preface to *Cinque romanzi brevi*, p. 16; on the same page she states 'I had conceived a profound loathing for direct speech.'
71. NG in an interview with Oriana Fallaci published in *L'Europeo*, 14 July 1963, p. 40, entitled 'L'Europeo interroga NG: Parole in famiglia'.
72. Preface to *Cinque romanzi brevi*, p. 16.
73. See her statement in ibid.: 'nostalgia is always accompanied by a desire to start writing', p. 17.
74. See in this context I. Thomson, 'Spinsters in Italy', *Independent*, 21 Dec. 1987, p. 14: 'Both [Compton-Burnett and Ginzburg] have composed books almost entirely of dialogue, conjuring up a whole world without going to the lengths of actually describing it: both employ a deceptively simple, anti-rhetorical prose which is sharpened, like the claws of a cat, with an ironical wit that is nicely feline'; see also note 160.
75. *La Grande Signorina* in *Never Must You Ask Me*, p. 89.
76. Ibid., p. 90; see also Pym, 'Finding a Voice', p. 383: 'Another author I came across . . . was Ivy Compton-Burnett . . . Of course I couldn't help being influenced by her dialogue, that precise formal conversation which seemed so stilted when I first read it – though when I got used to it, a friend and I took to writing to each other entirely in that style.'
77. Preface to *Cinque romanzi brevi*, p. 16.
78. *La Grande Signorina* in *Never Must You Ask Me*, p. 90.
79. Preface to *Cinque romanzi brevi*, p. 17.
80. P. Milano, 'NG: La vita come attrito', *L'Espresso*, 2 July 1961, p. 17.
81. G. Pullini, *Volti e risvolti del romanzo italiano contemporaneo* (Mursia, Milan, 1974), p. 194.
82. W. Mauro, 'Un romanzo di NG: *Le voci della sera*', *Il Paese*, 21 July 1961, p. 3.
83. B. Brophy, 'Onto the Cart', *New Statesman*, 2 Aug. 1963, p. 147.
84. G. Freeman, 'Fan Fare', *Spectator*, 2 Aug. 1963, p. 155.
85. J. Brooke, book review, *Listener*, 15 Aug. 1963, p. 249.
86. F. Antonicelli, book review, *Radiocorriere-TV*, XXVIII, no. 42, 15–21, Oct. 1961, p. 25.
87. G. Vigorelli, book review, *Tempo*, 22 July 1961, p. 62.
88. N. Sapegno, *Compendio di storia della letteratura italiana*, 12th edn

(3 vols, La Nuova Italia, Florence, 1959–60), vol. 3, p. 408.

89. This attitude extends beyond literary criticism to journalism and the media, e.g. news bulletins on state radio and television, where Italians use a highly specialised code familiar to any foreigner who has tried unsuccessfully to skim through a leading article or absorb the gist of a political report. In this context see Ginzburg's article 'Dell'acqua e del pane', *Belfagor*, XXXIX, no. 3 (1984), p. 333: 'How different is the language in which our laws are formulated from that of the man in the street, how far removed from everthing that ordinary people dream of, hope for, and seek . . . laws should be formulated in the same words we use when we speak of bread and water . . . when it comes to novels, poetry, the theatre, it's important to distinguish each time between impenetrable language which derives from laborious analysis, from genuine complexity of thought, and obfuscation, which is simply and solely a smoke-screen designed to conceal lack of inspiration . . . But when it comes to newspapers, to newspapers! Clarity is of the essence. People buy them and read them every day to learn and to understand what's happening in the world, and they must be easy to understand. And when politicians make statements they should be clear statements that anyone can understand, understand at once, clear as a bell . . .'

90. See her comments in 'Dialogando con Landolfi', *Corriere della sera*, 21 June 1975, p. 3, where she comments that the author's 'preciosity' of language succeeds in 'transporting words into the highest region of thought'.

91. Lennie, *Posso presentarle?*, p. 70.

92. See her comment in Baldini, 'Questo mondo non mi piace', p. 132; 'When I write I'm always afraid of not expressing myself clearly enough.'

93. Lennie, *Posso presentarle?*, p. 71.

94. Preface to *Cinque romanzi brevi*, p. 8.

95. Ibid., p. 12.

96. Toscani, 'Incontro con NG', p. 210.

97. ' "I temi che io avrei scelto" '. *Corriere della sera*, 3 July 1975, p. 1.

98. 'Un corteo di dinosauri', *Corriere della sera*, 6 July 1976, p. 3. See also her comments in the 1972 essay *Senza fate e senza maghi*, reprinted in *Vita immaginaria*, p. 163: 'nothing is more instructive than a style which is clear, fluent, and true to life'; also her statement in a note entitled 'Parole povere', *Tuttolibri*, VI, no. 12, 29 March 1980, p. 7: 'I believe we are undergoing a real crisis in communication; society is changing and writers and authors no longer know who they are writing for. There is undoubtedly a growing distrust in the power of words.' In this context it is interesting to note comments made by the anonymous reviewer of *Family Sayings* in 'Un-Italian Activities', *Times Literary Supplement*, 23 Feb. 1967, p. 149: 'Her style in so self-consciously stylistic a country, is a non-style . . . she writes conversationally (some say chattily) with an apparent simplicity that is in fact dense and suggestive; what she says seems transparent, but when you peer through it you find implied an almost disturbing richness. It is in this capacity to mean much while saying little . . . that her

quality and above all her originality lie.'

99. '"I temi che io avrei scelto"', *Corriere della sera*, 3 July 1975, p. 1; see also her statement in *My Vocation* in *The Little Virtues*, p. 54: 'My vocation is to write stories . . . things that are concerned only with memory and imagination and have nothing to do with erudition.'

100. 'L'intelligenza', *Corriere della sera*, 20 Oct. 1974, p. 3.

101. *Moravia* in *Vita immaginaria*, p. 25.

102. Cavalli, 'Intervista con NG', p. 10.

103. See her statement in Fallaci, 'L'Europeo interroga NG', p. 40, that 'a woman must write like a woman but should have the qualities of a man', which she defines as 'writing with masculine detachment and disinterest' without 'pretending to be a man oneself', a formula which encapsulates the essential ingredients of her style: the depiction of reality or truth through a form of narration in which memory and imagination combine in a climate of emotional participation. Fallaci comments on p. 41 that the difficulties involved in possessing the qualities of both sexes is one reason why there are fewer women who write and who write well than there are men.

104. Ibid., p. 36; see also her statement in *Portrait of a Writer* in *Never Must You Ask Me*, p. 163, that when writing in her youth she felt the need to 'hurry to reach a conclusion', and that since she was frequently unable to finish what she had started completion was the most important object of the exercise.

105. 'Fra guerra e razzismo', *Corriere della sera*, 25 May 1975, p. 3.

106. Preface to *Cinque romanzi brevi*, p. 10.

107. Biagi, 'Incontro con le protagoniste italiane'.

108. This interview, entitled 'Intervista alla scrittrice NG: "Mi sento il Bartali dell'editoria"', is published in *Tuttolibri*, n.s., VII, no. 269 (9 May 1981), p. 1. See also her statement in *Portrait of a Writer* in *Never Must You Ask Me*, p. 163: 'When he stopped writing he spent years without doing any. He had lost or forgotten his way to it . . . he felt he had betrayed his old plans and told himself that he had a duty to write again.'

109. Gasparini, 'Incontro con NG'.

110. Cavalli, 'Intervista con NG', p. 10. See also her statement in Lennie, *Posso presentarle?*, p. 69: 'When I work I work a great deal, a great deal, I sleep very little, I work hard.' Her claim in the same paragraph that she writes only when she feels like it needs to be seen in this context, despite the fact that she then adds 'Sometimes I go for years without writing, years and years', and we may note that Ginzburg had published two plays in 1970 and 1971, the date of this interview, as well as a book of essays. Likewise her claim in Baldini, 'Questo mondo non mi piace', p. 134, that 'When I write I always experience pleasure. If I don't experience pleasure I give up immediately' dates from 1973, the same year of the publication of her novel *Dear Michael*.

111. Cavalli, 'Intervista con NG', p. 10.

112. Lennie, *Posso presentarle?*, pp. 69–70.

113. She elaborates on this point in ibid., p. 70: ' . . . when I was about to finish I would think to myself: "How am I going to stand leaving

these places and these people?"' See also *Portrait of a Writer* in *Never Must You Ask Me*, p. 166, where Ginzburg describes how she felt 'sad and lost' on finishing a book and having to detach herself from the places she had described therein 'like a man who has to leave a town where he knows every street and house, and to which he is quite certain he will never return'.

114. Preface to *Cinque romanzi brevi*, p. 17.
115. Ibid.
116. Fallaci, 'L'Europeo interroga NG', p. 36.
117. Preface to *Cinque romanzi brevi*, pp. 17–18.
118. See the Author's Preface, p. 7, where she writes: 'There are also many happenings which I have remembered but have passed over in writing this book.'
119. Foreword, p. 7. She appears to have pursued this aim wholeheartedly, witness her comment that 'my relationships with these people have been similar to my relationships with the characters of my novels' in an interview with Lietta Tornabuoni published in *La Stampa*, 23 Jan. 1983, p. 3, entitled 'NG accusa in un libro l'autore dei "Promessi Sposi": Manzoni, il mostro di famiglia'.
120. See her admission that for some time she had felt her work as an author to be 'extinct, lifeless' in an interview with Carla Stampa published in *Epoca*, no. 1694, 25 March 1983, p. 103, entitled 'A colloquio con NG, autrice de "La famiglia Manzoni": "Confesso, la prima volta che lo lessi Manzoni mi annoiò"'.
121. Extract from the author's presentation inside the dust cover of the original Italian edition.
122. B. Levin, 'Domestic suffocation', *Sunday Times*, 9 Aug. 1987, p. 43.
123. Ibid.
124. See L. Visintin, '"La famiglia Manzoni" della Ginzburg vince il Bagutta', *Corriere della sera*, 26 Nov. 1983, p. 4, and L. Vergani, 'Bagutta-Ginzburg: l'amore per Milano', *Corriere della sera*, 27 Nov. 1983, p. 3; it is perhaps significant that the former recounts how during the celebrations Ginzburg was asked by one of the journalists present whether she saw her book as a novel or an essay. See also her comment in an interview with Antonella Amendola published in *Domenica del corriere*, 16 Feb. 1985, p. 57, entitled 'NG parla di sé e del suo ultimo best seller: "Vi scrivo da un mondo di gente randagia"': '*The Manzoni Family* is not really a novel, though I would like people to read it as they would read a novel . . .'
125. L. Portier, book review, *Revue des Etudes Italiennes*, XXXII, nos 1–4 (1986), p. 173, note 1.
126. Ibid., p. 175.
127. G. Pampaloni, 'I romanzi di Pomilio e della Ginzburg: Manzoni e dintorni', *Il Giornale*, 30 Apr. 1983, p. 3.
128. During her research Ginzburg discovered several previously unpublished letters by Manzoni in the Braidense Library in Milan; see G. Nascimbeni, 'A colloquio con la scrittrice in occasione dell'uscita del suo nuovo libro: Ginzburg: "Il mio Manzoni giù dal piedistallo"', *Corriere della sera*, 5 Feb. 1983, p. 3.
129. S. Romagnoli, 'Il lessico famigliare e i silenzi di casa Manzoni',

Rinascita, no. 21, 27 May 1983, p. 33.

130. See Nascimbeni, 'A colloquio con la scrittrice', who uses this comment as part of the title of his article.
131. Extract from an interview with NG entitled 'Gli scrittori e il teatro' originally published in *Sipario* and quoted in L. Marchionne Picchione, 'NG', *Il Castoro*, no. 137 (1978), pp. 85–6.
132. Ibid., p. 85.
133. Lennie, *Posso presentarle?*, p. 72. Her optimism may be excessive, witness the tendency in the Italian cinema not only to dub foreign films but also to replace the original soundtrack containing strong regional dialogue with one using standard Italian, with predictably grotesque results.
134. See note 89.
135. Lennie, *Posso presentarle?*, p. 72.
136. Extract from the author's Preface to *Ti ho sposato per allegria* in P. Grassi and G. Guerrieri (eds), *Collezione di teatro* (Einaudi, Turin, 1966), pp. 6–7.
137. An obvious example is her mother's frequent comment about liking cheese, one of a series of details that communicate her personality to the reader; see *Family Sayings*, p. 29.
138. Extract from an interview with NG entitled 'Gli scrittori e il teatro' originally published in *Sipario* and quoted in E. Clementelli, *Invito alla lettura di NG* (Mursia, Milan, 1972), p. 92.
139. Lennie, *Posso presentarle?*, p. 73.
140. Clementelli, *Invito alla lettura di NG*, pp. 95–6.
141. M. Garzonio, 'Ginzburg e Moravia, dalla letteratura al teatro', *Vita e pensiero*, no. 49 (1966), p. 1017.
142. Ibid.
143. J. Ricapito, book review, *Books Abroad*, vol. 48, no. 2 (1974), p. 351.
144. R. Radice, book review, *Corriere della sera*, 2 June 1968, p. 11.
145. E. Capriolo, 'La delicata storia di una moglie mitomane', *Vie nuove*, no. 21, 26 May 1966, p. 58; while pronouncing the language 'less resonant and thinner' than in Ginzburg's narrative writing Capriolo none the less sees the play as being successful as a dramatic entity.
146. Ginzburg herself has given some credence to this view by stating that in her first play nothing happens and that the play itself is devoid of meaning, apologising accordingly since 'the absence of meaning always produces disappointment, and rightly so', Preface to *Ti ho sposato per allegria*, p. 8.
147. D. Del Giudice, 'Commedie di NG: Le chiacchiere quotidiane', *Paese sera*, 5 Jan. 1973, p. 4.
148. P. Lucchesini, 'Gli ottimisti di Natalia', *Carlino-Sera*, 5 July 1966, p. 3.
149. M. Esslin, 'Approaches to Reality' in *The New Theatre of Europe* (Delta, New York, 1970), vol. 4, pp. viii–ix. Ironically Ginzburg's own comments reflect those of her less perceptive critics, describing Teresa's monologue as 'a structural error deriving from my inexperience ... I wanted to establish a background to the action, and could only do so through these interminable monologues'; see A. Blandi, '"L'inserzione" ... ritratto di una donna sbagliata', *La Stampa*, 22 Feb. 1969, p. 3, quoted in A. O'Healy, *A Woman Writer in*

Contemporary Italy: NG, typescript of Ph.D. thesis for the University of Wisconsin-Madison 1976, p. 146.

150. D. Wade, 'Grotesque Events', *The Times*, 27 Jan. 1973, p. 10.
151. Lennie, *Posso presentarle?*, p. 73; see also Ginzburg's comments in 'Filo diretto Dessi-Ginzburg', *Corriere della sera*, 10 Dec. 1967, p. 7, quoted in O'Healy, *A Woman Writer*, pp. 141–2: 'Lately I found I could only use the first person when writing novels, and I was bored with writing "I" all the time. I don't believe the novel is on its last legs but I do believe that in this day and age it's impossible to write other than in the first person; to use a third-person narrative in a novel has become impossible . . . writing plays is one solution to this problem as far as I'm concerned.'
152. *Portrait of a Writer* in *Never Must You Ask Me*, pp. 163, 165, 167.
153. Toscani, 'Incontro con NG', p. 211. It is perhaps no coincidence that in 1969 she should have written an essay evoking a 'black summer' immediately after the war when she was undergoing psychoanalysis; see *My Psycho-analysis* in *Never Must You Ask Me*, p. 50.
154. The essay was reprinted in *Never Must You Ask Me*; these extracts appear on pp. 55–7. The title refers to the novel by Gabriel Garcia Marquez.
155. Ibid., p. 57.
156. See her statement in ibid., p. 55: ' . . . even those of us who don't believe it breathe in the idea, submit to it, and suffer it, for it is a subtly contagious idea, and our present human society is oddly subject to contagion; true and false ideas spread and are confused above us like clouds . . . which means we can no longer distinguish the false from the true'; see also *L'unico libro di Elizabeth Smart* in *Vita immaginaria*, p. 39: 'The impulse to construct and organise carefully and in harmony with ourselves and with those around us seems to have vanished from the world . . . we feel like victims and victims don't construct things. Nowadays the novels we write are always or almost always written in a state of chaos and while weeping floods of tears.'
157. Toscani, 'Incontro con NG', p. 211.
158. See *Goffredo Parise* reprinted in *Vita immaginaria*, where she describes a feeling of self-pity because she can no longer undertake creative writing, and an awareness that although this is irrelevant 'when compared with the many many much more important things which should be happening and aren't' (p. 68) she is also conscious that the ability to write creatively was her only talent and feels humiliated now it has deserted her.
159. Baldini, 'Questo mondo non mi piace', p. 129. See also her statement in *Bergman* in *Vita immaginaria*: 'I don't like the age in which I am obliged to live. I don't know if I'd have preferred a different one because there's no way of knowing. What I do know is that I find this age hateful and hate it . . . the desire to tell stories seems to have died and become fossilized', pp. 41–2. Even bleaker are her comments in *Tonino Guerra* in ibid.: ' . . . when we think about starting a novel we're immediately overwhelmed by the feeling that what we invent will be squalid . . . Other people no longer exist. We're alone. We feel

we're standing alone and confronting universal solitudes. For reasons which I'm unable to understand writing novels and communicating with a world which we've invented and constructed ourselves is, nowadays, one of the most wretched and lonely activities one can undertake', pp. 61–2.

160. D. Davis, 'At the breaking-point', *Times Literary Supplement*, 4 Oct. 1985, p. 1115; see also I. Thomson, 'Finely-spun despair', *Sunday Times*, 19 Oct. 1986, p. 54, who speaks of 'a deceptively simple, anti-rhetorical prose'; see also note 74.

161. U. Dotti, 'Nuove lettere da Natalia', *L'Unità*, 15 Dec. 1984, p. 13.

162. The interview was published on 18 Dec. 1984, p. 7, entitled 'NG parla del suo nuovo libro: Ultime lettere di gente comune'; see also an interview with Patrizia Carrano published in *Amica*, no. 11, 12 March 1985, p. 38, entitled 'Lei ha vinto', in which Ginzburg states that in writing *The City and the House* she could no longer use the device of a first-person narrator as in *Dear Michael*, defining this device as 'a kind of concealed third-person approach'; likewise her comments in *Appunti sulla 'Storia'* written all of ten years earlier and reprinted in *Vita immaginaria*: 'In this day and age a novelist is as frightened by the thought of writing in the third person as he would be if confronted by a wild beast. He knows that all kinds of dangers lurk within the third person, within the word "he"', p. 102; the novel referred to in the title is by Elsa Morante.

163. Nascimbeni, 'A colloquio con la scrittrice'.

164. Amendola, 'NG parla di se', p. 57.

165. Ibid., pp. 56–7.

166. Davis, 'At the breaking-point'.

167. M.T. Giuffré, 'Sotto la parola cova la desolazione della vita', *Gazzetta del sud*, 29 Jan. 1985, p. 10.

168. *Portrait of a Writer* in *Never Must You Ask Me*, p. 166.

169. Del Pozzo, 'Letteratura/Il caso Ginzburg', p. 133.

170. Carrano, 'Lei ha vinto', p. 38.

171. Del Pozzo, 'Letteratura/Il caso Ginzburg', p. 131.

172. *Lessico famigliare no. 2: Il cocchio d'oro*, in *Corriere della sera*, 17 Aug. 1975, p. 8.

173. I. Quigly, 'The Low in Spirit', *Times Literary Supplement*, 2 June 1978, p. 607.

174. *My Vocation* in *The Little Virtues*, p. 58.

175. See her comments in *Appunti sulla 'Storia'* in *Vita immaginaria*, p. 107: 'A strange kind of hope seems to emanate from this bleak novel when all is said and done.'

176. *The Little Virtues*, p. 8.

177. Ibid., pp. 9–11.

178. Ibid., pp. 49–52.

179. Ibid., p. 53.

180. 'Elzeviri', *Corriere della sera*, 30 June 1974, p. 3.

181. The quotation is from a short untitled article by NG in the series 'L'autore si confessa', *Epoca*, XXV, no. 1260, 30 Nov. 1974, p. 86.

182. Ibid.

183. Ibid.
184. Toscani, 'Incontro con NG', p. 211.
185. Lombardi, 'NG', p. 7621.
186. D. Porzio, review of *Vita immaginaria* in *Panorama*, no. 450, 5 Dec. 1974, p. 19.
187. See respectively in *The Little Virtues* the essay of the same title, pp. 97–110; *Human Relationships*, pp. 75–95; *England: Eulogy and Lament*, pp. 21–8; in *Never Must You Ask Me* see *Old Age*, pp. 31–5; *On Believing and Not Believing in God*, pp. 143–53; in *Vita immaginaria* see *La condizione femminile*, pp. 182–90; *Gli ebrei*, pp. 174–81; *Infelici nella citta bella e orrenda*, pp. 199–203.
188. See respectively in *Never Must You Ask Me*: *Emily Dickinson's Town*, pp. 40–4; *The Actor*, pp. 120–4; '*Film*', pp. 117–20; in *Vita immaginaria* see *L'unico libro di Elizabeth Smart*, pp. 35–40; *Maledetta domenica*, pp. 47–51; *Bergman*, pp. 41–6; *Amarcord*, pp. 80–7.
189. *Vita immaginaria*, p. 227.
190. Lombardi, 'NG', p. 7619.
191. Ibid., p. 7618.

2 Female Alienation: Childhood and First Youth

Melancholy . . . is the prime characteristic of Ginzburg's fiction . . .[1]

The overwhelming sadness which led Natalia Ginzburg to compose her poem on the death of love at the age of twelve is the first known indication of her most striking characteristic: a preference for themes and situations that are elegiac if not uncompromisingly pessimistic. Once consciously identified five years later as a major stimulus for her creative writing it has rarely been abandoned, becoming something of a *leit-motif*, freely acknowledged by Ginzburg in her admission over forty years on that 'As a rule I create while immersed in sadness',[2] and leading her to focus her attention almost exclusively on the difficulties implicit in establishing and maintaining satisfactory human relationships, both within the restricted confines of the family unit (where parents and children seem to be inhibited rather than encouraged by their literal and metaphorical closeness) and in the area more traditionally associated with the art of the novelist: sexual passion.

Dissatisfaction, frustration, and a sense of alienation are almost invariably crucial to Ginzburg's characters, whose lack of fulfilment frequently brings them face to face with the realisation that they exist in a state of total solitude, unable to relate other than superficially and imperfectly to those around them. Children, unable to communicate with their parents during their infancy, find, when they have reached adulthood in their turn, that the world they inhabit is no nearer that of the older generation, whose principles for living are rooted in a past which has no relevance to the present and who in addition persist in treating their offspring as immature adolescents, thus ensuring permanent dissatisfaction on both sides; elsewhere those who have sought independence or who find it, for whatever reason, thrust upon them, discover in their sexual partner a fundamental incompatibility of spirit which frequently leads to the breakdown of marriage, and, subsequently, an isolation which is all the more distressing for having been temporarily relieved. As Clo-

64

tilde Soave Bowe has perceptively stated Ginzburg's writing demonstrates that 'Solitude . . . [is] the necessary condition of existence, even after people are entangled in the permutations of love relationships',[3] a state of affairs especially painful for women, traditionally encouraged to consider marriage as a goal rather than a point of departure for a new existence and who are thus often deeply disillusioned by the realities of married life. This preoccupation with failure, incompetence, and the more negative aspects of existence presupposes a deep pessimism which is counterbalanced by two further characteristics: a fulfilling sense of intimac that develops between the reader and the author's characters, to the extent that one feels one has known them all one's life, and the gradual emergence and consolidation of a keen sense of humour. The intimacy evolves through her attention to the minutiae of day-to-day existence, innumerable items of apparent trivia which are in reality deeply revealing in the light they throw on individual characters; the humour springs both from the fact that characters' attempts to realise themselves and to achieve their own aims are frequently absurd and nonsensical, and from Ginzburg's awareness that life often juxtaposes the sublime with the ridiculous, reproducing this accordingly.

Ginzburg's awareness of the difficulties implicit in establishing a positive rapport with one's parents[4] clearly derives from her own experience during a childhood which was largely unconventional by the standards of the time, while also being influenced by many of the basic attitudes towards one's offspring then routinely accepted as a matter of course. Thus there appears to have been no interest whatever expressed by either parent in her attempts at creative composition, whether during her infancy or at a later stage when this activity was clearly something more than a childish pastime. This thoughtlessness and insensitivity was typical of a time when 'physical health was considered very important but psychological health was not'[5] and which in Ginzburg's case led to her being kept away from primary school, a potential source of infectious diseases, her first contact with elementary learning being through private tuition. Aware that this state of affairs was unusual in relation to the activities of other children of her age she experienced her first feelings of alienation, uncertain whether her family was sufficiently wealthy to create its own life-style in the field of education and confused by frequent references in family discussions to the lack of money available for the necessities of everyday existence. This feeling of uncertainty and separateness was further enhanced by her realisation that despite having a Catholic mother she did not share the conventional Christian background of her peers, while at the same time lacking a corresponding Jewish context as her father was non-practising and the Levis had no contact with the local Jewish community; 'we were "nothing", my brothers had told me, we were "mixed", that is half Jewish and half Catholic, but in fact neither one thing nor the other: nothing',[6] something which Ginzburg has stated caused her deep embarrassment 'since my earliest days'.[7] When at eleven years old she entered secondary school and found herself for the first time obliged to mix with a group of children of her own age, all of whom had long since mastered the art of making friends and being part of a community, she was seized with panic at the sight of these superior beings who were able to understand and practise the complicated rituals of their environment and whom she felt she could never join on equal terms; their spontaneous gestures, so different from her own rigid immobility, their functional clothes, so different from those arbitrarily chosen by her mother and which immediately marked her as an outsider, her inability to understand simple arithmetic, all combined to convince her that she was condemned to live on a different plane in which incomprehension and incommunicability were the norm and solitude a natural and inescapable condition of existence. Unable to confide either in her father, too busy to have any patience with his youngest child, or her mother, who, insensitive to her daughter's anguish, brushed aside her complaints about unsuitable clothes, Ginzburg focused on the root cause of her unhappiness: her separateness, which already in her early years had led her to nurture 'the germs of pride and shame in myself', so that 'I felt growing in me, like a mushroom, the proud, humiliating conviction that I was different and therefore alone'.[8] Now, after her first contact with the real world outside the protection afforded by her family, she realised the limitations and shortcomings of her environment, conscious that she had entered a new phase of her life in which she would have to solve her problems alone:

> The image of my home, which was both hateful and dear to me, now appeared as a refuge in which I would soon be hiding but where I would find no consolation, because the sorrow of being friendless would pursue me forever, and everywhere. I would reproach my mother harshly for my overall, my satchel and my pen, but I would say no more. I wouldn't let her know that I had sat alone on my bench and that no one had addressed a single word to me. The reasons why my misfortunes had to remain secret were obscure to me; I knew, though, that the thought of

saddening my mother was not one of them.

For the first time in my life I didn't care whether my mother was pleased or sad; I was very far from her, although I had left her only recently and would see her again at home quite soon; I saw my life going ahead along roads where I could see none of the people I had so far had with me.[9]

Ginzburg's anguish at having to confront a world peopled by strangers and organised according to mysterious rules was inevitably a traumatic experience for a child who had never set foot outside her home unaccompanied before reaching the age of eleven, and whose sheltered upbringing had left her in total ignorance of the most simple domestic tasks such as dressing, tying shoelaces, lighting the gas cooker, or making a bed. Though essentially happy in this blissful ignorance she was none the less disturbed by her father's frequent scoldings, and distressed not only to hear him repeatedly describe her as a ninny but also to note that he held her mother responsible for this deplorable state of affairs and believed it could never be remedied. Strong feelings of resentment towards her mother, now seen as the source of her inferiority and the cause of her unhappiness, climaxed when she discovered she would have to walk to school and back again all by herself, a decision designed to shake her out of her childish torpor but also clearly another example of naive insensitivity. Not surprisingly Ginzburg reacted by cultivating feelings of contempt for her mother, refusing to answer her questions and making a point of leaving home without kissing her good-bye, speaking coldly and harshly to her when communication was inevitable, and despising the tears her mother shed when her older daughter, now married and living outside Turin, would go back home after visiting at the weekend. When, shortly afterwards, having been accosted in the street by someone she initially took to be a friend of her father's, Ginzburg realised she had unwittingly '"spoken to a stranger"'[10] who thereafter met her regularly and walked her to school, she consequently felt quite unable to speak to her mother about her feelings of guilt and fear, eventually realising that this first experience of exposure to danger was evidence of an all-pervading evil which lurked beneath the placid surface of life and deriving from that revelation an intense feeling of sadness which would never leave her:

I had known no sadness in my childhood; I had known only fear . . . but they were merely fears and disappeared quite easily . . . But now, behind the fear, melancholy had opened up . . . melancholy would follow me everywhere. It was always there, motionless, boundless, incomprehensible, inexplicable, like a very high, black, heavy, empty sky.[11]

Conscious that she had grasped a truth which was vital to understanding the reality of life and also profoundly depressing Ginzburg felt a deep envy for her peers, apparently well integrated into this world and so different from her parents, who were fossilised in their domestic routines and whose repetitive conversations 'about things of no importance whatsoever' in words of 'revolting banality' she now knew by heart.[12] Her proficiency in essay-writing, the one subject that appealed to her and in which she excelled, so that she would sometimes be asked to read her work to the whole class, brought her neither fame nor fortune; her class-mates despised her, calling her an ass and thus reinforcing her feelings of inferiority, while her mother, happy to announce to friends that Natalia was '"good at Italian"', at no time participated in her daughter's efforts, nor, as already mentioned, took any positive interest in her artistic development; 'she would glance casually at my homework, believing me to be studious . . . she also knew vaguely that I wrote poetry.'[13]

Ginzburg's feelings of resentment towards her mother, unable or unwilling even to consider her problems, much less help her to resolve them, were balanced by an equally strong conviction that she could expect no help from her father, a benevolent despot whose angry roars would regularly fill the house and who was unsparing in his criticism of everything connected with his younger daughter, to such an extent that 'Terror lay for me in my father's features'.[14] This combination of paternal antagonism and maternal insensitivity is clearly at the root of Ginzburg's short story *I bambini*, published under her maiden name in 1934 in the literary review *Solaria*, where her parents' characteristics are neatly inverted to produce a hen-pecked father, who, when not absent on business, creeps around the house in his slippers seeking refuge from his wife among the pots and pans in the kitchen, and a tyrannical mother who is constantly scolding and punishing her children while declaring she can no longer bear to put up with them. If this inversion is clearly a fictional transposition of Ginzburg's own domestic environment the story also reproduces – albeit in an extreme form – her feelings of bitterness in relation to both her parents' neglect of her true needs, beginning as it does with the short sentence 'They had always been frightened of her' (p. 66), a phrase which anticipates her description of childhood terror over thirty years later, and continuing, in the second paragraph, with an equally significant statement: 'They would sometimes wonder if there were any other children in the world who didn't love their mother' (ibid.). Ignored or rebuked by their parents the two infants at the centre of this story compare their stiff and unbending mother with the plump and homely Mrs Oppenheimer next door, whose children have a swing in their garden and whose delectable teas are so much more exciting than the simple bread and butter available in their own home, and are unable to reconcile the happy laughing pictures of domestic bliss in the family album with the reality of their day-to-day existence.

This austere and essentially unhappy life changes suddenly and unexpectedly one evening while the children's father is, as usual, away on business, and their mother receives a visit from her brother-in-law, Uncle Bindi. Packed off to bed earlier than usual, and unable to sleep, Giorgio and Emilia decide to amuse themselves by creeping back to the terrace to say good-night once more to their uncle, only to see their mother being passionately embraced by Bindi before eventually persuading him to leave. When she realises they have seen everything her first panic-stricken reaction is to rage against them and threaten them with boarding school, but the build-up of conflicting emotions is too much for her and she collapses in tears, at which point the children gather round her and she embraces them fitfully, telling them it has all been a game and begging them not to mention a word to anyone. The story ends on this note of reconciliation, with the children happily fantasising about a new loving relationship with their mother, who, they fondly imagine, will in due course reward their silence with an expensive present: a bicycle for Giorgio and a gold watch for Emilia. The irony of this situation is not lost on the reader, who, unlike the children, has no difficulty in seeing through the false glitter of the happy ending, which leaves open the question of the relationship between the two adults while making it clear that the mother's new affection for her offspring is hardly disinterested. In addition it is also apparent that, while the emphasis throughout this story is on the two children and their reactions to what they see around them, Ginzburg also has an implicit understanding of their mother, whose rapport with her husband is obviously unsatisfactory and whose isolation for long periods during his absence makes it easier to understand her behaviour, thus introducing alongside the more obvious theme of parental neglect that of marital incompatibility and female loneliness.

Although Ginzburg makes use of small children in several other short stories they are almost always marginal characters with roles of limited significance. Thus in *Un'assenza*, her 'first real story',[15] published under her maiden name in 1937 but written four years earlier, Maurizio's relationship with his son Villi is mentioned only briefly, being merely one of the factors which contribute to defining his character; in *Casa al mare*, also published in 1937 under the pseudonym of Alessandra Tornimparte, the role of Walter's unnamed child is purely functional and limited to two brief scenes which exemplify the antagonism between his parents; in *Mio marito* (1941) the narrator's awareness that her maternal feelings are somehow deficient similarly serves to highlight the growing realisation that her marriage is based on falsehood. In two other stories, however, children are once more at the centre of things: *Il maresciallo*, published in 1965, a fairy-tale for adults on the theme of illusion and reality,[16] and *La madre*, written in 1948 but unpublished till 1957. In the latter she once more describes a family crisis through the eyes of two children, still young enough to share their mother's bed at night and thus too naive to understand her emotional problems; though they are sufficiently perceptive to notice everything that happens around them they inevitably lack the ability to distinguish between trivial details and events whose implications the reader can recognise as deeply disturbing, thus ensuring the presence in this story of two distinct levels of reality. Like the mother in *I bambini* this similarly unnamed woman also neglects her children, but in a very different context, apparently more comforting and supporting but in reality even colder and more isolated. A very young widow, little more than a child herself, she inhabits a spiritual void in which the impossibility of establishing any fruitful communication with her children is paralleled by the equally rigid limitations of her aged parents, who refuse to accept that she still has emotional and sexual needs that cannot be satisfied in the essentially passive role which society has automatically assigned her on the death of her husband; as a result she exists in a kind of limbo in which her increasingly desperate attempts to find some sort of equilibrium emphasise more and more the difference between her disorganised existence and the solid conventions which regulate the daily life of her family. Dimly aware that all is not well with their mother the children marvel at her curious behaviour, so unlike that of a normal adult; she keeps strange hours, coming home late at night, often cries in bed, quarrels with their grandparents, who call her a bitch, and smokes a great deal. Totally undomesticated she never tidies her room, where her clothes are strewn about haphazardly and cigarette ash is scattered

70

everywhere; when they go shopping together she frequently embarrasses them by losing her way or leaving her gloves or her handbag on the counter, and is invariably palmed off with poor quality food, thus ensuring more trouble when she returns home. Her very appearance is disquieting; not only is she much younger than the mothers of their school-friends, she is also much thinner. Can they really have been carried in that small belly and fed from those tiny breasts? Quite clearly 'their mother was not an important person. The important people were grandmother and grandfather, aunt Clementina who lived in the country . . . Diomira the maid, Giovanni the consumptive doorman . . . all these people were important for the two boys because they were strong people, and you could trust them . . .' (pp. 397–8). Here too Ginzburg is drawing once more on her own experience of family life, as is evident from the comments attributed to her sister in *Family Sayings* over ten years later.[17]

When one day the children see their mother sitting in a café and holding hands with a strange man, 'her face happy, relaxed and happy, as it never was when she was at home' (p. 402), this merely confirms what the reader has known for some time: she has a lover, but is prevented by the rigid conventions which govern her position from acknowledging him openly. A trip to Milan by the grandparents to visit some relatives, which coincides with the maid's day off, gives her a chance to invite him home, and he makes friends with the children, who find him charming and are reluctant to go out and play after lunch; when their mother puts them to bed at the end of the day they see nothing strange in her suggestion to avoid mentioning him to their grandparents, 'who don't like having visitors in the house' (p. 404). Inevitably this guilty relationship based on subterfuge is doomed to failure, and when she is abandoned by her lover and once more feels alone in the world she can no longer bear the strain and kills herself, a gesture which elicits no sympathy from the community but merely sanctions the general view that she is a heartless deviant who has ' . . . selfishly left those two poor kids to fend for themselves' (p. 405). Shocked by what has happened the boys try hard to understand what lies behind their mother's actions, the older one guessing that Mr Max may have left town for good, but they are soon distracted, first by the thrilling new life they lead in the country at aunt Clementina's, and, subsequently, on their return home, by the well-regulated routine of life with their grandparents; this sense of security, together with the excitement of growing up, soon leads them to forget their mother and her problems, so that they eventually even forget what she looked like. The story ends with the first indication in the two lads of an adult awareness that their mother was something more than just a maternal figure, but they are unable to perceive the implications of this truth, not only because they are too young but, more disturbingly for the reader, because the adults around them appear to be equally incapable of delving beneath the surface and interpreting the situation with any degree of sensitivity. The irony of the conclusion recalls the end of *I bambini*,[18] and if the deliberate device in both stories of concentrating on the naive perception of young children clearly reflects the author's sympathy for a kind of outraged innocence the greater attention paid in this later tale to the mother, who dominates the action directly from the very beginning,[19] indicates Ginzburg's desire to focus on the difficulties facing an older age group – one composed of people who are nominally adult but whose emotional and intellectual development is at variance with their years, and who are thus quite incapable of organising their lives, unable to cope adequately with any degree of independence, and, almost inevitably, destined to become victims of their environment.

The first direct representative of this category is Delia, the narrator and protagonist of *The Road to the City* (written in 1941 and published the following year[20]), a young girl of sixteen living in a squalid peasant environment. Technically still a child she is old enough to claim a degree of autonomy and a kind of independence in a society where girls grow up quickly and are seen as eligible for marriage at an early age, but she has no suitors herself and is correspondingly restless and unfulfilled at home, where she and her three younger brothers are caught between her mother, a domestic drudge unable to control her brood and who is ignored by everyone, and her father, who describes the home as 'a madhouse' (p. 12), leaving it whenever he can to spend his free time in the city while constantly reproaching his wife for having failed in her maternal obligations. Delia can only think of following the example of her sister, who had married at seventeen and gone to live in the city, unable to grasp that escape from the family through marriage to a man one does not love is merely the exchange of one kind of emotional aridity for another, and if this inability to reflect on the implications of one's actions is to some extent natural in an adolescent it is equally clear that, as Aldo Capasso has perceptively stated, 'Delia receives the first important stimulus for her wretched development from having been born into a home which is both poor and disgusting',[21] a home in which there is no communication between parents and children and in which, despite the oppressive presence of the other members of the family, Delia is in effect totally alone.

Obsessed by the desire to get married Delia is only too pleased to encourage the attentions of the village doctor's son, a young man with status who soon tires of her but is forced into a shotgun marriage after she becomes pregnant. Exiled to her aunt's house in an even more primitive village, to conceal her shame while nego-tiations are taking place between the two families, she discovers a different but equally hopeless environment in which her cousin Santa, who is all of twenty-four years old, has never succeeded in getting married because her mother, 'who couldn't bear her and bawled her out all day long', has systematically prevented her from preparing her trousseau, preferring 'to keep her at home and tor-ment her' (p. 38). Despite being afraid of her mother Santa cannot bring herself to break away, unable even to subsist alone in the house if Delia's aunt has to go to town for the afternoon, and is clearly a willing victim eagerly participating in her own oppression, a negative example for her cousin of the perils of family life in rural poverty; in the same way her description of how she sees life after marriage to a local peasant, to whom she is engaged, is no more encouraging.[22] Clearly in this kind of context Delia's lot, however wretched, is the lesser of several evils; but she is none the less aware that it is the opposite of fulfilment, as she remembers the carefree days before her pregnancy when she would rush off to the city as soon as she woke in the morning, a period now over for ever and during which she had been impatient for her life to change but which she now realises was something akin to happiness. Here too there is a clear parallel with Ginzburg's own feelings as expressed in the essay *Winter in the Abruzzi*, written three years later after the death of her husband, in which she evokes their life together during his exile in Pizzoli and contrasts her hopes and dreams from that time with the suffering and emptiness that were to follow.[23]

The novel ends with Delia achieving her aim of moving from her deprived village to the prosperous city, where, like her sister, she leads an aimless life empty of all emotional substance and only superficially preferable to her dead-end existence at home. Her husband's parents do nothing to relieve her spiritual apathy; Giu-lio's father, eager to avoid a scandal, is only too happy for the marriage to take place, but there is no mention of his ever visiting the newly-weds, while his mother, distraught at what has happened, loses no opportunity to nag at Delia, rebuking her insensitively for her indifferent performance in labour, criticising the shape of her breasts, which are unable to suckle the baby, and, in due course, plotting against her with the help of her maid, a scheme which misfires only because by now 'Giulio was so much in love with me that he paid no attention to his mother or anyone else' (pp. 66–7). This late flowering of emotion on her husband's part is the one positive element in Delia's new life, and together with her acquired wealth and higher social status seems likely to guarantee her a degree of security for the future – but she is unable to respond in kind, dimly aware that her cousin Nini, now dead, had loved her disinterestedly for many years and that she too had loved him, though without realising it at the time; in addition it is quite clear that her child, whose unfortunate conception has determined her future and to whom she is largely indifferent, is unlikely to receive any more effective training for life from its mother than she has herself.

The cycle of parental neglect thus seems destined to repeat itself, albeit in less squalid surroundings and at a higher social level corresponding more closely both to Ginzburg's own background and to the setting for her next novel, *The Dry Heart*, written five years later and described by one critic as 'the most lucid example of self-analysis among Ginzburg's characters'.[24] Here too the protagonist is a young woman, nominally adult, and, indeed, possessed of an official degree of independence in that she is employed as a school-teacher in a large town some little distance from her native village, a fact which obliges her to spend the working week in a boarding-house rather than to commute day by day. Older than Delia and better educated she is none the less just as unsophisticated, just as immature, and if her parents inhabit a world likewise far removed from that of Delia's poverty-stricken family – her father a general practitioner and her mother a placid housewife – this has in no way encouraged the development of a meaningful rapport between the generations, whose life-style is characterised by an unthinking passivity which has no conception of obligations that go beyond the basic necessities of existence and has made the protagonist (who is never named) unable to contemplate any alternative to life within the family home. At no time does she mention friends of her own age still living in the village who might provide another dimension to her experience and so justify her unshakeable resolve to return to the domestic hearth every weekend, while it is quite clear that she has insufficient initiative to make any new contacts among colleagues at work, her daily routine consisting exclusively of journeys from her lodgings to her school and back again, evenings being spent alone in her room dreaming romantically of an ideal husband who will one day emerge from nowhere and make her happy for ever after. In these circumstances her return home every Saturday clearly represents a need for reassurance through contact with a familiar environment, but Ginzburg makes it equally clear that she derives no lasting benefit from this; lacking even the minimal stimulus required to prepare her classes and travel back and forth she sinks into a state of apathy which is almost catatonic. Despite noticing her constant silence neither her father nor her mother presume to question her about her activities during the week; he is only interested in playing chess with the vet and she is either participating in the game or occupied with her cooking, a narrowness and insensitivity reminiscent of the adults' reactions to the young woman's situation in *La madre*. When school breaks up and the protagonist finds herself spending long periods at home, in an atmosphere totally lacking any kind of emotional or intellectual stimulus, she perceives the emptiness of her life; however, this is not because of any sudden maturity of spirit but is the result of an obsession with a middle-aged bachelor she has recently met by chance through some mutual acquaintances and who has gradually released within her a previously unrecognised need for human contact and affection. Elusive and unwilling to communicate Alberto nevertheless spends long hours walking round town with her, listening to her childhood memories and unwittingly encouraging her expectations, with the inevitable result that she eventually decides she is in love with him. When he learns what has happened he is appalled but eventually agrees to marriage although he does not love her in any real sense, thus ensuring a disastrous outcome for this relationship, and, in due course, a common fate which, though more obviously destructive than the conclusion to Delia's misfortunes in *The Road to the City*, is no less inevitable.[25] Significantly the girl's parents are once more quite incapable of reacting to such an unsuitable match with any degree of intelligence and awareness, conscious only of the bridegroom's age and social standing.

Totally unprepared for the realities of married life, to the extent that she feels both frightened and nauseated at the thought of sexual intercourse, the protagonist soon finds she cannot accept her husband's reluctance to communicate his feelings, while she, conversely, is now seized by an unrelenting desire to understand him and to analyse her thoughts after years of unremitting silence. Alberto is both temperamentally unsuited to this kind of intense relationship and, in addition, anxious to conceal from his wife the continued existence of a long-standing affair with a married woman which leads him to absent himself from home at irregular intervals and to reproach the protagonist for the pressure she exerts on him. When she discovers by chance that Alberto's childhood friend Augusto has not accompanied him on a nostalgic visit to their old country haunts but is still in town she guesses the truth and is suddenly aware that 'our marriage was a big mistake . . . I felt like a guest in this house' (p. 93); however, she is unable to do anything to remedy the situation, taking refuge in a pathetic attempt to please her husband through her submissiveness and cultivating a spurious intimacy during long evenings in which he reads the newspaper while she knits in silence, offering him a 'cowardly and idiotic smile' (p. 107). Aware that her parents can be of no assistance to her, and indeed must be kept in the dark, she stops visiting them, while at the same time seeing less and less of the couple through whom she had met Alberto in the first place as he becomes increasingly unsociable; this growing isolation from the outside world intensifies her awareness that 'after our marriage I had let everything go' (p. 92). Her last chance to escape from her oppressive loneliness by, for instance, resuming her teaching, which she has foolishly abandoned once married, vanishes when she discovers she is pregnant.

This new development has no effect on Alberto, who continues to retreat ever further into non-communication while maintaining contact with his mistress, to the point where husband and wife abandon all attempts at maintaining a normal domestic routine and sleep in separate rooms. Now fully conscious that her marriage is a failure in every sense and that this failure is all the more unbearable in that, despite everything, she cannot stop loving her husband the protagonist transfers the full force of her pent-up emotions to her child, thus achieving a kind of fulfilment which turns out to be equally obsessive and equally detrimental.[26] Unable, because of her higher education and different social standing, to find contentment, like Delia, in material well-being, her reaction to the child is equally radical while being totally different in nature, and all the more inevitable for being entirely in keeping with the conventional belief that, as her husband tells her without a trace of irony, 'the main thing for a woman was to have a baby' (p. 94). Little by little the confines of her world contract until she is completely incapable of undertaking any activity that does not relate directly to her daughter, whose growth and general well-being become her sole reason for living and who instinctively responds to this constant attention by making ever-increasing demands on her mother's resources, keeping her up most of the night, throwing tantrums at meal times, and bursting into tears whenever left on her own, so that 'I had to take her with me, even into the bathroom' (p. 114). Totally absorbed by this unrelenting activity the protagonist no longer has time for anguished confrontations with her husband and realises that her feelings of jealousy have been superseded by more import-ant considerations; the result is a kind of reconciliation in which the couple resume sexual contact and the young woman reflects that 'our marriage was no better and no worse than the run-of-the-mill variety' (p. 116), conscious none the less that her relationship with their child is more a source of torment than of satisfaction, that the long hours she spends in her daughter's room leave her 'exhausted, as if from a battle' (p. 115), and that these claims on her attention must take precedence over everything else, even at the most in-opportune moments, such as during love-making. The strain in-volved in this all-consuming dedication to her maternal role sometimes proves too strong for her, and she experiences moments of rebellion, but these soon pass and she once more accepts her lot, convinced that 'when a woman has her baby in her arms nothing else should matter' (p. 108). There is once again here a clear parallel with Ginzburg's own experience of motherhood in the early 1940s, during which, as already mentioned, she experienced two successive pregnancies that, following a period of writer's block, effectively put paid to any chance of artistic development. Although she nowhere says so it seems clear from the evidence available that alongside the difficulties involved in rebuilding her life after the war, and which were in themselves sufficiently traumatic to make her 'totally de-fenceless and miserable',[27] she was also haunted by the memory of a period in which, like the protagonist of *The Dry Heart*, she was at one and the same time totally absorbed by maternal duties and con-scious that there could be other dimensions in her life, a feeling necessarily more agonising for a creative writer than for someone described somewhat patronisingly but also accurately as 'a poor little woman'.[28] Ginzburg's description of life as a young mother as recorded in the essay entitled *My Vocation* is appropriately anguished and clearly analogous to that of her character in the novel published two years previously:

> . . . my children were born and when they were very little I could not understand how anyone could sit herself down to write if she had children. I did not see how I could separate myself from them in order to follow someone or other's fortunes in a story. I began to feel contempt for my vocation. Now and again I longed for it desperately and felt that I was in exile, but I tried to despise it and

make fun of it and occupy myself solely with the children. I believed I had to do this . . . But I felt a ferocious longing within me and sometimes at night I almost wept when I remembered how beautiful my vocation was. I thought that I would recover it some day or other but I did not know when: I thought that I would have to wait till my children grew up and left me.[29]

If Ginzburg succeeded in transcending this period of creative apathy by gradually coming to terms with the different demands of her personality[30] and without any kind of domestic upheaval the same is not true of the young woman at the centre of *The Dry Heart*, whose simplicity leaves her no resources to draw on and who is ultimately destroyed by a lethal combination of unexpected disaster and a basic incompatibility in no way more bearable for being depressingly familiar. A temporary separation from her husband, during which she looks forward confidently to a new life open to new experiences, collapses in ruins when her daughter dies of meningitis during a trip to San Remo; in her anguish she feels the need to return to Alberto, who is equally distraught at what has happened. As she gradually comes to terms with her loss and feels able to face the world again he likewise begins to revert to his normal personality, paying her less attention and withdrawing once more into his shell, the old pattern of their life thus reasserting itself anew. But the young woman's suffering has made her less submissive than before, and when she learns that despite assurances to the contrary Alberto has re-established contact with his mistress she shoots him, a gesture which precludes any possibility of a new life for the protagonist, and it is clear from the final paragraph that she is about to turn the gun on herself.

It would be simplistic to blame all the unhappiness in this novel on the well-intentioned insensitivity of the protagonist's parents, who at no time exert any direct influence on their daughter's behaviour; throughout she makes her own decisions and decides her own fate. The fact remains, however, that like Delia and indeed like so many of Ginzburg's female characters she receives no training whatever for life and is clearly at risk from the moment she sets foot outside the family home, where her mentors appear to have no conception that life can exist other than as they themselves have experienced it, unable even to appreciate the potential difficulties involved in leaving the reassuring warmth of the rural hearth for the cold and loneliness of the big city. It is thus hardly surprising that their daughter automatically subscribes to the traditional belief that her ideal destiny is marriage and domesticity, resigns from her teaching post as soon as this seems within her grasp, and restricts the limits of her interests to the four walls of the family home, her situation being largely determined by the age-old conventions regulating women's place in Mediterranean society. In this context the protagonist is obviously symbolic of all females attempting to cope with the new stresses of urban life in the immediate post-war period when women were beginning to enter professions hitherto incompatible with their traditional role of wife and mother, and finding their upbringing not only useless but sometimes counter-productive. If it is certainly true that ultimately the young woman at the centre of this tale is 'guilty of having simply waited for something to happen . . . of allowing herself to be conditioned by her environment without attempting to influence that environment herself . . . a victim, yes, but a victim of her own laziness, totally absorbed by a relationship which turns everything to dust',[31] it is equally true that this kind of passivity is the logical outcome of the thoughtlessness characteristic of outdated attitudes among the older generation, and far more obviously so in 1962, when these words were written, than when the novel was first published fifteen years previously.

This fundamental awareness that there can, and indeed must, be more to life than a single well-worn path sanctioned by tradition and no longer relevant to contemporary reality is what distinguishes older people from those who survived the war while still young enough to reflect on their experiences and analyse them. As early as 1945 Ginzburg was already contrasting her open-ended existence in liberated Rome, where her funds were insufficient to cover both food and clothes, so that 'I still wear worn-out shoes . . . if I have any money I would rather spend it on something else as shoes don't seem to me to be very essential things', with the solid unbending life-style of her family living in the north, who 'utter cries of indignation and sorrow at the sight of my shoes'[32] and who still believe after everything that has happened that a respectable appearance and a strict domestic routine are more important than the pursuit of ideas or artistic activity, and this despite the fact that their daughter is turning thirty and old enough to know her own mind. Here too it was Ginzburg's inner resources which allowed her to transcend an unthinking obsession with motherhood and formulate an important distinction between providing warmth and domestic efficiency for one's children while they are young and allowing them the freedom which is their right when they have matured:

. . . my chidren live with my mother and so far they do not have worn-out shoes. But what kind of men will they be? I mean, what kind of shoes will they have when they are men? . . . I shall take care that my children's feet are always warm and dry . . . at least during infancy. And perhaps . . . for learning to walk in worn-out shoes, it is as well to have dry, warm feet when we are children.[33]

A year later she had refined this concept, stressing the importance of an open relationship with children based on truth and far removed from the well-intentioned artificiality of traditional forms:

Our parents and those older than us disapprove of the way we bring up our children. They would like us to lie to our children as they lied to us. . . . But we cannot do this . . . to children whom we have woken in the middle of the night and tremblingly dressed in the darkness so that we could flee with them or hide them . . . who have seen terror and horror in our faces. We cannot bring ourselves to tell these children that we found them under cabbages, or that when a person dies he goes on a long journey. There is an unbridgeable abyss between us and the previous generation.[34]

Four years after completing *The Dry Heart* Ginzburg published *Valentino*, whose eponymous protagonist is aptly described by Ian Thomson as 'a feckless young fellow'[35] and whose story is narrated by his sister Caterina, a girl inhabiting a kind of no man's land somewhere between the benevolent neglect shown the protagonist of *The Dry Heart* and the unthinking assumptions which characterise the attitude of the grandparents in *La madre*. In keeping with another Mediterranean tradition which favours male children at the expense of their female siblings Caterina is automatically relegated by her parents to the role of domestic drudge, and, as a result, doomed to perpetual spinsterhood; and though she is spared through living at home while pursuing her studies from falling unthinkingly into an unsatisfactory marriage, like the young woman in the earlier novel, this in no way excuses the behaviour of her parents, who simply take it for granted that she will permanently fulfil the role of unpaid servant. Caterina is aware of the injustice behind this discrimination but remains unmoved by it, at least at first, being too good-natured to experience feelings of resentment and, in addition, 'confident that sooner or later things would improve for me' (p. 20); however, these naive hopes are never fulfilled. When her father dies her mother is consumed with guilt at having neglected and disparaged him over the years and little by little sinks into apathy and depression, thus increasing the need for her daughter's presence; as she subsequently

80

develops arthritis this need intensifies, and when in due course she becomes bedridden there is clearly no further possibility of escape. While the old lady is still able to subsist on her own Caterina has the chance to spend a month at the seaside with her brother and his wife, but, ever willing to sacrifice herself, turns the invitation down, an act which at last releases within her feelings of indignation and brings her face to face with the reality of her situation, forcing her to acknowledge 'a yearning in my heart to be able to stride out alone and speak to someone who was not my mother' (p. 23). This spiritual awakening is, however, short-lived. When her mother dies Caterina is ridden with guilt at the thought of her earlier impatience, and recalls with no little anguish her pathetic attempts to secure some minimal relaxation from the constant strain of attending to the old lady's needs: 'I had loved her very much. I would have given anything now to be able to repeat those evening walks that had bored me at the time, with her long, slender, deformed hand resting on my arm. And I felt guilty for not having shown her more affection' (p. 24).

Reverting to her original role as passive observer of other people's lives Caterina goes to live with Valentino and his wife, where she witnesses the gradual disintegration of their relationship and suffers the indignity of finding herself engaged for a mere twenty days to a friendly eccentric who almost immediately asks to be released from his pledge for reasons which are only made clear later. She leaves her brother's house, now doubly unbearable, and spends some time in the country with a maiden aunt, another old lady with whom she goes for walks in the evening, reflecting that 'it was just like walking with my mother' (p. 44). When she learns that Valentino and his wife have separated and that he has been thrown out of the matrimonial home brother and sister take a flat in town, where they live off the money Caterina makes from her teaching and which is supplemented by a monthly allowance from her sister-in-law, whose feelings for Caterina remain unchanged and who realises she would otherwise have difficulty in making ends meet. Ever feckless, her brother makes no attempt to find work, and it is clear that Caterina will end her days acting as his nursemaid, having simply transferred her attentions from one relative to another without ever enjoying – other than during her all-too-brief engagement – any real emotional autonomy or independence.

The female narrator in this novel is clearly the mirror image of her opposite number in *The Dry Heart*, but the absence from her life of an insensitive husband and a demanding child hardly compensates for her wretchedly submissive existence; it seems equally clear that she too is in essence a victim of her circumstances, conditioned by her upbringing to accept a second-class role and similarly unable to rebel consistently against her fate. Once again it is the absence of dialogue between the generations which creates the climate in which this process can take shape; the phenomenon is not restricted to Caterina's family,[36] being consciously revived not only in the increasingly superficial conversations with Valentino's wife but also, more disturbingly, between brother and sister, who take care never to discuss the problems that have caused their life to turn out as it has. This thereby avoids the possibility of open conflict, but, at least for Caterina, in no way diminishes her frustration, rather the reverse:

> Our conversation is strictly limited to daily trivia, to our food or the tenants of the flat opposite . . . So there is no one to whom I can speak the words that most need to be spoken, about the events which most closely concern our family and what has happened to us; I have to keep them bottled up inside me and there are times when they threaten to choke me. (pp. 48–9)

In an essay published in the same year as this novel Ginzburg discusses the pernicious nature of silence, recalling how people of her age, when young, had seen through the rhetorical falsehood of the language of their parents' generation and resolved to communicate with a fresh clear style when becoming adults in their turn, only to find that while there is indeed no place in the new world for the ponderous and theatrical tones of days long vanished nothing has emerged as an adequate replacement, and the language of modern man is 'watery, cold, sterile . . . no use for writing books, for linking us with someone we love, for saving a friend'.[37] She is here clearly referring not only to the emotional grandiloquence of the Fascist period, doubtless absent from exchanges among members of her own family, but, in a more general sense, to the great gulf existing between parents and children in more formal times when there were universally accepted rules for bringing up one's offspring, and, similarly, rigid conventions regarding relationships between adults. If all this ensured that the scope for intimate communication was reduced to a minimum and restricted to well-defined areas of human experience it likewise provided fixed points of reference in a system purporting to have an answer to all human problems and designed to make life as simple and uncomplicated as possible. At one time youthful impatience with the limitations of established norms would inevitably mellow into a gradual acceptance of the need to conform to established social values, thus ensuring a basic similarity of attitude between adults of different generations, who all essentially shared the same beliefs; after 1945, however, attempts on the part of the older generation to recreate the old absolutes, rejected by younger people no longer able to believe in them, resulted in a basic incompatibility of spirit, as already mentioned, and a breakdown in communication between age groups who would previously have had little difficulty in establishing a common code of behaviour. The result is a dichotomy between two sections of the community, who, while continuing to live together, become increasingly estranged.

In this context the older generation's tacit assumption that their daughters will conform to traditional patterns in a world where these no longer have any meaning is likely to come into conflict with a new awareness among those same daughters of the many alternatives to such a pattern (as we shall see later); elsewhere, as with the female protagonists examined so far, this dichotomy will ensure that those who do unthinkingly attempt to live by their parents' standards find they cannot reconcile the principles behind these with a modern reality in which anything is possible and which they are unable to ignore. In these circumstances the obsessive introversion characteristic of the young woman in *The Dry Heart*, together with her equally obsessive desire to analyse her husband's every phrase in order to achieve communication with her partner, are both logical reactions to the confusion resulting from her contradictory situation; in the same way Caterina's acceptance of her parents' unthinking assumptions about her future and her subsequent willingness to take on an equally traditional role in relation to her brother are balanced in both cases by feelings of resentment which she cannot entirely eliminate.

Under these conditions the difficulties experienced by both sexes – but especially by women – in discussing matters of importance openly and honestly can be seen as similarly logical in that in less free times such matters would either not have arisen in the first place, or, in the event, have been dealt with – usually by men – according to a fixed set of conventions designed to eliminate uncertainty at its source and reduce discussion to a minimum, any feelings of frustration being carefully repressed in accordance with accepted norms. Now that these no longer apply, and there is less inhibition about acknowledging one's feelings, people have discovered that in a world which has had to recreate itself out of nothing language is first and foremost something functional, a practical means to a specific end and unsuited to convey the intimate workings of the emotions other than by recourse to outmoded expressions now devoid of meaning. In *Silence* Ginzburg suggests that the first artistic signs of this process of linguistic denudation can be seen as early as 1918 in Debussy's *Pelléas et Mélisande*, an opera written while the author was still suffering from the effects of the First World War and in which, she claims, the two lovers converse in language of the utmost banality: '("*J'ai froid – ta chevelure*")', so different from the text of nineteenth-century librettos full of resounding phrases such as '(Sconto col sangue mio – l'amor che posi in te)'.[38] Social activities associated with the post-war period, such as mass tourism, organised gambling, alcoholism, and promiscuity, are seen by Ginzburg as abortive attempts to blot out the unbearable consciousness that communication is no longer possible and that we are all condemned to live in perpetual silence, both within ourselves and in our relations with others, a feeling which can lead to despair, and, indeed, to death:

> Silence can become a closed, monstrous, *demonic* unhappiness; it withers the days of our youth and makes our bread bitter. It can lead . . . to death. Silence must be faced and judged from a moral standpoint. Because silence, like acedia and luxury, is a sin. The fact that in our time it is a sin common to all our fellow men, that it is the bitter fruit of our sick times, does not excuse us from recognising it for what it is and from calling it by its true name.[39]

Silence, whether in the literal sense, or, as is more usual, disguised under a veil of mindless chatter and a trivial preoccupation with domestic duties, is central to the problems confronting the youthful protagonists of Ginzburg's next book, *All Our Yesterdays*, published a year later in 1952. This is a long tale of approximately three hundred pages whose theme is ostensibly 'the story of two Italian families before and during World War II',[40] described rather gushingly by one critic as 'a wonderful novel about Italy and the Italians',[41] but which can be seen more accurately as a further depiction of the dangers of emotional naivety abandoned to its own devices. This theme is here given an added political dimension by being set in the perilous atmosphere of Fascist Italy at a time when the future of Europe hangs in the balance and youthful idealism, equally unprotected, is exposed to risks whose implications are no less disturbing. The book has many characters, as befits its length, but the main protagonist is an adolescent girl, Anna, the youngest of four children, whose youth and sex make her doubly vulnerable in a family where there is no effective parental control and thus nothing to safeguard its members from being led astray, whether emotionally or politically. Their father, a lawyer by training, has retired in order to write his memoirs, an obsessional activity that occupies him totally and is interrupted only by periods of depression during which he is plagued by self-doubt and so incapable of exercising any authority. His death while his offspring are still young leaves them entirely in the care of Signora Maria, an elderly lady originally their grandmother's companion and who has subsequently replaced their mother, a delicate woman unable to survive four pregnancies and who had died soon after Anna's birth. Absurdly conscious of her social status and ever-mindful of the exotic life she led in happier days Maria lives in a world of her own, which, though very different from that of the children's father, is equally removed from reality, and she is thus totally unsuited to act as their spiritual mentor. Full of boundless energy and ever anxious to do what is best for everyone, she cannot grasp that there are more important things in life than social decorum and making sure the house is clean and tidy; thus she is incapable of seeing or understanding more important matters taking place under her very nose. The father's uncompromising if ineffectual anti-Fascism is seen by her as no more than a tiresome eccentricity whose reasons she never presumes to investigate, and she has no inkling whatsoever that when, in the heady atmosphere of total freedom that exists after his death, Anna's elder brother Ippolito and two other young friends begin meeting regularly in the evenings they are planning left-wing activities involving the distribution of foreign newspapers hostile to the regime. One of the two friends is a boy who had once had a crush on Anna's older sister Concettina, and Maria is convinced that this is still the reason for his frequent visits, though he has long since ceased to admire her, and, with a similar degree of obtuseness, she deduces that he is also anxious to share their food because he does not get enough to eat at home. When later on this boy is arrested Maria is unable to understand the importance of the political context and announces that she would never agree to a marriage between him and Concettina because 'they had put him in prison . . . for swindling or smuggling. For smuggling watches, perhaps' (p. 63).[42]

If Maria's estrangement from everything substantial around her is ultimately no more than a mild irritant for these young men it proves little short of disastrous in relation to Anna, whose growing needs are totally neglected by her surrogate mother while her siblings are too preoccupied with their own interests to give her any real attention. 'Pale and indolent . . . and not very tall for her fourteen years' (p. 35) but at the same time romantic and gullible, she fantasises about helping her brother and his friends overthrow the Fascists but is kept well away from the sitting-room where they hold their meetings; she is treated like a child by all the family including Maria, who makes her wear dresses knocked up out of old curtains in order to save money on clothes. Good-natured and, like most of Ginzburg's female protagonists, lacking sufficient determination to assert herself,[43] Anna reveals an affability and a willingness to fall in with other people's wishes which already in her childhood mark her out as one of life's victims. Despatched to the house opposite on the day of her father's death she meets Giuma, a boy of her own age with whom she strikes up a reluctant friendship despite the fact that '[she] did not enjoy herself very much with him' (p. 27) and is regularly exhausted by his extravagant behaviour, so that 'her neck ached from so much nodding and her lips ached too, from pretending to smile' (p. 28). Sensing he can do as he pleases with her Giuma has no qualms about playing frightening games which involve tying her to a tree with ropes that cut deep into her flesh, games which end only when he and his family leave to spend the winter in Switzerland. When they meet up again some years later at Concettina's wedding breakfast, where Giuma has been invited because 'he was very smart and made a good appearance' (p. 83) Anna realises she is no nearer resisting his blandishments and accepts his offer to go to the cinema the next day, despite experiencing 'a great boredom, a great fatigue at being with him, the same boredom and the same fatigue that she had felt in the days when they had played together' (pp. 85–6), feelings further complicated by the fact that 'she felt for him a kind of pity and did not know why' (p. 86),[44] realising intuitively that he is very shy. As they see each other more frequently Giuma takes to using her as an outlet for his unhappiness at school, where his peers 'detested him, they turned their backs at once if he came up to speak to them' (p. 91), and at home, where he is reproached for his laziness. One day when he is feeling particularly low he kisses her, and, conscious that although no one can stand him he is the only person to pay her any attention, she becomes increasingly submissive towards him, pretending to believe everything he tells her, however absurd or incredible, and reviving old fantasies about manning the barricades, this time with Giuma, heroic and dashing and quite unlike his real self. It is only a question of time before he makes love to her in order to fill the empty spaces between words, and although Anna is by now well aware that 'something had got lost between them' (p. 109) she is none the less quite unable to stop seeing him, drawn despite herself to this wretched but lonely boy who no longer knows what to say to her. Inevitably she becomes pregnant, while in the world outside the Germans conquer Norway, Holland, and Belgium, invade France, and look like becoming masters of Europe; all the while Maria remains sublimely indifferent, totally absorbed by Concettina's new baby. Anna is briefly tempted to seek help from the old lady, the only adult she has access to, but realises this would be useless, aware that 'she would never be able to say anything to Signora Maria, she had thought of it for a moment but how foolish she had been to think of it' (p. 121). Giuma and his family leave town for their villa near Stresa while Anna and her relatives prepare to go off in their turn to the country; all too happy to make his exit Giuma has meanwhile given her some quinine to suck and a thousand lire to pay for an abortion, though neither of them has the slightest idea how to go about finding someone willing to perform the operation. On the day of their departure Anna's older brother Ippolito shoots himself, convinced that no power on earth can halt the German advance, a despairing gesture which Maria characteristically interprets as a sign that he has been crossed in love.

Totally alone now that Giuma is far away and apparently unwilling even to write to her, while her family, having pulled themselves together after Ippolito's suicide, are once more wrapped up in their own affairs, Anna experiences feelings of acute anguish at the thought that she has no one to confide in, and it is precisely when she is at her lowest, during a trip to the butcher's in the pouring rain, that she meets Cenzo Rena, an eccentric middle-aged friend of her father's who has visited them in the past on one of his frequent journeys round the world and is about to call on them again. Sensing that for the first time in her life she is in the presence of a mature adult Anna bursts into tears and tells him the whole story, gradually drawing sustenance from his presence and feeling 'as though she were washed clean by her tears, as though the fear and the silence had suddenly been discharged from her heart' (p. 145). Cenzo Rena is Anna's salvation, not only because the next day he offers to marry her and give her child a name, thus solving her immediate problem, but because in him she discovers an educator who can develop her mind and foster within her an awareness of the realities of life, of human relationships, and of social questions, all things far removed from her romantic dreams of revolutionary barricades and the fact that 'she had not yet thought of how she wanted to spend her life'

(p. 144). Her education begins within the hour as he tells her sternly that 'at sixteen a person ought to begin to know how he wanted to spend his life' (ibid.), and, subsequently, that 'until that day she had lived like an insect. An insect that knows nothing beyond the leaf on which it hangs' (p. 149), while conversely human beings have a duty to take the initiative and make decisions, acquiring courage little by little as they go forward, taking risks and overcoming fear, while 'anyone who was afraid of a cold shudder did not deserve to live, he deserved to hang on a leaf all his life' (p. 150). As the only character in this novel possessed of any drive Cenzo Rena is clearly a mouth-piece for the author's own views, here expressed directly rather than implicitly suggested as in her earlier work. The marked contrast between Rena's dynamic approach to life and its problems and the nebulous passivity of Anna's family, composed of 'grey colourless characters in the grip of a dismal apathy which saps all will-power, reducing life to a mechanical succession of events shot through with renunciation or defeat',[45] reaches its climax in the sequence where he announces their marriage to Anna's astonished relatives, whose angry protests at the apparent indecency of such a match so exasperate him that he kicks over a table in the sitting-room, breaking one of its legs. His subsequent explanation in private to Concettina naturally pacifies her while making her aware for the first time that she has her share of blame for what has happened and that the person carrying the greatest responsibility in all this is Maria, too wrapped up in her private little world to protect Anna or give her any assistance and naively convinced that Giuma's social status and long-standing friendship automatically place him above reproach.

The first part of the book ends with Anna and Cenzo Rena leaving for San Costanzo, his village in the depressed south, while Maria, having resigned herself to their wedding, worries about the social niceties of the situation. The second and final section is located almost entirely in San Costanzo and concentrates on the activities of Cenzo Rena, whose involvement with the problems of the local peasantry, neglected or exploited under the Fascist administration, becomes increasingly dangerous as the war continues and living conditions become progressively worse. If in this latter part Ginzburg is clearly concerned to shift her focus away from Anna's personal problems to provide a wider spectrum of events it is still largely through her eyes that we see things; we witness her gradual change from 'someone at the mercy of outside events who accepts everything that happens to her with resignation'[46] to a state of mind in which she passes from 'insect-like silence' (p. 170) and during which she is only interested in receiving letters from home and looking after her child, to identifying with her new environment and developing a positive relationship with her husband. Despite this, however, she remains basically the same person as before, as Rena tells her uncompromisingly, 'still just an insect, a little lazy sad insect on a leaf, he himself had been just a big leaf to her . . . she was very lazy, she was a person who stayed where she was put' (pp. 245–7). While it is perhaps an exaggeration to claim, as Pietro Citati has done, that Anna remains 'untouched by what happens around her and with her consciousness unaltered',[47] the reader is still left with the feeling that the absence of any training for life during her childhood and adolescence has combined with her natural indolence to form a kind of shell, which, while in no way protecting her from pain and suffering, none the less ensures the existence within her of a fundamental passivity that, paradoxically, allows her to survive the horrors of war to begin life again in peace time. In this sense her marriage to Cenzo Rena, who not only provides her with genuine warmth and affection far superior to anything she has known among her own kind but also broadens her intellectual horizon, is ultimately little more than a stroke of good fortune.

While we feel deeply for Anna and her problems there is undoubtedly a greater and more varied response called forth with regard to the social and political issues predominant in the latter half of the book in relation to her husband, and which will be discussed in a later chapter.

Notes

1. Adriano Seroni, 'Racconti di NG' in *Esperimenti critici sul novecento letterario* (Mursia, Milan, 1967), p. 83.
2. Cavalli, 'Intervista con NG', p. 11.
3. C. Soave Bowe, 'The Narrative Strategy of NG', *Modern Language Review*, vol. 68, no. 4 (1973), p. 790.
4. See the speech by Giorgio in *Paese di mare*, p. 172: 'Children don't need their parents. The less they have to do with them the better off they are.'
5. *Childhood* in *Never Must You Ask Me*, p. 58.
6. Ibid.
7. *White Whiskers* in *Never Must You Ask Me*, p. 135.
8. *Childhood* in *Never Must You Ask Me*, p. 59.

9. Ibid., p. 61. See also her statement in Maraini, *E tu chi eri?*, p. 119: 'What upset me was the feeling that no one in my family had any great love for me.'
10. *White Whiskers* in *Never Must You Ask Me*, p. 137.
11. Ibid., pp. 139–40. See also her statement in Maraini, *E tu chi eri?*, p. 120: 'My feelings of melancholy began the very year I started going to school.'
12. *Lessico famigliare no. 2: La luna pallidassi*, in *Corriere della sera*, 10 Aug. 1975, p. 8.
13. Ibid.
14. *White Whiskers* in *Never You Must Ask Me*, p. 131.
15. Preface to *Cinque romanzi brevi*, p. 5.
16. A group of children playing in a cellar are repeatedly visited by a police sergeant who tells them adventure stories about his life and becomes the focal point of their existence. When they tell an adult about him he no longer comes to see them, and a fight develops when one of their number voices what they all know but dare not mention: he does not exist. Adults break up the fight and close the cellar, thus putting an end to the children's meetings.
17. See *Family Sayings*, p. 102.
18. '. . . if she had loved them she wouldn't have taken poison . . ', p. 407.
19. As already indicated *I bambini* begins with a sentence reflecting the children's reactions to their mother: 'They had always been frightened of her', p. 66; *La madre* opens with the words 'Their mother was small and thin, and her shoulders were slightly bent . . .', p. 398.
20. Like *Casa al mare* this was published under the pseudonym of Alessandra Tornimparte at a time when no Italian editor would have risked being associated with the obviously Jewish name of Ginzburg.
21. A. Capasso, 'Romanzi della fatalità quotidiana', *La Nazione*, 25 Dec. 1947, p. 3.
22. '". . . when I marry I'll have to tie a handkerchief around my head and go out and sweat in the fields all day on a donkey"', pp. 41–2.
23. *The Little Virtues*, p. 8.
24. G. Manacorda, *Storia della letteratura italiana contemporanea 1940–1965* (Editori Riuniti, Rome, 1967), p. 321.
25. See Capasso, 'Romanzi della fatalità quotidiana': 'Both women are marked by fate and could not develop other than as they do . . .'
26. See Laura Ingrao's comment in her review in *Rinascita*, IV, nos 11–12 (1947), p. 352: 'There is only one escape for this woman: motherhood, which she embraces with all the energy of her loneliness and disenchantment.'
27. Preface to *Cinque romanzi brevi*, p. 14.
28. R. Frattarolo, book review, *L'Italia che scrive*, Oct. 1947, p. 205.
29. *The Little Virtues*, p. 62. The same point is made in more general terms and at greater length in *Human Relationships*, ibid., pp. 90–2.
30. See her statement in *My Vocation* in ibid., pp. 62–3: '. . . the feeling I then had for my children was one that I had not yet learnt to control. But then little by little I learnt . . . I still made tomato sauce and semolina, but simultaneously I thought about what I could be writing.'

31. M. G. Amadori, 'NG ultima crepuscolare', *La fiera letteraria*, XVII, no. 4, 28 Jan. 1962, p. 4; see also Michele Sovente's comment in *La donna nella letteratura oggi* (Esperienze, Fossano, 1979), p. 72: 'She cannot conceive of her existence without a man by her side.'
32. *Worn-Out Shoes* in *The Little Virtues*, p. 9.
33. Ibid., pp. 10–11.
34. *The Son of Man* in ibid., pp. 51–2.
35. Thomson, 'Spinsters in Italy'.
36. This is most obvious in her mother's reluctance to receive her daughter-in-law's administrator, who brings the family a monthly allowance, so that 'I always received him alone in the drawing-room; my mother stayed in the kitchen with the door shut and never allowed me to mention the envelope; yet this was the money that fed us every day', p. 23.
37. *Silence* in *The Little Virtues*, p. 70.
38. Ibid., p. 69. The Italian, there given in a rather mild English translation, can more properly be rendered by a phrase such as 'My bloody death will atone for my guilty passion'.
39. Ibid., p. 73.
40. T. G. Bergin, 'Italy Only Yesterday', *Saturday Review*, 5 Jan. 1957, p. 14.
41. S. Stallings, 'A Novel of Italians in a World at War', *Herald Tribune Book Review*, 13 Jan. 1957, p. 4.
42. Maria's comments on the African campaign are similarly short-sighted: '. . . the old man had gone much too far in his anger against the Fascists, because in the end they had taken Africa, where later on they meant to grow coffee', p. 37.
43. Geno Pampaloni comments in his review in *L'approdo letterario*, Oct.–Dec. 1952, p. 90, that 'Anna is very like the female protagonists of Ginzburg's previous stories; indeed she is basically the same person'.
44. Angus Davidson translates *pena* as 'distress'.
45. R. Tian, 'Cronache letterarie', *Il Messaggero*, 3 Apr. 1953, p. 3.
46. M. C. Innamorati, 'Tutti i nostri ieri', *Il mattino dell'Italia centrale*, 8 Apr. 1953, p. 3.
47. P. Citati, book review, *Belfagor*, vol. VIII (1953), p. 363.

3 Female Alienation: Girls and Older Women

> Ginzburg's aim is to communicate the essentially painful absurdity of life.[1]

If Ginzburg's main interest in the four novels so far examined has clearly been in female protagonists occupying an inferior position who are victims of other people's insensitivity and the social conventions which regulate human relationships, negative forces to which they further contribute through their own short-sightedness, she is also fully conscious not only of the reassurance supposedly provided by traditional female roles but also of the attractions of an independent life-style for those who have sufficient means to pursue it and who believe they can disregard the limitations which bind others less fortunate than themselves. In almost every case, however, both these alternatives also prove equally unsatisfactory.

The first example of a character willingly conforming to type is provided by the unnamed narrator of *Mio marito*, a short story written as early as 1941 whose protagonist, a woman of twenty-five long resigned to spinsterhood, marries a rural doctor twelve years her senior who visits her family with a view to purchasing some land they own and subsequently and unexpectedly asks for her hand. Despite not having any feelings of love for him she accepts his offer, determined to make a good life for both of them, only to find that he has been motivated by a vain attempt to escape from an obsessive infatuation with a local peasant girl, a discovery which inevitably leads to their progressive estrangement, and, ultimately, to her husband's suicide, which leaves her totally disorientated and at a loss to know how to spend the rest of her life. A less dramatic but equally significant variation on this theme occurs in *All Our Yesterdays* in Concettina, for whom the most important thing in life is a range of pretty clothes and a string of platonic boyfriends, one of whom will one day become her future husband. She has no interest in her studies, and when she presents her graduate dissertation on Racine, which is only twenty-five pages long, it is, not surprisingly, rejected, despite being 'bound up in a big album tied with red tapes' (p. 61).[2]

Her friends and siblings console her by telling her she will surely get married soon and thus have no need to graduate, but are shocked when shortly afterwards she announces her engagement to a wealthy young man 'who always came to take her out in his car' but whom everyone knows for an active Fascist who 'went round in a black shirt in processions' (p. 74). Fortunately for all concerned he turns out to be a harmless conformist who knows nothing about politics and cares even less, but if Concettina's willingness to disregard the principles she has nominally shared with the other members of her family in favour of a conventionally good marriage appears to be no more than a confirmation of her essential superficiality of character it is subsequently revealed as something more disturbing: a total identification with accepted norms of behaviour and attitude. Soon she is suggesting that the Fascists must be given credit for improving communications between cities by building roads and bridges; and when she returns, appropriately pregnant, from her honeymoon, and in due course gives birth, it becomes clear that her interests are now totally restricted to things maternal, all other considerations having been firmly and definitively discarded, so that 'with Concettina it was now quite impossible to hold a sensible conversation, all she could talk about now was milk and babies' (p. 138). The irony in all this is that Concettina's increasingly close adherence to conventional patterns of behaviour does not in any way bring her satisfaction or peace of mind but rather the reverse, with the result that she suffers more acutely from the horrors of war, has nightmares about fleeing into the unknown to protect her child from German invaders, and in due course emerges embittered and disgruntled into peacetime, pitied and despised by her siblings, who all agree 'the important thing was *not* to be like Concettina' (p. 293).[3]

Totally different but equally unfulfilled is the protagonist's city cousin Francesca in *The Dry Heart*, who has over-reacted to traditional restrictions by becoming outrageously promiscuous. Throughout the novel she appears as a completely free agent who comes and goes as she pleases, leaves home when she can no longer stand her mother's constant nagging, and frequently encourages Alberto's wife to abandon him and start a new life. It is clear, however, that she has achieved emotional independence only after much soul-searching and no little anguish, conscious that there is something within her which makes her radically different from the established norm:

'Oh, I've had a lot of men,' she said . . . 'What kind of a girl am

I?' I said to myself. 'I must be a bitch if I like to change so often . . . I still thought I ought to marry and be like everyone else. Then little by little I learned to make life less of a tragedy. We have to accept ourselves for what we are.' (p. 111)

Despite having her freedom Francesca is still not convinced that she has the right to live as she wishes, and her basic insecurity is revealed in the remainder of this exchange:

'Am I a bitch?' she asked.
'No, you're not a bitch,' I said. 'But you'll be alone in your old age.'
'What the devil do I care about that? I'll kill myself when I'm forty.' (ibid.)

while earlier on in the same conversation she has stated with equal forcefulness that '"If ever I had a baby I'd kill myself, for sure"' (p. 109). At one point she attempts to achieve some degree of stability by rejecting her lovers and turning her flat into an artist's studio; here she devotes herself exclusively to painting pictures whose chaotic nature are clearly indicative of her unchanged restlessness of spirit. However, this soon passes, and at the last we see of her she has gone back to her old life, which she realises intuitively may eventually destroy her.[4]

Less extreme by nature but similarly dissatisfied with the conventional patterns of middle-class married life is Alberto's longstanding mistress Giovanna, who visits the protagonist on two occasions and tells her frankly of the difficulties which have led her to seek fulfilment elsewhere:

'I was on poor terms with my husband from the start . . . we haven't anything to say to each other and he thinks I'm silly and queer . . . He . . . at first . . . made dreadful scenes, but finally he got over it and we settled down to tolerating one another . . .' (p. 126)

Despite having found a long-term partner in Alberto Giovanna has been unable ever to live with him, thus making it impossible for them to grow together and adapt to each other's character; the result, as she admits, is an imperfect relationship which they are now in any case too old to alter but which might have brought them greater satisfaction had things been different in their youth. However, unlike Francesca, who seems determined to spend the rest of her life sailing increasingly close to the wind, Giovanna has come to terms with her problems and is able to compromise with her ideals, and, while clearly not a happy woman in a real sense, can live a life in which she is never exposed to danger or anguish, a life in which she can plan her wardrobe from fashion magazines and order her days as she thinks fit. A similar picture of quiet pessimism and a willingness to be content with one's lot emerges from Ginzburg's analysis of Maddalena, Valentino's wife, an energetic landowner whose uncompromising lack of sex-appeal[5] is amply compensated by a boundless self-confidence and an intense will-power which make Caterina realise from their first meeting that 'she intended to marry Valentino come what may' (p. 11), unable to grasp that he is only interested in her money. Fully occupied in running her large estate she none the less manages to produce three children in between dealing with fractious peasants and keeping her administrator up to the mark, happy to have exorcised her youthful fears that she would always be too unattractive to find a husband and raise a family, occasionally quarrelling with Valentino because of his reluctance to pursue his studies but still unaware of the truth. Gradually their marriage deteriorates as she begins to appreciate his true nature; when she tells Caterina that it is only their children who keep them together it is clear she has come to despise him and that her joy at having banished the spectre of loneliness has been no more than a temporary illusion, finally shattered for ever when she learns that Valentino's real instincts are homosexual and that he has for some time been involved in a furtive relationship with her cousin Kit, whom he has driven to commit suicide. Unable to bear him any longer Maddalena expels her husband and resigns herself to a life of solitude; no longer possessing the energy to deal directly with her business affairs she changes her life-style completely and makes a conscious decision to spend her days '"darning socks and looking after the children and sitting down a lot"' (p. 46), adapting her image to this new role so well that Caterina is astonished, on first visiting her after Valentino's departure, to see her looking 'all of a sudden . . . very old . . . a little old lady' (p. 45). If it is Maddalena's undiminished will-power which allows her to survive the emotional shock she has undergone and use her resources intelligently to create an acceptable context for herself she is, like Giovanna, far from being a happy woman in absolute terms, as is clear from her momentary breakdown while telling Caterina what has happened and her injunction to leave immediately and never return, an untypically cruel gesture which she immediately negates by calling her back and embracing her while they both weep copious tears. In the final picture Ginzburg gives of her she is described as 'very fat and her hair is completely grey; she is an old lady. She occupies herself with her children, taking them skating and organising picnics in the garden . . . She spends whole afternoons at home . . .' (p. 48).

This sharp contrast between youthful dynamism and middle-aged resignation, adumbrated in *The Dry Heart* but now more fully developed in *Valentino*, confirms the presence of a new element in Ginzburg's writing: a sympathetic understanding of the problems facing older women, now no longer seen simply as negative figures unable to discharge their maternal responsibilities adequately but also as victims themselves of that same naivety which is so detrimental to their offspring, and just as exposed to the suffering deriving from unsatisfactory human relationships. Herself now in her mid-thirties and newly married she was clearly in a position to take stock of her life both past and present, realising she was rapidly approaching middle age, and thus, inevitably, beginning to identify with members of the older generation; this is clear from an essay published two years later (in 1953) and entitled *Human Relationships*, in which she looks back on her experiences from earliest infancy to maturity, tracing a pattern of development familiar to many of her readers – from the bewildered incomprehension of young children confronted with the adult world, through the complexities of working relationships with school-fellows and the pain that springs from adolescent rejection of one's background, to marriage and the creation of one's own family, where the pattern is destined to repeat itself notwithstanding the greater degree of sophistication which modern adults have acquired and their desire to avoid making the same mistakes as their parents.[6] This theme is developed in the essay entitled *The Little Virtues*, published in 1960, in which Ginzburg pin-points the difficulties involved in establishing a meaningful communication with one's children, contrasting the naive presumption of previous generations with the well-intentioned but largely fruitless attempts of her contemporaries:

> Education is only a certain relationship which we establish between ourselves and our children, a certain climate in which feelings, instincts and thoughts can flourish . . . In our relationships with our children it is no use our trying to remember and imitate the way our parents acted with us . . . They were authoritarian towards us in a way that we are quite incapable of being . . . a dialogue was impossible because as soon as they suspected that they were wrong they ordered us to be quiet; they beat their fists on the table and made the room shake . . . it was a

time of strong and sonorous words that little by little lost all their substance. The present is a time of cold, submissive words . . .'[7]

Despite these problems Ginzburg is convinced that it is indeed possible for parents to communicate with their children provided they allow them a certain independence of spirit in which they can retain their natural love of life, a spontaneous instinct whose preservation she sees as the most important aspect of parental duty, and which in due course will encourage the development of a vocational interest that will polarise the individual's random aspirations and give a meaningful structure to his or her existence. The greatest threat to such a development is the absence of a corresponding interest among the older generation, whose lack of creative drive frequently leads to an obsessive rapport with their offspring in which the young person's aims and hopes are ignored or actively opposed in favour of alternatives which appear more useful or more attractive to parents who have not realised their own ambitions:

> . . . if . . . we do not have a vocation, or if we have abandoned it or betrayed it out of cynicism or a fear of life, or because of mistaken parental love . . . then we cling to our children as a shipwrecked mariner clings to a tree trunk; we eagerly demand that they give us back everything we have given them, that they be absolutely and inescapably what we wish them to be . . . we want them to be entirely our creation, as if having once created them we could continue to create them throughout their whole lives . . . as if we were not dealing with human beings but with products of the spirit.[8]

Clearly it is the absence of a vocational interest which is responsible for much of the misfortune and unhappiness afflicting Ginzburg's younger female protagonists, who are victims either of passive obtuseness, or, more obviously, of active obstructionism on the part of those who have neglected their own opportunities for the greater security offered by conventional patterns of existence or short-sighted selfishness. At the same time those members of the older generation who find themselves at variance with their children's desires, like the grandparents in *La madre* and Francesca's mother in *The Dry Heart*, or who realise they have wasted their life, like Delia's mother in *The Road to the City* or Caterina in *Valentino*, are similarly frustrated; while those past their first youth anxious to fulfil themselves on more than one level are likewise forced to admit defeat, like Maddalena in *Valentino*, or, more dramatically, the character at the centre of Ginzburg's next novel, *Sagittarius* (published in 1957), who is both 'decidedly neurotic',[9] 'an extreme example of conventional attitudes, a walking cliché',[10] and, in equal measure, typical of Ginzburg's 'poor women driven onto the sidelines of the life they would love to inhabit fully'.[11] In contrast to her previous technique Ginzburg here chooses to have the story recounted not by this main character but by her daughter, and although this inevitably makes for a certain degree of artificiality[12] it has the advantage of allowing her to describe with great precision both aspects of the character's personality as she alternates between her role as obsessive mother, in keeping with the pattern established in Ginzburg's earlier work, and prospective business woman, anxious to widen the confines of her domestic routine and live a more exciting life.

Needless to say she is unsuccessful on both counts, greatly disappointed in her daughters, who, though very different from each other, are equally unwilling to submit to her wishes, while her naive attempts to break into the commercial world are a total disaster. On the home front she is frustrated by the apparent passivity of the narrator, a school-teacher who, having moved to the city three years earlier to take up her appointment, is determined to maintain her independence and refuses to live with her mother when she too comes to town; a shy serious girl with no social pretensions, uninterested in the frivolities of fashion, lacking any male admirers and with no friends other than the girl she shares her flat with, she is clearly a character modelled on Ginzburg's younger self,[13] while her other daughter Giulia, the picture of domesticity and submission and far more attractive, is also supremely apathetic, unable to make conversation, never opening a book, and falling asleep at concerts, hardly ever leaving the house and apparently quite unconcerned that the young men she meets while on holiday are bored stiff with her indolence and put off by her vacuous smile. With considerable subtlety Ginzburg succeeds in conveying the limitations of these three lives, allowing the reader to sympathise with the daughters' irritation at their mother's unflagging interference while at the same time stressing the narrowness of each individual's view of her existence.

Possessed like Maddalena of a boundless energy, but infinitely less intelligent and totally dominated by an inflated view of her own potential, the narrator's mother decides that her move to the city will mark the beginning of a new era in her life in which all the projects she has planned for years will finally be realised. She dreams of entering a world of intellectual stimulation where cultural questions are debated at length and artistic matters are at the centre of people's attention, but she is unable to find any such environment in the small provincial community where people talk about trivialities at café tables and the members of the local cultural centre are all elderly gentlemen who fall asleep during lectures, unable to maintain their interest. Anxious to be of service to her two older sisters, who have never married, she decides to inflict her presence on their small china shop, which caters exclusively for retiring elderly ladies like themselves, only to upset their genteel routine with her forthright manners and being more of a nuisance than an aid as she wanders through the place filling the air with cigarette smoke while occasionally bumping into things and breaking them. At once touchingly enthusiastic and impossibly oppressive in her desire to improve other people's lives while being herself at the centre of things she lacks a specific focus for her activity, her dispersive spirit revealing a degree of vulnerability more appropriate to an adolescent discovering her true personality than to a middle-aged woman supposedly in control of her life and able to fend for herself.

Unable to breathe new life into the china shop, whose dusty atmosphere she finds too gloomy, and ever more restless at the impossibility of participating in any intellectual or artistic activity, she becomes increasingly depressed with the emptiness of her life while still hoping that despite everything she will somehow be able to open an art gallery in the centre of town, a project which is clearly totally unrealistic. Here the problem is not so much the absence of a vocational interest as an inability to define that interest rationally and adapt it to the reality of a given context: namely, the absence in the subject of any cultural training which can justify such grandiose aims, coupled with their essential irrelevancy in a small provincial town whose inhabitants are largely indifferent to such matters. Too naive to understand any of this[14] the narrator's mother is easily tricked into parting with her life's savings by an unscrupulous adventuress she meets at the hairdresser's and who encourages her in her illusions by suggesting they pool their resources to set up the gallery, subsequently disappearing with the money. Meanwhile Giulia has finally put paid to any hopes of a wealthy match with a young man of good family by agreeing to marry an impoverished Polish refugee whose medical talents her mother does not appreciate, conscious only of his unattractive appearance and lack of poise. Totally absorbed by her new friend Scilla, whose activity as a painter increases her unthinking enthusiasm, she also fails to notice that Giulia's sudden and unexpected attachment to this lady's seductive daughter is a significant indication of her true nature, confirmed when she uses her subsequent pregnancy as an excuse to terminate any sexual contact with her husband.

Throughout this novel Ginzburg loses no opportunity to stress the absurdity of the mother's behaviour, her every comment and every action being consistent with an image of scatter-brained simplicity, pretentious snobbery, and insensitive meddlesomeness. At the same time it is equally obvious that she is invariably animated by the best possible intentions in her relationships with others, and, likewise, that her aspirations are, in themselves, perfectly proper despite being totally unrealistic. If in one sense she deserves her fate she is also clearly deserving of pity as one of life's victims, unable to defend herself against superior forces only too keen to take advantage of her vulnerability. The conclusion stresses this aspect, emphasising once more the author's new tendency to sympathise not only with younger women eager to live a life of their own choosing, here represented by the narrator, but also middle-aged females unable to understand the world they live in and destined for a rude awakening. Drugged by her false friend the mother comes round in an empty apartment in which, little by little, she realises what has happened to her and is filled with despair, a moving sequence in which the author clearly identifies with her anguish. Weeping convulsively she returns home, crossing the city on foot because 'if she took the tram people would see her crying, and she would not . . . take a taxi because she now felt as poor as a church mouse' (p. 127), eventually collapsing in hysterics in her bedroom. She has more hysterics the next day after the local police reproach her because 'despite all her grey hairs, she had acted with the circumspection of a four-year-old' (p. 128), and the estate agent supposedly handling the purchase of the art gallery claims to have no recollection of the deal, while a subsequent visit to one of Scilla's rich acquaintances reveals that, far from being on intimate terms with this lady, Scilla had merely worked for her as a part-time dressmaker. Conscious that her hopes and dreams are now well and truly over she resigns herself to a future of quiet domesticity, but even this is denied her; the news that Scilla's daughter has been shot by her jealous Sicilian husband provokes a brainstorm in Giulia, who seems to be on the point of losing her mind, and although there is no specific link between this event and her subsequent death in childbirth it is perhaps not unreasonable to suggest that the two may be connected. The closing paragraph provides the final touch in its description of the mother, who, 'suddenly very old and careworn,

100

gazed at this unknown infant with dull, misty eyes . . . eyes in which the old brilliance was now drowned in a veil of tears' (p. 134).

When Ginzburg completed this novel in 1957 she was in her fortieth year and conscious that she had reached a watershed in her life, now definitively leaving youth behind her and entering a new era. Her awareness of the significance of this particular time is clear from an essay she wrote many years later, in 1971: 'When they reach forty women begin to wonder how they can avoid turning into that ridiculous irksome and wretched thing which people call "a middle-aged lady"',[15] a telling phrase which explains the care lavished on the character at the centre of *Sagittarius*. If none the less her next novel, written four years later in 1961 while she was in London, appears to be a throwback to earlier preoccupations with wasted youth and domestic repression this is not as surprising as might at first seem when viewed in the context of her state of mind; as already indicated she had in the mean time suffered from writer's block and was able to dispel this only by giving way to feelings of nostalgia for Italy and things Italian. At the same time she was experiencing the influence of Ivy Compton-Burnett, and in addition, as is clear from this same essay, she had made a conscious effort not to wallow in self-pity over the intimations of her mortality: 'In order to be able to go on living with themselves without being overcome by horror they must decide to forget how old they are and carry on living while hiding their age away in a secret place which they take care never to go near'. Filed away but not forgotten this theme was to emerge anew some years later with increased vigour, as is clear from the conclusion of this paragraph: 'However they know that their age exists, hidden away in that dark place, and does not simply exist but increases day by day like a poisonous weed.'[16]

Thus in *Voices in the Evening*, one of her best-known works, Ginzburg concentrates once more on a young middle-class woman, Elsa, living with her family in a small industrial centre and whose emotional fulfilment is frustrated by the well-meaning but ultimately destructive activities of her mother, Matilde. Like her opposite number in *Sagittarius*, and in contrast to the neglectful passivity of most maternal figures in Ginzburg's earlier work, Matilde is the embodiment of parental dedication while at the same time being totally unaware that her daughter is not simply a younger version of herself but a separate human being, with distinct needs and aspirations very different from her own. Elsa narrates how the confines of her narrow domestic world temporarily expand to include a delicate attachment to a young man from the same area, only to contract again, condemning her to perpetual spinsterhood, when she realises that the formalisation of their relationship through a public engagement has destroyed their ability to communicate freely and genuinely with each other, and gives him back his ring. If the limited size of the community in which Elsa and her family live, and in which there is scant room for privacy of any kind, is itself sufficient to inhibit any attempt at creating an independent life-style Matilde is undoubtedly the prime representative of this petty world, where traditional conventions regulating human relationships are seen in absolute terms which make no allowances for spiritual or psychological development, and the pattern of human existence flows on unchanged from one generation to the next. Twenty-seven years old and a university graduate Elsa still lives with her parents on the outskirts of town, where she spends her days sitting by the stove warming her hands and relying for intellectual stimulus on the girl next door, who occasionally calls and chats about what's on at the local cinema. Elsa's only other diversion is trips to town to run errands for the family, and her need to have an excuse to leave the house at all not only confirms the supremely stagnant atmosphere of her home[17] but also provides a pointer to something the reader only learns later: that she has for some time been having an affair with Tommasino and meeting him twice a week in a rented room in town, thus revealing an aspect of her personality which her mother cannot even conceive of, as is clear from her forthright denial of a rumour that Elsa and her lover have been seen holding hands in a café and which Matilde defines as incredible.[18] The immediacy of this reaction is typical of someone whose obsessive preoccupation with the trivialities of a routine existence effectively excludes any serious consideration of the fundamental problems of life, and her total absorption by things domestic, to which she devotes an unquenchable vitality, is ultimately destructive of all self-knowledge and all fulfilment outside the narrow scope of day-to-day living. Tirelessly energetic and full of good will Matilde clearly possesses considerable potential, but has unthinkingly chosen to embrace the traditional role of wife and mother, thus unconsciously inhibiting a natural talent that could have produced impressive results if directed towards some more ambitious vocational interest but which has instead been channelled into a narrow furrow where it can only find release in obsessive small talk; this is never more strikingly rendered than in the opening and closing chapters, where a conversation between mother and daughter is soon revealed as being in reality an extended monologue wherein Elsa's participation is minimal, frustrated by an endless flow of shallow chatter ensuring that no true communication can take place. Significantly Matilde at first reproaches her daughter for her lack of response,[19] but makes no attempt to discover its cause, her interests being strictly limited to what is immediately accessible to the five senses or impinges on her sense of social propriety. The result is inevitably a feeling of emotional aridity and intellectual immobility far more repressive than any straightforward authoritarianism, all the more so since it springs from genuine affection and takes the form of benevolent concern.

It is Matilde's obtuse exuberance, both symbolic of conventional values and depressingly real in its constant immediacy, which in due course denies her daughter any chance of emotional fulfilment. Consciously aware that Elsa would be better off married than single[20] it never occurs to her that a woman who has reached maturity in the post-war period may have a different interpretation of this state; and it is Matilde's behaviour which proves crucial in the progressive disenchantment which overtakes Tommasino at the prospect of accepting the role of formal fiancé, and, subsequently, respectable husband. His first tentative appearance within the family circle, a delicate moment of considerable importance in its far-reaching implications, becomes simply another opportunity for Matilde to take the floor and deliver a stream of mindless verbiage in which she enquires at length about the health of his relatives, chatters about her married children, who have long left the area, and gives the young man an extended account of her recent visit to the doctor. Predictably this reduces him to a position of inferiority, and when he is later invited to dinner the greater amount of time available and the more intimate atmosphere appropriate to a family meal allow Matilde to marshal a more intense and elaborate barrage of trivia, directing a constant flow of tiresome questions at her guest, paying little heed to his answers, and switching arbitrarily from one boring item to another. Her attitude to Tommasino himself is throughout shamelessly patronising, as if he were still a child needing advice and attention, and it is clear from her reactions to her husband's discreet attempts to make things a little more interesting for her victim that she has no idea what he is talking about.[21] When the two lovers acquire the status of an engaged couple Matilde takes over the relationship completely, obliging them to concentrate exclusively on the domestic aspect of their forthcoming marriage and forcing her presence on them as much as possible, so that eventually the relationship ceases to exist other than in formal terms. The further necessity of providing the lovers at all times with a chaperon in order to satisfy conventional rules of propriety inhibits not only physical contact between them, but, far more seriously, any kind of real communication, as their secret visits to the room in town are now replaced by long evenings in the parental home where the constant presence of a third party makes it impossible even for them to talk naturally to each other. This effectively poisons their relationship, which in turn leads to an increasing feeling of oppressive emptiness and a rapid deterioration in the quality of their rapport.

The result of these increasing pressures is inevitable: the destruction of ' "something very slight, very fragile, ready to break up at the first puff of wind" ' (p. 156). The formal termination of the engagement produces a nervous collapse in Matilde, who has not the slightest inkling of any connection between this separation and the kind of life she symbolises, which has destroyed with its oppressive sterility the delicacy, as of a hothouse plant, of an irregular relationship forcibly distorted when placed under the spotlight of social scrutiny. When she recovers Matilde has no hesitation in resuming her benevolent tyranny over her daughter; at the last we see of her she is still encouraging Elsa to play tennis, and suggesting without the slightest compunction that if the family moves to a different locality she can share a room with her maiden aunt, thus destroying the only element of independence her daughter still possesses. In this final dialogue Elsa's total silence, now taken for granted by her mother, is more eloquent than any protest or complaint, and the story of her progressive absorption by a warm but stifling family environment which gradually extinguishes all opportunity for self-assertion is well characterised by Paolo Milano's description of the book as 'a trickle of blood that turns into a lethal haemorrhage'.[22] At the same time it is clear that Matilde's freedom to exercise her unwittingly destructive power is in large measure dependent on the absence of any opposition from her victim, apparently all too willing to contribute passively to her own emotional disintegration and thus to a large extent responsible for her own plight. In this sense Elsa is clearly another example of an older woman seeking fulfilment within the traditional patterns of female behaviour and finding these totally unsatisfying.[23]

Elsa's unthinking stagnation in the bosom of the family, already mentioned, an attitude typical of middle-class values in Mediterranean society, is Ginzburg's first detailed picture of the harmful effects of this entity, whose strangulatory force is manifest throughout the novel, not only in relation to Elsa's abortive relationship with Tommasino but also in connection with other characters still to be mentioned. This theme, touched on in her earlier work but not previously explored in depth,[24] here provides a further example of female alienation, now seen as applying not only to young girls whose education is neglected by their parents, to young wives and mothers unable to cope with their obligations, and to self-assured but naive ladies of independent means, but also to women mature in years but still conditioned by traditional attitudes in an environment where these reign supreme and thus determine individual destinies. In this context an interesting and significant parallel to what Olga Lombardi has called 'a grey lifeless female fate'[25] is provided by Elsa's friend Giuliana Bottiglia, whose mother, no different from Matilde in her unthinking simplicity of spirit, marries her off to a young man who is rumoured to be a homosexual drug addict but whose status as a general's son makes him nevertheless perfectly eligible in the eyes of society; the result, while very different from Elsa's permanent spinsterhood, is inevitably no more fulfilling .

While Ginzburg's description of Elsa's gradual surrender to her role as willing victim is clearly the most striking aspect of this book, occupying as it does the whole of the second half of the novel, she is also clearly keen to present further examples of female sacrifice in her portraits of four other women; all are equally frustrated in their attempts to achieve their respective goals, albeit in very different ways, and all 'unable to transcend the confines of a grey existence within the family, or, if able to make an adventurous escape, doomed in advance to pay a high price for the privilege'.[26] Thus in addition to touching on Giuliana Bottiglia, Elsa's friend from next door already mentioned, the author also devotes a considerable amount of space to Tommasino's four siblings, who are examined at length in the first part of the novel and of whom two are women, the final example of female misfortune being provided by the wife of their brother Vincenzino. Gemmina, the oldest of the four De Francisci children, now in her forties, is unmarried and clearly destined to remain so, having seen the man she loved in her youth unable to respond to her feelings and keen to marry someone else. Possessed of a sound business sense and keenly intelligent Gemmina has suffered from being supremely unattractive in appearance in an environment where women are prized mainly, if not solely, for their beauty, her intellectual skills totally eclipsed by the fact that she is tall and thin with short hair and a face which is 'long and narrow, all chin', complemented by a mottled complexion and, in later years, the signs of 'an old rash' which has left 'livid marks' (p. 42). Unable to find fulfilment in the small community and broken-hearted after her rejection she goes off to live in Switzerland, where she works in a tourist agency, returning only after the end of the war to grow old alone in the family house she has inherited from her parents, never entirely reconciling herself to her condition and nostalgically recalling the days of her youth when she had hoped for a better future. Her destiny is especially ironic in that despite her mental agility and her athletic prowess, which allowed her as a girl to go rock-climbing at weekends with the man she loves in secret, she is essentially a traditional woman who wants nothing more than to get married and raise a family, and her efforts to ingratiate herself with her unsuspecting companion only reinforce his view of her as a kind of honorary male whose stamina he admires but whose femininity he is never remotely conscious of. His astonishment when she eventually confesses her feelings for him is total, and determines her reluctant renunciation of domestic fulfilment for a life devoted to community work, the modern equivalent of traditional withdrawal to a convent; however, her sacrifice in rejecting emotional and sexual activity is clear from the fact that she appears constantly discontented and seems to derive little satisfaction from her achievements – building a hospital, setting up a general store, organising charity teas – frequently complaining of how tired she is, and, as she grows older, revealing the traditional defects characteristic of 'old maids': avarice, self-interest, and snobbishness. She too is essentially a willing victim who collaborates in her own misfortune, refusing to make a new life for herself in a more progressive environment, and, instead, foolishly returning to her roots, where, as she must know only too well, she has no chance of finding a suitable partner before reaching middle age and becoming doubly ineligible for marriage, her independence being maintained through her spinsterhood at the expense of emotional isolation.

Just as Giuliana can be seen as the mirror image of Elsa so Gemmina's younger sister Raffaella is a very different but equally striking example of female impoverishment. A forceful young girl with a strong political awareness she joins the partisans to engage in guerrilla warfare during the German occupation and finds complete fulfilment in a life-style even more energetic than Gemmina's and which is not restricted to weekends. When she reappears after the liberation wearing trousers, a red handkerchief round her neck, and a pistol strapped to her waist she is the very image of the liberated woman, proud of her Communist principles and anxious to apply them unreservedly in peace time. A jolly and uncomplicated person who enjoys charging down ski slopes and 'thumping everyone on the back with her hands heavy as lead' (p. 75) she is described at one point as 'a boisterous hobbledehoy' (p. 73) whose love of life is manifest in everything she does and says, but who little by little realises that party politics after 1945 are infinitely more complicated than blowing up bridges and establishing a common front against an enemy invader. Increasingly disillusioned by the conflicts fragmenting the left-wing opposition and which she does not really understand she resigns from the Party and joins a splinter group consisting of only three people in the whole area, burning up her surplus energy by buying a horse and building a new house to live in. Gradually she is reabsorbed by the unchanging routine of her new life and begins increasingly to adapt to conventional norms, eventually going so far as to marry an ex-Fascist who still has reverence and affection for Mussolini and whom she has known since her first youth. When in due course they have a child she retreats completely into full-time maternity, no longer interested in anything other than her son's welfare and obsessed with his material needs. Apparently content and fully occupied in looking after Pepè she has in reality attained tranquillity by systematically renouncing all intellectual or idealistic considerations and confining herself to one single area of existence, which she correspondingly focuses on unremittingly with results that are deceptively reassuring but essentially artificial.[27] If pressures to return to something approaching normality are stronger for Raffaella than for Gemmina her experiences while living rough for an extended period have been so far removed from any civilised life-style as to provoke in her the desire to contribute to a new improved society within her community; it is clear, however, that when she realises how her aspirations are incompatible with the reality of post-war life her only protection against profound disillusion is to embrace traditional values, which are ready, as always, to provide a context that will give life some meaning and guarantee an acceptable role among one's fellows; Gemmina's sacrifice of her emotional potential is thus balanced by her younger sister's interment of her social and political beliefs.

Their sister-in-law Cate, a pretty blonde girl from a nearby village, is yet another victim of convention and unthinking adherence to social norms, in her case the proverbial good match designed to ensure a stable future which instead leads to frustration and unhappiness. Although she does not love Vincenzino she agrees to marry him because 'he was so good, if a bit melancholy, and that he must therefore be intelligent', further stimulated by the fact that 'he had plenty of money and she had none' (pp. 69–70). Unable to participate in her husband's intellectual interests she soon becomes bored with married life, regretting the happy days with her large noisy family, now replaced by long silent evenings during which both parties realise they have nothing to say to each other, and even longer days in which she mopes about the house and weeps. Encouraged by Vincenzino to visit her family more often she begins to meet people outside his limited circle of social contacts, their estrangement gradually becoming transformed into something more substantial as Cate is briefly unfaithful, attracted by an itinerant musician relatively unimportant in himself but symbolising a definite emotional break with her husband. She soon becomes increasingly promiscuous, something which inevitably leads in due course to their separation, and it is only much later that she realises that the placid unexciting existence she had led during the early part of her marriage was a kind of happiness that can never be recaptured and which she has chosen to abandon for a life which has given her only bitterness. Although largely a victim of her own thoughtlessness she too, in her own way, has been conditioned by the values of her community, where poor country girls think themselves lucky to attract the attention of local gentlemen while at the same time being too passive to appreciate the opportunities for expanding their range of interests once they have been admitted to their husband's world. There is no hint here of the violence and squalor which characterise Delia's family life in *The Road to the City*, but Cate's background is clearly a more respectable version of this primitive environment where material needs are paramount and the complexities of human relationships remain unimagined.[28] In addition it is also abundantly clear that at no time does she receive any help with her problems from her husband, whose character will be examined in a later chapter.

The pessimistic implications of this unrelieved catalogue of female misfortune are only slightly relieved by Ginzburg's sketches of two other women who appear to have avoided a similar fate but whose lot is no more reassuring for the reader. One is Pupazzina, the girl Nebbia marries in preference to Gemmina, a mindless creature whose interests go no further than the contents of her wardrobe and the furnishings of her home, conscious only of her status in the small community, 'being anxious to play the lady' (p. 49). Like Concettina in *All Our Yesterdays* Pupazzina is perfectly content with her vegetable-like existence until the outbreak of war, when her husband is killed by Fascist activists; although we are not told how she recovers from this there seems little doubt that once normality has been restored she has resumed her placid existence, instinctively restricting her interests to the more superficial aspects of life and thus effectively resembling those members of the older generation who, like Matilde and Signora Bottiglia, maintain a naive innocence far removed from the disenchanted awareness of their offspring.

More interesting but also more dubious is the exotic Xenia, a Russian refugee whom Mario, the third of the De Francisci brothers, meets while on a business trip to Munich and promptly marries. Uncompromisingly foreign, to the point where she is unable even to speak Italian, and infinitely more sophisticated than Pupazzina, Xenia spends her husband's money like water, buying a large house, which she furnishes with exquisite taste while hiring a small army of servants to run it, ordering her clothes from distinguished Parisian couturiers, and spending her days painting and sculpting in a studio she has established on the ground floor. Notwithstanding her total lack of sex-appeal, which shocks her father-in-law,[29] Xenia makes her husband happy, and is thus a positive influence; despite this, however, there are suggestions that her whole image is fraudulent, a deliberate creation designed to impress her husband and his relatives while guaranteeing her a life of leisure. These suspicions are reinforced – though never specifically confirmed – by Mario's subsequent death at the hands of an incompetent Swiss doctor, specially imported to treat a stomach complaint, and whom Xenia later marries, thus ensuring her continued reliance on a wealthy partner and suggesting all manner of underhand activities in the interim ranging from adultery to murder. She too, however, achieves fulfilment only by going outside the accepted norms of female behaviour, and although there is no indication that, like Gemmina, she finds this a source of stress, it is clearly her ambiguously eccentric personality which determines the success of her life, a fact whose pessimistic implications further underline the limitations of this environment, characterised by 'the mediocrity, the illusions and false hopes, the spiritual and intellectual, and human even, dessication to which people are condemned',[30] and which form the background to 'a desolate family saga lacking the strong colours of the epic and showing instead . . . shattered fragments of daily existence and the precariousness of life rooted in domesticity'.[31]

If *Voices in the Evening* is on one level another confirmation of Ginzburg's inherently pessimistic view of the female condition it also provides additional evidence, albeit indirectly, of her growing sympathy for older women, first apparent in *Sagittarius*, as mentioned earlier, and now developed a stage further. While the reader cannot fail to respond first and foremost to Elsa's progression from initial loneliness through temporary fulfilment to a final isolation more painful than her original ignorance, a process in which, as already indicated, Matilde plays a crucial part, it is also noticeable that unlike Caterina in *Valentino* at no time does Elsa consciously experience any feelings of rebellion or indulge in any open criticism of her mother's oppressive influence. This is clearly not solely the result of passive conditioning but also derives from the fact that, like the mother in *Sagittarius*, Matilde is always full of good intentions, anxious to do her best for her offspring, and simply too naive to realise that all her efforts are counter-productive. Despite the impossibility of any real communication with her mother[32] Elsa never loses sight of the fact that Matilde loves her dearly, and, indeed, returns this love, as is apparent from the many small details concerning the old lady's appearance, her gestures, and her mannerisms; while the final sequence, where Matilde, in her ceaseless babbling, makes increasingly absurd attempts to understand the reasons behind Elsa's broken engagement, is not only an added torment for the poor girl but also one more childish attempt to provide consolation, thus making it doubly impossible for her daughter to come up with any response. Ginzburg is clearly highly aware of this illogical but deeply visceral link which binds daughters to their mothers even when there appears to be no common ground between them and no dimension in which their minds can meet. In Elsa she provides an impressive example of this curious phenomenon in which natural affection triumphs over the need for self-assertion, even at the cost of total self-sacrifice. With the benefit of hindsight it is quite obvious that for Matilde she drew in large measure on her own relationship with her mother, while Elsa correspondingly represents an extreme amd more pessimistic version of herself, or, more accurately, of what she might have become if unable to develop her creative talents in an area which, as already mentioned in Chapter 2, was of little or no interest to her parents. In *Family Sayings*, published in 1963, she furnishes an extended picture of her mother, Lidia Tanzi, whose naive enthusiasm for life and intense attachment to things domestic are at one and the same time her greatest failing and her lifeline through the troubled times of Fascism and the destruction of the Second World War.

As already indicated in Chapter 1 *Family Sayings* is not really a novel in the accepted sense, being in effect a kind of autobiographical collage of events and experiences relating to Ginzburg's life from her earliest childhood to the time of her second marriage and her return to Rome to join her husband. Openly described in the Author's Preface as a story 'not in fact my own but rather . . . the record of my family' (p. 7),[33] the book begins with a succession of sketches and anecdotes about her father, to whom she returns at frequent intervals, together with portraits of relatives past and present, in brief outlines which give us the measure of their personality, and friends of the family, similarly caught in their most revealing and characteristic attitudes. The book thus covers a wide area of experience and an extended period of time, building up little by little a colourful and lively picture of a small community which has had more than its fair share of eccentrics and whose members, all fiercely individualistic, none the less share a deep-rooted sense of family feeling, still as strong as ever in Ginzburg and her siblings.[34]

At the centre of this family is Ginzburg's mother Lidia, a forceful lady whose world is confined to the domestic hearth and whose close attention to the problems of day-to-day living unfailingly absorbs all the other considerations which inevitably impinge on her through her husband and her children. Apparently lacking any capacity for mental or intellectual analysis Lidia in fact possesses a natural acuteness of perception which, while expressing itself largely in a context of relentless triviality, allows her to grasp the essential truths about people's basic needs and ensures she is able to organise her life as she thinks fit, regardless of any criticisms she may receive. Thus she has a genuine affection for her mother-in-law, a tight-fisted old tyrant who 'shuddered at people who were not Jews, as she did at cats', realising that beneath this selfish intolerance 'she was as innocent and simple as a baby at the breast' (p. 14), and has no hesitation in standing up to her husband's irrational antipathy for her piano teacher on the grounds that '"He is very good to his little girl. He is very kind, and teaches her Latin. He is poor"' (p. 89), heedless of whether or not he is any good at his job. In choosing her friends, however, Lidia is quite ruthless in her desire to remain at all times a free agent, quite insensitive to the conventions which regulate social intercourse in polite society and require regular contact between friends and acquaintances; thus a lady she meets on holiday and whom she discovers lives in the same city is cultivated assiduously while she has no one else to occupy her attention but dropped completely as soon as the family returns to town, since 'Either she saw people every day or she had no wish ever to see them again . . . She was always afraid she would get "fed up" with them and was

afraid that people would come and call when she wanted to go out'
(p. 16). In the same way she carefully chooses her friends among
women younger than herself whom she can gently dominate and
who are happy to defer to her when organising how to spend an
afternoon.

Lidia's registration as a medical student in her youth confirms she
is not without intelligence or talent, but her decision to give up her
studies in order to get married makes it clear that her true calling is
the traditional role of wife and mother; at no time is there any
indication that she takes the slightest interest in her husband's
medical work, despite the fact that it is this very activity that
brought them together in the first place – indeed when he attempts
to tell her about his tissue cultures she pays him scant attention,
causing him to lose his temper. When not occupied with things
domestic her greatest joy is to recall incidents from her life in
boarding-school or to tell anecdotes about her eccentric relatives,
activities which her husband angrily describes as '"talking rubbish . . . playing theatres!"' (p. 28), while her frequent comments
on food are similarly defined as monotonous or vulgar. Despite her
natural perspicacity Lidia has clearly chosen, like Raffaella in *Voices
in the Evening*, to 'bury her thoughts about the world outside the
home, though in her case there is no hint that in this way she is
somehow coping with disillusion or unhappiness. She rather resembles Matilde in her essentially simple approach to life, her
boundless energy finding fulfilment in caring for her loved ones, and,
when unable to concern herself directly with one of these, indulging
in long and even more trivial conversations with her maid Natalina,
or, in later years, her grandchildren and their wet-nurses. She is
indeed a kind of honorary child herself,[35] fascinated by the naive
confidence of childhood, which she shares, while also being aware of
the advantages of being an adult, which, as already indicated, she is
able to exercise in her own quiet way. Any free time Lidia has is
spent in appropriately childish activities such as taking a tram to the
terminus and then riding back again, ostensibly to distract her
daughter but it is clear she derives as much satisfaction from this
outing as does the young Natalia; in the same way her choice of films
is restricted to those suitable for young children, thus ensuring she
never comes into contact with any serious application of this medium. When during the family's holidays, invariably spent in some
obscure mountain retreat, she is deprived of her circle of friends, or
when some years later her older children have left home and she
finds herself unable to communicate with the growing Natalia,

112

already developing her own artistic interests, Lidia complains of being bored, her husband tells her brutally that this is '"because you have no inner life"' (pp. 15 and 72). It is clear that she is quite insensitive to anything which does not relate in some way to her personal interests and emotions, something also apparent from her constant repetition of old stories, to which her husband reacts in the same way as Elsa's father in *Voices in the Evening*.[36] This tendency to interpret everything in relation to family and friends also extends to more traditional art forms, such as literature and painting. Thus Lidia reads Proust and enjoys him greatly but has been quite unable to penetrate the complex mind of 'someone who was very fond of his mother and his grandmother . . . and as he could not stand noise he had the walls of his room lined with cork' (p. 50); in the same way she visits art galleries when away from town but is not really interested in painting, while none the less enjoying the work of Felice Casorati because she knows him personally and 'as she thought he was handsome she liked his pictures too' (p. 51). Once again it seems clear that this kind of attitude is what inspired such details in *Voices in the Evening* as Matilde's admittedly much grosser reaction to her daughter's copy of *Cat on a Hot Tin Roof*: '"Oh, poor creature"' (p. 125).

If Lidia's superficiality is clearly an impediment to any kind of adult relationship it is in large measure compensated by her equally boundless curiosity, which, as Ginzburg herself states, 'never rejected anything but fed on every kind of food and drink' (p. 50), thus indirectly stimulating those around her to pursue in depth subjects which briefly fill her with enthusiasm before 'she got bored and gave up' (p. 45), full of admiration for those of her friends who have enough dedication to continue undistracted. This all-embracing enthusiasm evidently springs from an inherent goodness of disposition which cannot conceive of anything as rigid as a scale of values in which one interest is followed in preference to others, especially if this involves a reduction in the amount of care and attention reserved for the family. Ultimately it is clearly this fundamental dedication to her flesh and blood, supreme example of her basic generosity and devotion, to which Ginzburg responds in the wealth of detail she provides concerning Lidia, whose every manifestation, however naive, reveals an unflagging desire to ensure that all is best in relation to her children. This in turn guarantees the release within the reader of a degree of affection which makes it easy to understand how Ginzburg soon overcame the resentment she had felt towards her mother when a child, and, when sufficiently mature to realise the extent of Lidia's emotional involvement with her family, also grasped that her essentially dispersive spirit could never, whether consciously or otherwise, be a serious impediment to her daughter's intellectual or artistic development.

The result is a subtle amalgam of affectionate indulgence and perceptive awareness in which Ginzburg is able to stress the comical implications of her mother's restricted field of vision without ever losing sight of the fact that all she says and does is an expression of limitless maternal love. Lidia's affection for her brood is indeed such that she finds it quite normal to state that ' "The only people I like are my children. I only enjoy myself with my children!" ', but it is noticeable that even this supreme declaration of her feelings finds its expression in an essentially superficial context in which she is praising her son Gino's good looks and goes on to say that ' "When my children have new clothes to wear I love them more" ',[37] a phrase she repeats word for word when she is visited by her elder daughter Paola. Conscious only of the intensity of these feelings she is unable to conceive of any other claims on her children's affections, and is genuinely upset when, after having returned to live in Turin, Paola makes new friends and occasionally prefers to go out with them instead of visiting her mother, at which point 'she . . . thought that Paola did not love her any more' (p. 101); in the same way she is quite unable to understand how her youngest son Alberto has changed from ' "a little lamb" ' with ' "such pretty curls" ', whom she used to dress up in lace, into a young adolescent who comes home dirty and in disarray after playing football, ' "lies on the bed with his boots on and dirties the bedspread" ' and ' "smokes and knocks the ash on the floor" ' (p. 59).

Lidia's unfailing ability to reduce all life's manifestations to their most superficial aspect is especially striking in her reaction to her second son's activity as a political conspirator. When during a routine search of a car on the Swiss border it transpires he is carrying anti-Fascist propaganda he escapes arrest only by jumping fully clothed into the river and swimming to the other side, surviving simply because a sympathetic customs officer prevents his colleague from shooting at Mario while he is in the water; however, this crucial detail appears to have made little impression on Lidia, who is instead worried that he has dived in without first removing his overcoat, and she sees Mario's exile from his life and work in Italy solely in relation to the inevitable alterations in his eating habits.[38] When as a result of Mario's flight the whole family is placed under suspicion and the house raided by the police Lidia is immediately alive to the domestic implications of their hunt for subversive documents, and as the young Natalia leaves for school 'my mother slipped into my satchel envelopes with her bills because she was afraid that in the course of the search they might be seen by my father and he would scold her for spending too much' (p. 89). After 1945 the incessant debates about different types of left-wing ideology are similarly seen in a strict personal context; thus the Socialist Giuseppe Saragat is seen as a doubtful character since '"he has a face with no colour to it"' (p. 149), while Communism is a serious threat because '"if Stalin takes away my servant, I shall murder him. How could I manage without a servant, when I am no good at anything?"' (p. 150).[39]

The powerful, if limited, emotions behind everything Lidia perceives and comments on create an atmosphere of stability and reassurance for her offspring which persists well past their childhood; indeed it is only after the armistice in September 1943 and the subsequent German occupation that Ginzburg, now doubly exposed to grave danger through her husband, realises that she can no longer rely on Lidia for any kind of support: 'I received a letter from my mother. She too was frightened and didn't know how to help me . . . I saw that in future I might have to protect and look after her. For she was now very old, weak and defenceless' (pp. 137–8). The events of the next two years leave her even older and more fragile – 'disasters depressed and disheartened her, shortening her step, once so vigorous, and carving deep hollows in her cheeks',[40] a phrase recalling the narrator's mother in *Sagittarius*, who appears 'suddenly very old and careworn' (p. 134) at her daughter's death-bed; but this similarity is more apparent than real in that although Lidia's world has been turned upside down, and far more radically as a result of the war, she possesses within her the ability to transcend fear and suffering, however intense, to recreate her own simple context in which domestic life is born anew, tomorrow is another day, and there is always something to engage her attention and stimulate her interest. Unlike her counterpart in the earlier novel, who is left disconsolate and heartbroken, Lidia once more reveals a natural acuteness of perception which has already prompted her, at an earlier stage, to accept that her children will leave home as they grow older, and therefore 'She had padded and protected her life so that she did not feel the shock of that separation' (p. 117); now likewise this allows her to put her son-in-law's death behind her and make a fresh start, aware that there is nothing to be gained from brooding over past misfortunes and lamenting one's lot. In this sense, as Ginzburg realises, she effectively regains a youthful confidence which contrasts sharply with her years and augurs well for her future:

> . . . my mother went back to living in the world as best she could, happily, for she had a happy nature. Her spirit could never grow old, and she never came to know old age, which means withdrawing into oneself, lamenting the break-up of the past. My mother looked upon the break-up of the past without tears, and did not mourn it. (pp. 140–1)[41]

This pessimistic definition of old age adds a discordant note to the general warmth of what is otherwise a tribute to Lidia Tanzi and her ability to triumph over life's misfortunes, once more revealing Ginzburg's increasing consciousness of life's inevitable process of change and decay, which now competed for her attention alongside her original themes of parental neglect and youthful disillusion. Coupled with this feeling, indeed directly linked with it, is a tendency on Ginzburg's part to identify with her mother, noticing that as she herself grows older there are increasing similarities in their behaviour. The first direct expression of this feeling occurs in an essay entitled *He and I*, written in 1962, in between the composition of *Voices in the Evening* and *Family Sayings*, a fact which is clearly not without significance:

> I am very untidy. But as I have got older I have come to miss tidiness, and I sometimes furiously tidy up all the cupboards. I think this is because I remember my mother's tidiness.

Her subsequent comment in the same paragraph that 'My tidiness and untidiness are full of complicated feelings of regret and sadness'[42] shows a distinct uneasiness about the implications of this identification and provides a striking contrast with the passage in her essay *Childhood*, written seven years later, in which, as already mentioned in Chapter 2, she recalls her entry into secondary school as a moment of total break with her family and her mother in particular.[43] If this essay, together with *White Whiskers* from 1970,[44] is clearly designed to identify and isolate a moment of truth during her formative years, it is equally clear that, now in her late forties, Ginzburg was aware of being well past her first youth and faced with the increasingly close approach of old age.

Notes

1. P. Citati, 'Il mondo di NG', *Il Punto*, no. 34, 24 Aug. 1957, p. 14.
2. She is aptly described by Soave Bowe, 'The Narrative Strategy of NG', pp. 792–3, as 'a masterly refinement of the characteristic female, vain and mediocre . . . idle and slow-witted . . .'.
3. Angus Davidson translates *assomigliare* as 'to look like'.
4. 'She said . . . I shouldn't be surprised if I read in the paper one day that [a new lover] had strangled her in her sleep', p. 142.
5. She is mercilessly described as 'short and fat' with 'tortoise-shell glasses' behind which lie 'hard, round eyes. Her nose was shiny and she had a moustache . . . her . . . hair . . . was black streaked with grey, crimped and untidy. She was at least ten years older than Valentino', p. 10.
6. See *The Little Virtues*, pp. 75–95.
7. Ibid., pp. 98–9.
8. Ibid., pp. 109–10; see also the comment by Monique Jacqmain in 'Montherlant e NG: identità di vedute pedagogiche', *Rivista di letterature moderne e comparate*, vol. 24 (1971), pp. 63–4: 'clearly paying too much attention to one's children is merely an exaggerated manifestation of a natural desire to protect them from life's dangers, but Ginzburg also sees it as, deep down, a sign of boundless selfishness, or alternatively a form of distraction for someone whose life has been a failure or who has failed to realise his youthful hopes.'
9. Thomson, 'Spinsters in Italy'.
10. P. Sergi, book review of the collection entitled *Valentino*, in *Il Ponte*, Dec. 1957, p. 1884.
11. A. Bocelli, 'Racconti della Ginzburg', *Il Mondo*, 8 Oct. 1957, p. 8.
12. Ginzburg herself describes this novel as being 'too contrived'; see Preface to *Cinque romanzi brevi*, p. 16.
13. This is especially noticeable when the narrator informs us that she has 'secretly scribbled verses in exercise books since I was a child', p. 70, and that 'I had written little poems as a child and my essays had been read by the whole school', p. 87.
14. Pina Sergi aptly describes her as 'congenitally immature' in her book review, p. 1884.
15. *Le donne* in *Vita immaginaria*, p. 124.
16. Ibid.
17. 'My mother . . . hardly ever goes down to the town. Aunt Ottavia says to her, "Why don't we go to the town sometimes?" And my mother says, "What for?"', p. 113.
18. '"Impossible," said my mother, "just imagine to yourself whether Elsa would let her hands be held by a man in public"', p. 144.
19. 'She said, "Couldn't we sometimes have the miracle of a word from you?"', p. 15.
20. '"For a woman marriage is the finest destiny, a happy marriage"', p. 133.
21. Matilde's random and disparate pronouncements not only in this sequence but throughout the novel are a striking example of Ginzburg's method of characterisation; as Claudio Varese states in 'Due

scrittrici nell'ultima rosa', *Il Punto*, 24 June 1961, p. 9: 'Rather than construct a character or describe him or explain his feelings the author brings him into focus for no longer than is necessary, and . . . has him say, almost in quick succession, isolated phrases which are a kind of obsessive commentary on a given situation, and it is from those phrases that personalities, feelings, and events take shape.'

22.   Milano, 'NG: La vita come attrito'; the same article also contains a telling reference to Matilde's 'endless babbling, which sullies her daughter's days like the droning of a radio which can't be switched off'.

23.   See Italo Calvino, 'NG o le possibilità del romanzo borghese' in *Almanacco della terza pagina* (Carusi, Rome, 1963), p. 178: 'The narrator of *Voices in the Evening* is like so many other young women of her previous work . . . used to living on the sidelines, preordained victims of other people's selfishness.'

24.   Caterina's situation in *Valentino* is similar to Elsa's but she is much younger, being still a student at the beginning of the story, while her family, though likewise middle-class, is very short of money, two facts which would in themselves make it impossible for her to leave home; on the other hand Francesca in *The Dry Heart* has deliberately turned her back on the domestic hearth, stating quite unambiguously that ' "I've had enough of family" ', p. 110, and ' "Families are a stupid invention" ', p. 114.

25.   Lombardi, 'NG', p. 7613.

26.   F. Virdia, 'Tre romanzi brevi di NG', *La fiera letteraria*, XII, nos 31–32, 4 Aug. 1957, p. 1. The reference is to previous works but is equally applicable to *Voices in the Evening*.

27.   'I said, "Do you think Raffaella is happy with Purillo?" He said, "No, I think she is profoundly unhappy . . . but takes care not to admit it to herself, so as to be able to live" ', p. 152.

28.   Significantly the only time Cate appears content during her marriage is after the birth of her children, when she 'was busy and had stopped crying. She did not go so often to . . . her home village' (p. 72), the demanding task of looking after growing babies being seen as part and parcel of normal female activity and so one which she can discharge quite adequately.

29.   'She was small, thin and harassed-looking. Her face was so powdered that she looked dusty . . . When she took her gloves off there appeared two thin, slender hands covered with scars', p. 62. Her father-in-law's reaction is to comment ' "How can Mario bear to go to bed with her?" ', p. 67.

30.   S. Pacifici, book review, *Books Abroad*, vol. 36 (1962), p. 193.

31.   W. Mauro, 'Un romanzo di NG'.

32.   Her relationship with her mother recalls the comment by Danilo in *All Our Yesterdays*, p. 39: 'As for our parents . . . as soon as they have finished bringing us up we have to begin bringing *them* up, because it is quite impossible to leave them as they are.'

33.   See Chapter 1, note 19.

34.   The anonymous reviewer of this novel in an article entitled 'Spartans and Sufferers', *Times Literary Supplement*, 14 June 1963, p. 419, com-

ments that 'In a domestic setting she can see (and make us see) a political or social attitude, a way of life, a whole world of moral and spiritual implications, conflicts, loyalties . . . the sheer blessed tedium of family life has seldom been so feelingly, clearly, lovingly put across with a sharper ear for the sound of it'; see also W. Trevor, 'Remembering Well', *Listener*, 2 March 1967, p. 298: 'Miss Ginzburg's real characters snap into focus at her bidding and remain with one afterwards'.

35. Vittorio Lugli describes her behaviour as characterised by 'enfantillages' in 'Cronaca domestica', *Il Resto del Carlino*, 18 June 1963, p. 3.

36. ' "I have heard this story so many times," my father would bellow . . .' (p. 23); see also the last sentence of the novel on p. 177, which is almost identical; ' "You have told this story to me millions of times," said my father . . .', *Voices in the Evening*, p. 137.

37. D. M. Low translates differently on p. 48.

38. In Switzerland Mario has a mistress who weighs less than six stone 'because he only liked women who were very thin and very elegant', p. 73; on hearing the news Lidia 'put her hands together and said, "I wonder if that skinny girl friend of his will give him something to eat"', p. 84.

39. At her simplest Lidia is a perfect symbol of traditional womanhood, inhabiting what Donald Heiney has called 'a feminine world . . . in which tea-pots and the making of babies are important, but politics, business, and war are not: or, more precisely, in which politics, business, and war are recognized as affecting the destiny of all, but not susceptible of female control . . . The narrating consciousness takes refuge in a world of trivia, but the trivia are in some way elevated to the archetypal'; 'The Fabric of Voices', *Iowa Review*, Fall 1970, p. 92. Here too the writer's comments, while referring specifically to one text (*Voices in the Evening*), are also valid in a more general sense.

40. D. M. Low translates differently on p. 139.

41. Typical of this refusal to mourn what is inevitable is Lidia's behaviour when her own mother dies, and, despite being deeply grieved, she buys a red dress instead of a black one, explaining to Paola that ' "My mama could not bear black clothes, and she would be very happy to see me in this lovely red dress!"', p. 141.

42. *The Little Virtues*, p. 43.

43. See Chapter 2, notes 8–9.

44. *Never Must You Ask Me*, pp. 129–40.

4 Female Alienation: The Sere and Yellow Leaf

> I don't see life as something having continuity. I believe
> everything is falling to pieces . . . I don't believe the
> world is moving towards something, I feel it's rushing
> into a void.[1]

It seems clear that between 1962 and 1971 Ginzburg began to take
stock of her experience in a period during which she could contemplate both her past and her future while temporarily isolated from
both the extreme points of life. By 1968, the date of her essay entitled
Old Age, she was into her fifties, and, it would appear, bitterly
resentful at having passed the half-century:

> We are becoming what we never wanted to become, that is, old.
> Old age was something we never wanted or expected . . . we feel
> no interest in old age . . . we are advancing towards a grey zone
> where we will become part of a grey crowd whose doings will not
> fire our curiosity or our imagination . . . We hate old age with
> every fibre of our being and refute it.[2]

With a sharpness of perception more cutting than that of any
youthful observer she states uncompromisingly 'Old age is bored
and boring; boredom generates boredom, propagates boredom
around it'.[3] No longer able to believe in communication between
different generations, as she had once confidently proclaimed in *The
Little Virtues*,[4] Ginzburg now describes the world around her, in
which children grow up at 'dizzy speed', as 'incomprehensible',[5]
and is so conscious of her inability to relate to what she sees around
her that she doubts whether she will be able to go on writing. In her
despair she even goes so far as to suggest that old age begins as soon
as one gives birth to children, reiterating the impossibility of establishing any kind of adult relationship with one's offspring: 'At the
very moment of their birth old age struck us down like a disease
which we feel can never be cured. In addition to old age we have also
been overcome by terror, terror of a kind we had never experienced
before',[6] while specifically comparing the 'indecision, insecurity,
and terror' she experiences in relation to her children with the

120

feelings of 'indecision and terror'[7] her generation had perceived in their own parents in years gone by, a pattern which recalls her description of adolescent resentment written seventeen years previously.[8] In *Le donne*, from 1971, the ironic self-disparagement already quoted in Chapter 3[9] is followed by a more frightening projection of what may happen in old age and which clearly represents the author's real feelings of anguish as she imagines women of her generation forcibly expelled from a society which until then has been happy to accept them: 'In fact they may not even still have an arm-chair to sit in in their old age. They may have nothing left at all, and will end up sitting on a street corner clutching an empty tin can with their white hair flowing unkempt all round them.'[10] Three years later in the essay *Vita immaginaria* she speaks of 'old age overwhelming us like a hurricane' and defines it as 'switching on the light but still remaining in the dark'.[11] The bleakness of these pronouncements is aptly described by Rita Signorelli Pappas as 'a stunned reaction to ageing and its attendant feelings of insecurity and despondency',[12] while Lietta Tornabuoni likewise underlines how Ginzburg's world at this point in her life is 'quietly appalling; the past has either been renounced or can no longer be recaptured; the future offers no hope; and the present is unbearable'.[13]

In this context Ginzburg's attitude to her grandchildren is inevitably quite different from the free and easy approach typical of her mid-thirties, when, as we read in *Family Sayings*, her mother would reproach her for not paying enough attention to her children's clothing;[14] thus her visit to the United States in 1967 is, in complete contrast, characterised by what she herself calls the need 'to lecture, complain and insult' her son and his wife because of their apparent insensitivity to their child's needs at a time when parents had an unshakeable faith in Dr Spock,[15] thereby recreating exactly the same pattern of incomprehension between generations.[16] In *Le donne* Ginzburg provides an ironically touching account of her attempts to rationalise these feelings, and describes her obsessive preoccupation with finding an adequate number of rubber pants for her grandchildren, thus reproducing in virtually identical terms her own mother's concerns in the late 1940s:

Old women's heads are full of uncertainties. At times they find these new methods of bringing up children absurd . . . at times they feel that they themselves are in the wrong and have always been in the wrong. Despite being mortally tired they rush off to the chemist's to buy half a dozen pairs of rubber pants because

121

the ones they've been handed along with the children are few in number and falling to pieces. They find these rubber pants unbearable, but since the children are obliged to wear them at night they feel there ought at least to be a good stock in the house . . .[17]

This gradual identification with her mother's restricted view of life reaches its climax in *Housework*, written in 1969, which contrasts her past and present attitudes in a detailed picture full of references, both direct and indirect, to her own upbringing:

Being unable to sleep, the old mother gets up while it is still dark . . . She would like to start the housework . . . As a young woman she was lazy and untidy; as she grew older she acquired a mania for tidiness and a sort of gloomy love for housework . . . the mother goes into the bedrooms: with grim, wild delight she strips the beds that have already been made . . . her own mother couldn't have imagined the possibility of living in a house in which maids didn't wash the floor every day. But maids don't exist today . . . The mother wonders, as she washes the floors furiously, why she does these things, which may be pointless and humiliating; whether she does them in memory of her own mother, or out of some dry, lunatic pleasure . . .[18]

Ironically her own children have nothing approaching the patience Ginzburg had with her mother's life-style, but tell her quite plainly that 'Housework . . . is an excuse for her failure to do other things, nobler things like reading, taking an interest in politics, or cultivating her mind',[19] but she appears to have lost interest in all these things, now caring only about her family, sentiments which echo Lidia Tanzi's claim, already mentioned, to enjoy herself only with her children.[20]

Ginzburg's plays, all written between 1965 and 1971, are, as one might expect, less extreme in their pronouncements, comprising a range of female characters which include people both young and middle-aged, thus allowing the author to maintain her original interest in youthful victims alongside her more recent attention to the problems of older women. The theme of her first, *Ti ho sposato per allegria*, is, as the title implies, marriage, its main character a young woman who has run away from home in a squalid rural community to seek fame and fortune in the big city, where she hopes to become a film star. Like Delia in *The Road to the City* she naively believes she cannot fail to find fulfilment in an urban environment, but, similarly lacking any training for survival in a radically different society, she is equally vulnerable, and – given her need to fend entirely for herself

122

– even more ripe for exploitation. Forced to compromise with her high expectations by accepting employment as a shop assistant Giuliana falls head over heels in love with a neurotic married man separated from his wife, who, after refusing at length to sleep with her, eventually makes her pregnant, at which point he disappears without trace.[21] Once more alone, unable to find work, and with her money running out, she is saved from destitution by a chance meeting with her lover's wife, Topazia, a dynamic photographer who takes her under her wing, pays for her abortion, and generally supports her until leaving for America on an assignment, thereby plunging Giuliana once more into what looks like an inevitable downward spiral in that she has still not learned how to subsist on her own initiative. This time her salvation is provided by Pietro, a wealthy lawyer who takes her home from a party where she has passed out after too much drink, and spends the next ten days with her, after which he agrees they should get married. The play opens a week after their marriage and focuses on a period of two days during which Giuliana talks incessantly, whether to the maid Vittoria, who is given a detailed account of her life beforehand, to Pietro, with whom she engages in long rambling conversations which emphasise their apparent incompatibility, or, in due course, to her husband's mother, an elderly lady who strongly disapproves of their relationship and whose reactions are portrayed at length in Act Three. Despite being crucial to his wife's survival Pietro is essentially a marginal character in this play; Ginzburg's main interest throughout is clearly in the interaction between Giuliana's totally anarchic approach and the conventional norms which regulate the lives of those around her, a contrast between radically opposing life-styles which has great comic potential and provides infinite scope for a series of confrontations which reach their climax in the meeting with her mother-in-law.[22]

Unlike most of the young protagonists of Ginzburg's earlier work, desperately unhappy as a result of their inability to cope with their problems, Giuliana, however bleak her situation, possesses an innate confidence which never entirely abandons her and which allows her to pass through the most distressing situations emotionally unscathed, ever hopeful that something will happen to change things for the better.[23] Apparently unaffected either physically or mentally by her abortion she is sufficiently buoyant, despite the increasing precariousness of her position, to attend the party where she meets her future husband, and, likewise, to contemplate something as serious as marriage with the same spontaneous thoughtlessness that has characterised her every previous action. Totally unable to profit from experience or learn from her mistakes Giuliana remains quite unchanged by whatever happens to her,[24] and it is this inability on her part to penetrate below the surface of events or relationships which constitutes the comic mainspring of the play, since at no time does she realise that Pietro is completely captivated by her erratic personality and will ensure she enjoys permanent security, delighted as he is to enjoy the company of a woman who is the antithesis of his staid middle-class family or his dry professional colleagues. At the end of Act Three Giuliana is no nearer appreciating her good fortune and is still wondering whether their rapport will survive – in between being distracted by trivial matters such as her husband's desire to wear a hat or whether the maid's previous employer had a swan's down on her dining-room table – still, like Delia, unaware of the reality of her situation, but with the important difference that in her case it is its essentially positive characteristics which she is unable to recognise, something much more ironic in its implications.[25]

If the most obvious appeal of this work clearly stems from Giuliana's scatter-brained personality and its effect on those with whom she comes into contact the play also has a serious dimension which is perhaps less immediately apparent. Thus on one hand it provides a disturbingly accurate picture of the dangers to which naive country girls are exposed when suddenly finding themselves alone in a large urban environment; on the other, the comparatively large amount of space devoted both directly and indirectly to maternal figures clearly confirms Ginzburg's strong interest in this category, none of whose representatives appears to have achieved any degree of serenity in her declining years. The most important is Pietro's mother, whom Giuliana ironically describes in the first few moments as 'the life and soul of the party' (p. 16) and who is discussed at length before her appearance on stage in Act Three, at which point she immediately reveals herself as an unbearable old tyrant perpetually at odds with the world around her and determined at all costs to find fault with everything she sees before her. As the Act progresses it becomes clear that this old lady is a walking symbol of middle-class values, firmly entrenched in her role as defender of conventional norms and aggressively anxious to impose her will on all those she suspects of having escaped into a more liberal life-style. Like Matilde in *Voices in the Evening* and Lidia in *Family Sayings* her terms of reference are essentially domestic, but unlike these characters she is also unpleasantly militant in her behaviour, shamelessly exploiting any circumstances and even inventing non-existent problems to increase her range of complaints. Totally self-centred she cannot conceive that Pietro has married Giuliana because it suited him to do so, convinced instead that he has acted in this way 'to make me suffer. To flaunt your lack of principles' (p. 69) since the marriage has not been solemnised in church, proclaiming her belief as an orthodox Catholic but happy meanwhile that her friend's son has not married the woman he is living with because she is 'a whore' (p. 53). Inevitably she has strong views on literature, dismissing a recent best-seller as being 'full of dirty words' (p. 64) but adding immediately that she never finished cutting the pages; her political views are likewise uncompromisingly reactionary, their context being limited to the detrimental influence of Marxist ideology on the availability and quality of domestic help.

If Ginzburg is clearly aware of the absurdity of such an obsessively restricted attitude to life and to human relationships she is also equally conscious that this appalling old lady, whose defects she parades unsparingly before us, is also deserving of sympathy in that her personality is in large measure the result of her past experience. Pietro's mother is not only a source of irritation to those about her but also a genuinely unhappy woman unable at her time of life to live peacefully and serenely within the context society has assigned her. As Pietro himself informs Giuliana in a speech where the lightness of tone which characterises their exchanges is temporarily abandoned:

> My mother, poor woman, was beautiful when she was young, and elegant, and took it very badly when she started to grow old. She got quite neurotic about it. Then, during the war the house she lived in was bombed flat. Then she lost some of her savings, not a lot, but enough to make her very frightened of being poor. Now when she wakes up in the mornings she frequently cries and feels distraught because she's afraid of being poor . . . Then a few years back my father died, and that was a great blow for her. And my sister isn't married yet and this upsets her greatly. And now I've gone and married you, a girl whom she's never heard of but whom she imagines as some sort of tigress. (pp. 38–9)

While it is undoubtedly true that, as Giuliana comments, 'These are not real disasters', it is also true that, as Pietro perceptively informs her, 'she suffers just as much from them as if they were' (p. 39), something which transforms this character from a mere grotesque into a recognisable human being whose problems clearly relate to Ginzburg's increased awareness of the negative aspect of old age. In addition her status as a mother gives her an added importance which Pietro and Giuliana openly admit in the final scene of the play, after the old lady has at last taken herself off and left them to reflect on the far-reaching implications of her relationship with her son, an individual whose personality, though radically different, must none the less be seen as springing in some way from her own:

PIETRO   . . . pyschoanalysis teaches us that we behave as we do because of our relationship with our mother.

GIULIANA   How strange that is! These mothers lurking there in the depths of our life, at the very root of our existence, hiding there, so important, so crucial to our very being! We forget about them while we're busy living, or we disregard them; yes, we think we've cut all our ties with them, but we never really cut them completely. Your mother's completely dotty and yet she's determined the way you are! You wouldn't think she was capable of determining anything, but she's determined the way you are!

PIETRO   That's right, she has. (p. 72)

Here too there is an obvious link with Ginzburg's sensitivity to things maternal and her tendency to identify with a figure whose inability to understand or communicate with her offspring is not simply an expression of narrow-minded obtuseness but also a kind of perverted expression of deeply-rooted emotional ties that spring from a blood relationship and have paradoxically contributed to the formation of the young person's character. In Pietro's case this has led him into marriage with a woman who, while being the complete antithesis of his mother, nevertheless shares with her an irrepressible tendency to garrulousness; in the same way Giuliana's total inability in any situation either to take the initiative or defend her position through some kind of positive effort is a perfect reflection of *her* mother's role as passive victim to her husband's neglect and abandonment, while her anarchic attitude to life and her scatter-brained approach to practical problems is clearly an echo of her mother's eccentric behaviour:

My mother collects old newspapers, she has tons of them under the bed and under the furniture . . . And in the evening she locks herself in the kitchen and stays there locked in until two in the morning . . . And if anyone goes to the kitchen door and tells her to go to bed she loses her temper and shouts and screams and refuses to open the door. (pp. 37–8)

126

It is especially ironic that while reacting against their family background[26] these young people have unwittingly chosen to live in a context which has recognisable links with their origins, a phenomenon which can be seen as the artistic equivalent of Ginzburg's awareness of the increasing similarity between her own behaviour as she grew older and that of her mother. Even more ironic is the fact that, like her characters, she too seems unaware of this link; witness her claim in the interview with Raffaello Baldini that when writing for the theatre 'I wanted to invent characters who were totally different from myself',[27] and, in a similar declaration to Claudio Toscani, 'For me the essence of theatre is to give life to characters who are unlike myself',[28] meanwhile realising, as already indicated in Chapter 1, that 'evidently there was some deep need within me to move in this direction'.[29] It seems clear that the author's deliberate creation of characters whose outward manifestations are far removed from her mother's simple and essentially tranquil temperament has obscured the true motivation behind her work at this stage of her life while none the less indicating its true nature through the emphasis on maternal influences, while her own dejection at the prospect of having to cope with the problems of old age is similarly apparent in the relentless discontent typical of the elderly females in this play; in addition to the two mothers[30] Ginzburg also provides thumb-nail sketches of Pietro's maiden aunt, who is confined to a wheelchair and who reacts to her nephew's marriage with a nervous collapse, and Virginia, a friend of his mother, whose husband's recent death appears to have plunged her into near-penury and whose children's life-style she is similarly unable to understand or appreciate. Despite this Ginzburg is sufficiently objective to realise the humorous implications of these two contexts in that Aunt Filippa is also revealed as 'a nasty gossip' (p. 41) and Virginia as a tight-fisted old crone whom Pietro describes as 'quite unbearable' (p. 60); while in the final scene the young couple, once more alone, agree that although mothers are 'very mysterious' and 'very important' they are also 'extremely boring' and that 'while continuing to love them we can none the less tell them gently to push off and leave us in peace' (p. 74).

There is a basic similarity of plot in *The Advertisement*, written only a few months later. Here too the protagonist, Teresa, is the product of a loveless marriage and has left a similarly squalid rural environment to become a film star at Cinecittà. Attractive and anxious to please she has no shortage of men eager to enjoy her favours, and does indeed succeed in working briefly as an extra on a film set.

Here, one day during her lunch break, she meets Lorenzo, who, realising his good fortune, loses no time in picking her up after work, taking her out to dinner, and spending the night and the next three days with her, during which time 'we did nothing but make love, sleep, smoke, and eat cans of corned beef' (p. 12). At the end of the third day Lorenzo goes out, ostensibly to buy cigarettes, and does not return, meeting up with Teresa again only by chance and all of six months later, during which time she has given up hope of breaking into films and has taken a job as a hairdresser's assistant. His convoluted explanations for having disappeared without trace, quite possibly genuine, are deeply offensive to Teresa, who realises that someone who can forget her as soon as he sets eyes on a friend and who tells her to her face that '"You're not a person yet – not to me at any rate"' (p. 14) has simply used her as a sex object and has no qualms about telling her so. Conscious, possibly for the first time, that she has been humiliated, Teresa interprets the strength of her outraged feelings as a sign of love, and when Lorenzo attempts to drive off and leave her after having once more taken her out to dinner she climbs into his car and inveigles him back to her flat, an action which marks the beginning of a steady relationship that initially seems to satisfy both parties and which in due course leads to marriage, though only when Teresa discovers – wrongly, as it turns out – that she is pregnant.

Like Giuliana in the earlier play Teresa has acquired a husband quite by chance, and, in addition, appears to have no doubts about the feelings that bind her to her partner. The outcome of this relationship is, however, quite different, thus making *The Advertisement* a far more sombre work; it has its root cause in the fact that Teresa's efforts to capture and retain Lorenzo after their second meeting are motivated not by love, as she naively imagines, but by wounded pride, while he, far from being diverted by her muddle-headed approach to life, as Pietro is by Giuliana's, finds her chaotic behaviour increasingly irritating in the long term, especially since he too has been motivated not by love but, as he himself explains in Act Two, by pity and a desire to help her:

> I came to live with her because I was sorry for her . . . I wanted to cure her anxieties and throw light on her confusion . . . Instead of curing her anxiety I felt myself involved in it . . . I was losing my breath, my reason . . . a horrible sensation (pp. 30–1)

Lorenzo's attempts to educate his wife once their relationship has acquired some degree of stability are a complete failure in that

Teresa is quite incapable of any intellectual activity[31] while also being totally incompetent in the domestic sphere, her obsessive need for constant confirmation of her husband's feelings expressing itself in insatiable sexual demands, this being the only level on which she can communicate. As his patience grows shorter and her insecurity increases conflict becomes inevitable, and leads equally inevitably to a separation which reduces Teresa to hysterical neurosis and causes her to relive with increasing strain the phases of her broken marriage. The long speeches addressed in Act One to Elena, who has come to rent a room, are the equivalent of Giuliana's monologue to the maid Vittoria in the first Act of *Ti ho sposato per allegria*, but if they contain a similar sequence of grotesque incidents which are superficially comic the pain they reflect and the progressive deterioration of Teresa's personality make this a far less amusing piece of theatre. When at the end of Act Three Teresa learns that Elena, with whom by now she has established a genuine friendship, is about to leave her to live with Lorenzo, who has become her lover, the violence which has been lurking beneath her hysteria since the beginning bursts forth in a pistol shot, murder being the traditional revenge for betrayal.

Even at this moment of crisis Teresa's emotional dependence on Lorenzo is such that she immediately phones him, begging him to come round and help, a revealing gesture that indicates the degree to which she is dominated by her feelings.[32] He is clearly in one sense the source of all her misfortunes in that by accepting her invitation to move in with her, and, subsequently, to get married, in both cases for the wrong reasons, he has deluded her into believing that despite their fundamental incompatibility this relationship can flourish and survive. He is, however, by no means the only pernicious influence on Teresa, who, like Giuliana before her, has experienced more than her fair share of unhappiness during childhood: a violent father who refuses to believe she is his child and who regularly beats her mother, another pathetic victim unable to stand up for herself and soon reduced to acting as nursemaid to her husband's invalid father in addition to looking after the farm. Constantly snubbed by her own father, who refuses to have her in the house, Teresa is unable to satisfy her increasingly frustrated need for affection through her mother, who is too easily dominated by more forceful relatives to have any time for her daughter. Teresa's reaction, understandably, is to despise this willingness to function as unpaid servant to all and sundry, eventually running away from home because 'I didn't want to end up like Mother' (p. 11), this apparently simple phrase acquiring a greater significance than she realises in the light of her subsequent availability for sexual activity when she moves to Rome; technically promiscuous, Teresa is in fact still searching for the affection she has not received as a child. However, she is unable to perceive that the ease with which she accepts men's attentions automatically ensures they despise her; at the same time her belief that an emotional rapport necessarily implies male domination is clearly related to her mother's obsequiousness, which Teresa is unconsciously reproducing despite being 'angry and humiliated' at her mother's attitude to life and human relationships (ibid.). Once again the observant reader can perceive a specific link between the generations which makes it clear that Teresa's failure to establish an adult rapport with Lorenzo is the inevitable result of a deprived childhood, while her inadequacy as a human being stems directly from her parents' neglect, whether intentional, in her father, or, more importantly, as a result of her mother's congenital incapacity. As in *Ti ho sposato per allegria* Ginzburg adds depth to the play by also showing how maternal influence does not merely determine the behaviour of her main character, but, similarly, conditions that of her partner; Lorenzo's mother, a wealthy snob, at no time attempts to discipline her son and seems content to see him wasting his intellectual talents by living like a playboy, meanwhile wasting no opportunity to denigrate his wife, whom she describes as having 'hands and feet like a cook' (p. 17). Unaware that by neglecting her son's professional obligations she has fostered his enduringly adolescent attitude to life and life's problems, thus in her turn ensuring that he is unfit to undertake any activity involving long-term commitment, whether emotional or academic, she has also, more obviously, alienated his affections by her unswerving devotion to class-consciousness; this is clear from Lorenzo's comments that in beginning a steady relationship with Teresa he was not only responding to feelings of compassion for a fellow-creature in need, as already indicated, but also intent on doing something 'to annoy my mother . . . to live with a girl who was lonely, and poor, and bewildered . . . a girl who came from a completely different world from the world of my family' (pp. 30–1). His mother's antipathy for Teresa is thus inevitable, and if, after their separation, the young woman's anguished accusations that she and her daughter 'were the ones who turned Lorenzo against me . . . because I was poor' (p. 23) are clearly somewhat simplistic, the family's constant opposition to their marriage has ensured that she is left with no one to turn to in her hour of need.[33]

If husband and wife are thus effectively predestined for unhappiness as a result of their upbringing the same is also true, albeit in a different way, of the third protagonist, Elena, whose naivety is established from the beginning and who is clearly a variation on the standard theme of the innocent abroad. As she describes her parents to Teresa in Act One it soon becomes apparent they are in the same mould as the protagonist's in *The Dry Heart*: the father a lovable work-shy old man, only interested in socialising with the guests in his boarding-house, the mother tirelessly engrossed in domestic and culinary activities, both too busy to attend to their daughter's needs or to warn her against the dangers implicit in giving in to one's feelings without analysing them beforehand. Anxious to find a quiet room where she can pursue her studies away from the noisy life-style of her relatives' home Elena responds immediately to Teresa's extended account of her misfortunes, which begins as soon as she sets foot inside Teresa's home, never pausing to reflect that she will be even worse off in the company of an obsessive talker whose emotional demands are unrelenting and whose needs are clearly going to monopolise the relationship. Ironically enough it is precisely Elena's willingness to be manipulated by Teresa which destroys both women, in that by accepting to move in with her Elena creates within the bonds of friendship the same kind of insidious dependence that Lorenzo had fostered in sexual terms, thus ensuring that Teresa finds herself humiliated by the two people most dear to her. Elena's ingenuous receptiveness likewise makes it inevitable that she should fall in love with Lorenzo, a man whose charm is displayed at length in Teresa's interminable account of their relationship and whose appearance in the flesh in Act Two completes the process of seduction, a process unwittingly initiated by the person who stands most to lose by it and which destroys the most innocent of the three characters concerned.

Wider in scope than Ginzburg's earlier play *The Advertisement* provides examples of three distinct age groups: elderly mothers, unable or unwilling to educate their offspring adequately; mature, or, rather, supposedly mature adults incapable of sustaining a long-term relationship; and the youthful simpleton whose good nature proves to be her undoing. In her next play, *Fragola e panna*, written a year later in 1966, we once more find three categories of female victims, each committed to a situation which is essentially negative and which cannot be altered other than superficially. The main protagonist, Barbara, an illegitimate orphan, is clearly another victim of parental neglect, or, more accurately in her case, of neglect by her alcoholic grandmother, who has nominally brought her up but has never paid her the slightest attention.[34] Totally lacking in judgement she becomes the victim of the first man to notice her: her future husband Paolo, who impregnates her when she is only sixteen and thus precipitates a shotgun marriage which she soon realises is insufficient for her emotional needs. Five months after the birth of their child Barbara runs into Cesare, a middle-aged lawyer whom she had first met while dealing with legal formalities in relation to land inherited by her husband; they become lovers, a relationship clearly destined to be short-lived and that, while having no effect on Cesare's life, which continues unchanged in all other respects, completely destroys that of his youthful mistress, who finds it increasingly difficult to relate to her husband or be satisfied with the pattern of her existence, both now revealed as depressingly squalid. When the affair is discovered Paolo reacts predictably, first by losing his temper and then forgiving his wife, who agrees to terminate the relationship; equally predictably she is unable to keep her promise and re-establishes contact with her lover, who has now grown tired of the whole business and is increasingly reluctant to engage in tearful meetings at the corner café. Meanwhile Paolo is becoming more and more despondent at his wife's behaviour, eventually suffering a nervous breakdown during which he alternates between weeping uncontrollably and beating Barbara with increasing ferocity; this in due course moves her to leave him and turn for help to Cesare, whom she sees as responsible for the breakdown of her marriage and who had at one time told her she could move in with him if things got too difficult, his wife Flaminia being fully aware of their relationship and quite unconcerned, as their marriage has long ceased to have any practical significance. Act One shows the meeting between these two women at Cesare's country villa, during which Barbara tells Flaminia the background to her situation, only to discover that her lover's wife, while confirming the open nature of her marriage, is none the less totally unwilling to take Barbara in, informing her brutally that Cesare no longer has any interest in her and that on returning from a business trip to London he will ensure he never has to set eyes on her again. Deprived of her lifeline Barbara agrees reluctantly to spend a few days in a convent, and is taken there by Flaminia's sister Letizia, who on returning to the villa receives a phone call informing her that Barbara has decamped from there also and has hitched a lift back to Rome, where, it subsequently transpires, she has fetched up at the hairdresser's; meanwhile Cesare has arrived from the airport in a foul mood, and

132

reacts to the confusion resulting from Barbara's appearance by reassuring his wife and sister-in-law that there is no cause for alarm since all this is a joke rather than a tragedy; Barbara will console herself by eating up to ten strawberry ice-creams, as he has seen her do in the past, and everything will sort itself out somehow. In any case if she has by chance lost her head and committed suicide 'I've had enough, I'm fed up with the whole thing. If she wants to chuck herself in the Tiber that's just too bad' (p. 158).

Here too, as in the earlier plays, Ginzburg has created a character whose misfortunes are the direct result of her own irresponsibility but who has also been deprived of all training for life, and whose nature is consequently that of an overgrown child acting on impulse without imagining the consequences. At forty years old Cesare is clearly a father-figure whose superior social status and prosperity are irresistible to a simple working-class girl who has drifted into marriage and motherhood almost without realising it, but whose entertainment value is strictly limited, especially since, as Letizia tells her sister in Act Two, 'I don't know what Cesare can have seen in that girl. She's not the least bit pretty' (p. 148). Ironically enough it is this same essentially unstructured attitude to life which allows Barbara to survive a confrontation which could have been traumatic, and to pass through initial bewilderment and momentary despair to relaxing at the hairdresser's, thereby revealing an astonishing range of quickly changing moods which are another indication of her basically childish approach to the business of living. At the end of the play her problems are no nearer a solution than at the beginning, and if the only three alternatives open to her all appear unthinkable – returning to her husband, who may kill her in his righteous anger, going on the streets to make ends meet, or committing suicide as a last resort – it seems clear that in reality nothing truly dramatic or tragic will impinge on this life, and that Barbara will continue to drift along, coping as best she can and somehow surviving. This casual, unreflective approach to life is clearly typical of the anarchic attitude of the hippy generation in the mid-1960s, and if Barbara's context of primitive domestic conflict is in truth far removed from that of the middle-class drop-out both undoubtedly have in common the refusal – whether deliberate or not – to plan their lives according to a recognised pattern, instead following their inclinations unswervingly and naively undertaking obligations which subsequently turn out to have unexpectedly far-reaching consequences. As Letizia says in Act Two, 'Young people nowadays don't know which way to turn, and decide to get married the way other people decide to buy themselves an ice-cream. Then they produce children. And they're a push-over for the first unscrupulous smooth-talker that comes by' (p. 157); it seems clear that on one level this play is a criticism of the unbuttoned spirit of the times from someone who, however sympathetic to young people's problems, found herself essentially at variance with the philosophy of total freedom then current throughout the Western world.

If Barbara clearly represents a topical variation on the now familiar figure of the naive female, unable to cope with the pressures brought to bear on her, her rival Flaminia is no less frustrated and unhappy despite being in all respects her complete antithesis. Well established both socially and economically, with no practical problems to disturb her and no obligations other than those she may choose to create herself, she appears to lead a near-perfect existence in which her every need is catered for while she relaxes in her luxurious country villa, a woman who has chosen to embrace a traditional female role and is now reaping the benefits. Unfortunately this conventional middle-class package also has a darker side in its reliance on the age-old distinction between passive dependence in a wife, deemed to have achieved total fulfilment in the domestic sphere, and the independence of her husband, whose professional activities outside the home provide ample opportunities for repeated acts of infidelity which his partner is supposed to be unaware of or to ignore, men being traditionally seen as inevitably promiscuous by nature. Unable to accept this Flaminia has grown increasingly bitter over the years, and has only succeeded in maintaining some sort of emotional stability by deliberately stifling her feelings for her husband, a long-term process which, as she tells Barbara in Act One, has involved much suffering and anguish. Now no longer a young woman and lacking any resources of her own on which to draw, whether emotional, professional, or intellectual, she vegetates miserably in her gilded cage, describing her daily routine in terms which form a striking contrast to the supposedly serene sophistication of their open marriage as reported by Cesare:

> Now I no longer have any men buzzing round me. I've lost my looks. I live in the country. I look after the flowers in the garden. I read to pass the time. I'm bored to tears. I play the piano a bit. I wait for Cesare to come home, and when he does he tells me about his girl friends. Does that sound like a good life? It's a bloody awful life, I can tell you. If I try to think of a time in my life when I was happy I have to rack my brains and go back years, years. (p. 143)

Flaminia has clearly been duped by the conventions operating in her environment, and her discovery that the pattern she has unquestioningly adhered to does not automatically guarantee happiness or fulfilment has come too late. In her own way she is as much a victim as Barbara, of whom she is in effect the mirror image. It is typical of Ginzburg's ability as a dramatist, and, more fundamentally, as a perceptive observer of human behaviour, that it should be the confrontation with Barbara – probably the first of Cesare's mistresses to appear before Flaminia in the flesh – that causes her to break down, destroying in a moment the mask of patient resignation she has built up over an extended period and bringing her face to face with the true squalor of her position. Her reaction, postponed by the need to find a practical solution to Barbara's immediate problem, is no less extreme for having been delayed; it bursts forth on the arrival of her husband, who ignores her completely in his irritation at being confronted with this sordid business and almost immediately loses his temper, causing Flaminia to go into shock as she obsessively repeats Barbara's lament: 'Where can I go now? I don't know which way to turn' (pp. 152, 155, 156, 157) while the colour drains from her face and her body temperature drops to the point where her sister describes her as being 'as cold as ice' (p. 157). At the same time she is intensely conscious of two things: the contempt she feels for her husband's despicable nature, and, alongside this, the fact that Barbara, despite the seriousness of her position, is none the less infinitely more fortunate in that her life is characterised by passionate feelings of various kinds, while Flaminia is suspended in a kind of passive limbo from which there is no escape. As a result she is racked by contrasting feelings of shame, anger, and disgust, even invoking death in a moment of supreme despondency. Inevitably this moment of truth passes, and the play ends with things still unchanged: Letizia, the voice of reason, convinces Flaminia that nothing serious has really happened, while her sister agrees that 'life doesn't change, it always stays the same, bloody awful' (ibid.), once more resigned to her fate. Ginzburg's compassion for this character, who dominates the whole of Act Two, is clearly indicative of her sympathy for women who have spent their life conforming to the rules laid down by society only to discover the essential inadequacy of those rules when they have become too vulnerable to react against them; if her own situation in the mid-1960s was, fortunately, very different, her decision to concentrate on Flaminia in this final Act while excluding Barbara from the characters on stage is symptomatic of a greater degree of identification with a woman whose age-group and domestic context are nearer her own.

Similar in age but very different in status from Flaminia is the third important female character in this play: the servant Tosca, a comic figure whose chatterbox personality provides surface entertainment as she attempts to monopolise the conversation and restrict it to domestic duties, even when serious matters of life and death are being discussed. Beneath this narrow surface, however, Tosca is in reality a sensitive individual anxious to communicate with her fellow creatures while being at the same time deeply conscious of her inferior social position, which restricts any such communication to the field of cooking and cleaning; as a result she is deeply offended by Flaminia's complete lack of interest in both these activities and her insensitivity to the fact that Tosca has no fellow servants to provide companionship, while the hours she has to keep make it impossible for her ever to travel to town, even on Sundays. We learn at the end of Act One that she has been a servant since childhood, something which implies a lifetime of economic and social exploitation; it comes as no surprise to discover at the same time that she has also been deprived of any instruction in the wider aspects of life, becoming pregnant at an early age by 'a scoundrel who never showed his face again' (p. 147) and never finding a husband. Deprived and unfulfilled, Tosca repeatedly complains about her employer's neglect in between regularly announcing her intention to seek a more satisfying position elsewhere, but it is obvious she will never graduate from this state of perpetual subjection, the most she can hope for being an improvement in her conditions of service. She too has been conditioned by society to accept a subordinate role, one which her working-class origins have made even more oppressive than that assigned to Flaminia, but it is clear that both women are essentially victims of the system that has shaped their lives. Barbara has been just as radically affected by the climate of her generation, apparently more liberated and easy-going but ultimately no less relentless in its judgement on her behaviour. If Letizia, seemingly stable and full of initiative, appears to confound the obvious deduction that a woman's lot is not a happy one, it is noticeable that she too is at least in part conditioned by her environment, unable to give Barbara sanctuary herself, as she would wish, because her husband and mother-in-law are both 'old-fashioned people, and very conventional' (p. 145), an apparently insignificant remark which, when seen in context, might well encourage the feeling that this play is more uncompromisingly feminist than either

The Advertisement or *Ti ho sposato per allegria.*

La segretaria, written six months later in 1967, is a more complex play with a larger number of parts than in Ginzburg's earlier work and in which she also devotes more space to male as well as female characters, the most striking being one – Edoardo – who never appears on stage but whose influence on three of the five main protagonists is crucial to the course of events; it conditions both their behaviour and that of his wife, another off-stage presence whose decision to leave Edoardo eventually leads to his suicide and the definite severance of the links, both emotional and economic, that bind him to the other characters. These consist of a married couple, Nino and Titina, who live in genteel poverty in a country villa outside Rome together with Nino's sister Sofia and their maid Perfetta, each of whom is soon revealed as quite incapable of coping with the practical demands of day-to-day living, or, much less, of making long-term plans which have any hope of coming to fruition. Perfetta's inadequacies, the direct result of a recent operation for appendicitis, mean she can only partially discharge her duties, something which creates further difficulties in an environment in which everything material appears to be gradually deteriorating and there is insufficient food for the family's needs, since Nino, described as 'a pathological shirker' (p. 172), is incapable of facing up to his responsibilities as a landowner and thus providing for his wife and two children; meanwhile Titina, obsessed, like so many of Ginzburg's mothers before her, with her babies' claims on her attention, is terrified at the thought that she might be pregnant yet again. This general inability to organise one's life adequately extends to Sofia, who spends all day and part of the night sitting at her typewriter translating third-rate crime novels into Italian for a publisher – Edoardo – whom she knows has no funds available to pay her but with whom she is in love despite all her claims to the contrary. Sofia is married to Filippo, but she left him long ago, and although rumour has it he is now a successful businessman with European connections she has lost all touch with him and derives no advantage from his new-found wealth; quite clearly it is only a question of time before these three characters are reduced to living entirely off Titina's mother, who has already lent them money on one occasion and is still naive enough to hope they may eventually pay it back.

Into this gently disintegrating world[35] comes Silvana, a young girl claiming to have been sent by a mutual acquaintance to act as Nino's secretary but in reality the mistress of Edoardo, who is planning to leave his wife to move in with her, Nino having agreed to put her up in the interim. Though willing in principle to do anything required of her Silvana is quite incapable of discharging any domestic duties effectively, let alone acting as secretary, and her cheerful unruffled incompetence immediately provokes fierce feelings of animosity in Titina, who is increasingly agitated by her new pregnancy and the indifference with which it is received by both her absent-minded husband and her doctor, a long-standing friend who appears equally incapable of exuding any human warmth. Her sudden departure for distant parts to visit her dying mother, while removing the most obvious source of conflict among those present, does nothing to resolve the difficulties implicit in Edoardo's relationship with Silvana, who at one point takes an overdose of sleeping-tablets; this precipitates a crisis between her lover and his wife, both summoned to the girl's bedside by Sofia, who is too distraught to realise the consequences of her actions. By the time Silvana has recovered Edoardo's wife has left him, at which point, aware that in reality he has not the slightest desire to start a new life with his young mistress, he dismisses her and shoots himself. This inevitably creates chaos; it causes Titina, who has now returned from burying her mother, to go into premature labour, while Sofia, now at last able to confess her unrequited love for Edoardo, is heartbroken, conscious that none of them has lifted a finger to help him in his hour of need. Silvana, who has decided to put some order into her life by marrying the doctor, is, in her turn, sufficiently moved by what has happened to reject this practical solution to her problems, and the play ends with her decision to leave the next morning on her motor-scooter 'with the road before me and no need to think about anything' (p. 213), while Sofia tearfully phones a friend to tell her the news, commenting that 'people throw their life away as if it were something worthless' and that 'life treats us like dirt and we return the compliment' (p. 214).

If this play is uncompromisingly bleak in both its plot and its range of characters it also represents a return to Ginzburg's earlier technique of focusing her attention on more youthful females whose personalities have been shaped by the influence of their dominant parents or whose life-style has been conditioned by their emotional relationships; it is tempting to suggest that her recent creation of a woman – Flaminia – with problems distressingly close to those of her own generation had been too uncomfortable an exercise to warrant further direct analysis of this age-group. Be that as it may the women in this play are clearly no more able to achieve emotional fulfilment than those in Ginzburg's earlier work, each being in her own way a victim of loneliness and solitude, and, as such, no better off than the middle-aged protagonist of *Fragola e panna*. Most like her in this respect is Sofia, ostensibly on the fringe of the action but in reality having the largest part in the play, and, we may therefore assume, of particular interest to the author. Sofia is a fiercely independent woman anxious to earn her own living and embarrassed at having to live off her brother and his wife, sufficiently strong-willed to take the initiative when it comes to terminating sexual relationships which have grown stale but at the same time quite unable to maintain any degree of self-sufficiency, whether emotionally or economically; all the while she is desperately in need of human warmth and affection, two familiar characteristics which guarantee the failure of all her liaisons and remind her regularly of her inability to modify a life-style which is essentially counter-productive. The upheavals occasioned by the arrival of Silvana, the spurious secretary, oblige her to take stock of her situation and admit that her forceful personality and self-assuredness, amply demonstrated in the numerous phone calls she makes throughout the play, are little more than a cloak for a basic insecurity deriving from the fact that 'it's really awful to be separated from one's husband as I am; I'm neither a spinster nor a widow' (p. 180), a telling phrase which reveals an inherently traditional feminine nature totally at variance with the realities of modern life and reminiscent of the deprivations afflicting Flaminia in the earlier play. Sofia is sufficiently intelligent to realise the full implications of this incompatibility, at one point informing the doctor – a child-hood friend and erstwhile lover – that 'what I find most unbearable is what's real. Perhaps I'm one of those people who can't stand reality', a confession which causes her to panic momentarily and, again like Flaminia, exclaim ' Where can I go now? Where on earth can I go?' (p. 183), unwittingly anticipating the moment in Act Three when her equilibrium is definitively shattered by the news of Edoardo's death and she tearfully announces she has nothing left to live for.

If Sofia's frustrations as a lonely woman unable to achieve a long-standing relationship clearly mark her out as one of life's victims it is equally clear that Titina is in no way fulfilled by her marriage to Nino, and is indeed in some ways worse off than her sister-in-law in that she is obliged to cope with all the responsibilities of her status while apparently lacking any of the benefits. Unable to communicate with her husband, who is more interested in the health of his horse than in Titina's well-being or her state of mind, she is fully aware that everything around them is falling apart, both literally and metaphorically, while being quite unable to prevent it. Like Sofia, however, she has herself contributed to her own misfortune, in this case by refusing to practise contraception; as a result she already has two children and is now pregnant for the third time before she has got her strength back, a fact which terrifies her and leads her to think she may be on the verge of a nervous breakdown.[36] Though biologically an adult Titina is still very much a child at heart and essentially incapable of an independent attitude to life and life's problems; despite being at daggers drawn with her mother, as Sofia at one point coldly reminds her, Titina has a highly romantic and quite inaccurate memory of her life at home, invoking her 'little room' (pp. 170, 200) with pots of geraniums on the window-sill, becoming hysterical when she hears her mother is dying, and going into mourning when she returns from her distant village after the funeral. Outraged by Silvana's casual life-style she looks back wistfully to past times when 'families still existed . . . each family was like a kind of enclosed shell; now they don't exist any more and people come and go as they please' (p. 200), conscious that the younger generation have a wider range of options to choose from – it is hardly surprising that in the circumstances she should externalise her resentment by being increasingly abusive to an outsider who typifies the freedom she herself has never had. Equally naive and immature is Isabellita, Edoardo's wife, who is 'daft as a brush' (p. 190) but has no difficulty in adapting to her husband's increasingly desperate situation, though unaware, despite everything, that he no longer loves her until she discovers his infidelity, at which point she immediately abandons him because 'I'm an old-fashioned woman . . . I can't stand being cuckolded' (p. 196), thereby setting in motion the train of events which lead to his suicide.

Silvana herself is in some ways less unfortunate than the other women in this play in that she eventually makes a conscious decision to abandon this crumbling family for a new life in the world outside, but it is clear that she has no resources to draw on – outside her motor-scooter – and thus runs the risk of finding herself even worse off as a result. Like the youthful rebels in Ginzburg's earlier plays she has left home to escape from an intolerable domestic situation, here involving an eccentric father, a neurotic bed-ridden mother, and four unruly younger brothers, a destructive package whose appalling details inevitably ensure we look on her with sympathy. However, with characteristic irony Ginzburg shows her as equally

140

destructive in her new relationships with those around her, unaware of the damage she does through a casual attitude typical of 'those girls who are around nowadays and who don't have any real feelings or any future to look forward to' (p. 190), 'girls who have a screw loose, who have no idea how to behave, who have no heart, no feelings, no memories to draw on' (p. 203). Apparently self-sufficient and impressively resilient in her approach to life Silvana is in reality deeply disturbed as a result of her unsettled upbringing;[37] unable to bury her feelings indefinitely she reacts when they eventually surface by taking extreme measures at both ends of the emotional spectrum, first by attempting suicide and then, after her recovery, by agreeing to marry the doctor, whom she does not love, because 'he seems a very reasonable and sensible person' (p. 205) and 'I don't know what else to do. I've nowhere to go' (p. 207), words which once more recall those spoken by Flaminia in *Fragola e panna* while also being reminiscent of Cate's feelings in *Voices in the Evening*. At the end of the play her awareness that, like everyone else, she has her share of responsibility for the death of her ex-lover Edoardo impresses on her that human relationships inevitably involve some degree of suffering, and that her growing affection for Sofia will thus add to her unhappiness unless she makes a complete break while still able to do so; by the same token the absence of any genuine feeling on her part for Enrico the doctor clearly means that her prospective marriage would be a meaningless gesture while also creating a context in which, like her mother before her, she risks becoming entrapped by maternity. Her escape to a life on the open road free from responsibilities and commitments is thus essentially a romantic flight away from reality which can only lead to further disillusion and conflict.

Disillusion and conflict are likewise at the centre of Ginzburg's second collection of plays, *Paese di mare e altre commedie*, published in 1973, in which two full-length works are accompanied by shorter compositions for an increasingly reduced number of characters. If these plays appear initially to herald a move away from the pessimism of her earlier work for the theatre in their insistence on the humorous absurdity of much human behaviour, while also focusing once more on characters who are mostly in their prime, it soon becomes clear that their deceptively comic surface conceals an acute awareness of the wretchedness of much human endeavour and the realisation that while depression and incommunicability may be especially noticeable among the middle-aged or the socially disadvantaged they are equally rife among the middle classes and those with intellectual pretensions; all this provides further proof of the author's increasingly grim view of the human condition. *Paese di mare* itself, the first in chronological sequence, is perhaps the most austere of Ginzburg's plays, focusing as it does on two young couples who are both in their separate ways totally disaffected. Debora, married to Marco, is a rich girl who has fallen on hard times and realises her husband will never succeed in holding down a job; despite this she continues to live a life of idleness, sleeping late and buying expensive clothes which she absent-mindedly abandons in the various hotels or rented apartments she and Marco drift in and out of as they move from place to place, ostensibly so that he can improve his chances of permanent employment but in reality because he is incapable of settling into a routine and unable to maintain good relationships with his colleagues. If Marco is typical of a certain kind of ineffectual male (whose characteristics will be examined in the final chapter) Debora is clearly no better, unable or unwilling to help her husband achieve a more adult approach to his commitments and content to adopt instead the traditional role of a nagging wife whose constant reproaches merely add to the general dissatisfaction which is at the core of this marriage. When the play opens the couple have just arrived in a sleepy seaside town where Marco hopes to obtain work from an old friend – Alvise – whom he has not seen or been in touch with for all of nine years and who is now the owner of a local factory; they soon discover, however, from a couple of Alvise's friends who call on them unexpectedly, that his marriage to the wealthy but feckless Bianca has long since fallen apart and that as a result of his wife's constant infidelities compounded with systematic drug abuse he is on the verge of bankruptcy and his factory in total disarray. Bianca's sudden departure for Rome after a particularly violent scene with Alvise and her subsequent suicide put paid to any hope of a reunion between Marco and his old friend, who sends him word that he is too distressed to see him; the play ends with Marco and his wife once more heading for the open road with another vague prospect of a job opening, this time in Florence. By this time Debora has developed a strange liking for the dilapidated villa they have been renting, and established cordial relationships with Alvise's friends, Gianni and Bettina; this is in complete contrast to the contempt and intolerance she had shown on arrival, an ambiguous development confirming her husband's belief that she is unreliable and dispersive while also revealing her inability to help him face the truth about himself.[38] As in *La segretaria* the behaviour of the characters in this play is largely determined by the activities of

142

people who never appear on stage but whose actions are crucial to plot development and eventually decide the fate of those we see before us, a skilful device which loses nothing by being here applied over a smaller area; in addition the play acquires further depth through Ginzburg's creation of these two couples as mirror images of each other, in that while Debora's unhappiness stems largely from Marco's unreliability and general feebleness of purpose it is the neurotic Bianca, whose wealth has proved more of a curse than a blessing, who has ruined her husband Alvise both emotionally and economically.

If the overall greyness of this play leaves little room for surface humour, here limited to the more ridiculous aspects of the young couple's life-style, there is greater scope for this element in *La porta sbagliata*, a longer play written a mere six months later and focusing on four young people who exemplify various types of personal and professional failure; all are adversely affected by unsatisfactory relationships with their mothers and all apparently incapable of an adult approach to the business of living. Principal among these is Angelica, a neurotic woman who is feigning anorexia nervosa in order not to have to confront feelings of failed motherhood and existential *angst* and who ruthlessly exploits her husband Stefano, constantly at her beck and call, while capriciously manipulating all those around her on the grounds that she has to be humoured in order to cope with her disability. Unable to form satisfactory human relationships of any kind Angelica has divorced her first husband, a headstrong extrovert, and married Stefano, a shy and submissive intellectual with whom she finds it equally impossible to communicate; she is similarly incapable of establishing any kind of positive rapport with her daughter by her first marriage, whose absence she laments but whose presence she finds intolerable. As the play progresses it emerges that although Angelica is indeed supremely egoistic, unscrupulously using and abusing the good will of her husband and friends, she is also genuinely unhappy and thus at least in part deserving of sympathy. Clearly a person of heightened sensibility she has artistic talents which at one point had blossomed to the extent that she was exhibiting her paintings in Paris and attracting the attention of Kokoschka; however, unable to cope with her emotional problems, whether sexual or maternal, she has now abandoned her vocation in a totally unsuccessful attempt to come to terms with her feelings while having no resources to draw on either within herself or among those around her, a situation which ensures that she lives in a constant state of frustration and self-loathing. If the precise reasons for this conflicting state of affairs are never spelt out it is quite clear from the long telephone conversations she and Stefano have with her mother throughout the play that at no time has this elderly lady provided any moral support or encouragement in relation to her daughter's work, being solely concerned with details of domestic trivia and established norms of middle-class behaviour; as we have seen, this is a short-sighted attitude typical of Ginzburg's portrayal of the older generation and which, we may deduce, has created a favourable climate for Angelica's subsequent inability to reconcile the different claims made on her, eventually prompting her to forswear her creative potential in favour of a more conventional female life-style, only to find she is even more unhappy as a result. Angelica has in effect betrayed her vocation, something we know Ginzburg sees as an act of supreme folly,[39] and is thus to some extent her own worst enemy, but she has clearly been largely conditioned first by her family background and subsequently by her choice of husbands, both in their separate ways quite unable to understand her and equally incapable of helping her resolve her problems; at the same time it is clear that like Pietro's mother in *Ti ho sposato per allegria* Angelica's is a good woman, genuinely concerned about her daughter's ill-health and anxious to provide what she naively thinks are useful suggestions for improving the situation, unable to realise that helpful hints on cooking and cleaning are not only irrelevant but indeed counter-productive when dealing with an identity crisis, or, as in Stefano's case, with a bad case of writer's block.

Stefano's mother, for her part, is equally unaware of the difficulties facing her son; however, unlike Angelica's, who bombards the young couple with interminable phone calls, she never makes contact on her initiative, and it is always Stefano himself who calls her to indulge in conversations which are, if anything, even more trivial and dispersive than those with his mother-in-law. These calls afford much scope for comic effect in his accounts of recent domestic developments, invariably at variance with the information he provides for Angelica's mother, whose personality, equally limited but more forceful, he rightly deduces calls for a totally different approach. When Angelica's first husband Cencio announces his desire to remarry and move back into the house she and Stefano are occupying the couple are faced with the need to find alternative accommodation while having no funds to cope with this new crisis, a situation which can only be resolved by borrowing money from Stefano's mother, who is thus revealed as crucial to their social survival. Her anguished reaction to his phone call appealing for help gradually reveals her to be both distinctly well-off, and, at the same time, absurdly fearful of ending her days in destitution; here we have a further example of Ginzburg's perceptive understanding of elderly female sensibilities which is not only once more reminiscent of Pietro's mother in her first play but which also recalls the sheer terror associated with old age discussed in *Le donne* and described at the beginning of this chapter. Meanwhile things are further complicated by the arrival of Cencio's pregnant mistress, whom he blithely unloads on Stefano and Angelica following a road accident, thus forcing them to deal with her when she has an attack of appendicitis in the middle of the night – a problem which is made worse by the fact that the girl can speak only Hungarian. At the end of the play the apathy and inefficiency which have characterised their behaviour throughout remain unaltered, while the two elderly mothers-in-law have, on the contrary, responded to the Hungarian's unexpected needs by visiting her in hospital bearing helpful gifts, and, even more importantly, using influence to ensure she is well treated during her stay. If on one level this provides further confirmation that the older generation is able to respond only to problems which fall within its own terms of reference it is equally clear that within this (admittedly restricted) area of experience its members are able to act with a sureness and a confidence totally lacking in their younger and more sophisticated offspring, whose artistic and intellectual superiority is quite useless when it comes to dealing with the practical problems of everyday life.

The disadvantages of such a limited view of life, superficially comic in the case of these old ladies, are more bitingly expressed in two further maternal figures who are, likewise, physically absent from the scene but who have conditioned the fortunes of their children, friends of Angelica and Stefano who are clearly drawn to their company by a similar sense of aimlessness and dissatisfaction with their lot. One is Tecla, a mixed-up typist who has spent years in analysis and whose feelings of guilt in relation to her working-class background have been compounded by her mother's unshakeable conviction that she has improved her status and her bank balance not by hard work but through prostitution; this destructive short-sightedness is paralleled in a different but ultimately no less extreme context by the stubborn refusal of Giorgio's mother to come to terms with her son's creative potential by providing an environment in which he can develop his talents. Unable to enjoy any privacy at home Giorgio has ended up selling socks and stockings in the family shop, an activity which bores him to tears, while Tecla, despite having become economically self-sufficient, is incapable of achieving emotional fulfilment, whether sexually or in any other way, to the point that 'when I open my eyes in the morning I'm overcome by remorse and feel I'm being eaten alive' (p. 115).

The last two plays in the collection, both short compositions limited to a single act, are also largely concerned with neurotic or scatter-brained females, the short amount of space available ensuring that the emphasis is more concentrated than in the longer works in this volume. Both focus on a young woman whose immediate problems are now seen no longer as deriving from their maternal connections but, more directly, from their relationships with their partners, in both cases an unsuccessful artist whose inability to achieve recognition in his chosen field creates a stressful climate which encourages destructive patterns of behaviour. The first, *Dialogo*, written in 1970, presents Marta, a young mother unable to cope with the needs of her child now that her husband Francesco, a budding novelist, has been sacked from his job, something which has cut their economic lifeline and reduced them to living in a squalid two-room apartment where Francesco will quite clearly never finish his great novel. Overawed by the life-style of their prosperous friends Michele and Elena the couple live in hope that they may yet improve their situation through this useful contact, which so far has only produced some vague suggestions concerning Francesco's closing chapter and the possibility of a job as a television interviewer for his wife. Restless and depressed by all this Marta screws up her courage to the point where she can confess that she has drifted into an affair with Michele and is planning to leave her husband to live with him, taking their child with her; but the truth is hardly out when it is ironically revealed as quite unnecessary by the news of Michele's unexpected departure for Spain, an event which forces both partners to confront the inadequacy of their relationship in a painful exchange which is interrupted by a request from Michele's manservant that they should look after his master's dog during the family's absence.[40] The play ends with the couple's conflicting reactions to this, Marta crying out that she cannot bear to look on the animal, which will not only be a constant reminder of her abortive affair but will also create further problems in their pocket-sized flat, while Francesco accepts with enthusiasm something which will fill up his empty days.

If the immediate cause of Marta's infidelity is largely the appalling conditions under which her husband is forcing her to live, and

146

which show no real sign of improving, it is also clear that she is by nature an inconclusive person lacking in perseverance and out of touch with reality. During the course of the play we learn that she left high school without completing her diploma in order to study ballet, which she also subsequently abandoned; that despite their lack of funds she is planning to buy an expensive bed for their daughter in preference to a standard model at less than half the price; and that she travels everywhere by taxi because she is too lazy to find out about bus routes, thereby ensuring a further drain on the family purse. In this context her willingness to admit that she is scatter-brained and that 'when I think I'm in love with someone I can't make sense of anything any more' (p. 39) not only confirms her basic inability to think straight or to plan ahead but also implies that she likewise has her share of responsibility for what has happened, and suggests that the crisis she and her husband are undergoing is just as much her fault.

La parrucca, written eight months later in January 1971, is a monologue consisting of a frantic phone call from a hotel bedroom by a distraught woman who needs help to pay the bill. Like Marta this unnamed female is married, in her case with two children, to a struggling artist, this time a painter whose work, though cautiously praised by the critics, is selling very badly. Holed up in a small village off the motorway following the breakdown of their car on a trip from Rome to Todi, a trip which they hope will lead to a large sale of Massimo's paintings, she rings her mother in Milan while he takes a bath, and during her conversation we learn that the marriage has broken down, that unknown to her husband she is pregnant by another man, and that she is planning to make a new life with him despite the fact that 'he doesn't want to. He doesn't have the time. He's got no room for me in his life' (p. 183). These depressing facts emerge alongside some typically absurd trivia and lead to an amusing anticlimax in which, after having shouted the truth about her condition through the bathroom door, the protagonist discovers that her husband has left via the balcony for his breakfast some time previously and has thus not heard a word. The play ends with her hysterical threats to destroy his paintings, from whose sale the couple derive their income and whose disposal has prompted them to make the trip in the first place. Here the failure of the couple's marriage appears to derive less from their lack of means than from a fundamental flaw in their relationship; as the play progresses it becomes clear that while desperately needing his wife's moral support Massimo is at the same time unable to accept the fact that she does not like his work, and has reacted by growing increasingly impatient with her, to the point where he has recently attacked her physically and made her nose bleed.[41] If all this inevitably encourages feelings of sympathy for the wife this reaction must be tempered; for she is also, like Marta in the earlier play, an unthinking creature, whose sharp tongue and unconcealed contempt for her husband's paintings have contributed to the deterioration of their rapport, while her obsessive desire to move in with a lover who has made it obvious he does not want her is a clear indication of her irresponsible approach to human relationships, further demonstrated by her illicit pregnancy.

Although dealing with different age groups and a wide range of human relationships of different kinds all Ginzburg's plays focus, both directly and indirectly, on characters who are unable to satisfy the emotional and spiritual needs of the person closest to them, whether sexual partner or offspring, and whose well-being is supposedly their dearest aim; frequently, as we have seen, this is because of an inability to grasp the essential fact that strong emotional attachments do not necessarily imply a common philosophy of life or common aims. In this context we may see *Ti ho sposato per allegria* and *Paese di mare* as being at opposite ends of the emotional spectrum in that in both cases Ginzburg presents us with a situation where a fundamental incompatibility between partners determines the quality of their relationship, respectively for better and for worse, while in *Fragola e panna* she shows how the passage of time coupled with the experiences people undergo changes personalities to the point where a relationship once actively enjoyed or passively accepted can become intolerable. Elsewhere the plays occupy a middle ground somewhere between these two extremes in which we witness characters who either attempt unsuccessfully to improve an unsatisfactory state of affairs, as with Teresa in *The Advertisement*, Titina in *La segretaria*, and the various maternal figures in *La porta sbagliata*, or, alternatively, persist in behaviour which can only worsen a situation which is already desperate, as with Marta in *Dialogo* and the unnamed wife in *La parrucca*. These characters and others like them have in common an inability to realise the need for change in their approach to human relationships, and it is tempting to conclude that this is, at least to some extent, due to their feminine nature: specifically, in that they are either hide-bound by traditional attitudes which they are incapable of transcending, or, on the contrary, have rebelled against a conventional life-style only to find that they are equally incapable of self-sufficiency, both literally and metaphorically, in what is still very much a man's world, in which case the only solution is a deliberate rejection of all emotional involvement, as with Silvana in *La segretaria*.

In 1973, two years later and all of ten years after her last novel, Ginzburg published *Dear Michael*, a semi-epistolary work in which the author's characteristic pessimism is for the first time relieved by the suggestion that relationships which have grown stagnant may be able to take on a new lease of life once attempts have been made to transcend the conventional norms which regulate human behaviour in favour of a more realistic approach to problems of communication. Despite being in many ways 'another despairing cry of desolation'[42] the book thus represents a positive hope that the estrangement typical of so much human contact in post-1968 Europe might ultimately be surpassed and replaced by something more genuinely in keeping with the concept of emotional harmony; in this context *Dear Michael* is clearly the end product of a deepening pessimism which has its roots in Ginzburg's awareness of her advancing years, as indicated at the beginning of this chapter, and which is then extended to the younger generation, whose life-style, apparently uninhibited and stimulating, she sees as being in reality empty and meaningless, but with whom some sort of rapport is none the less possible. In her essay '*Cuore*', written in 1970, she recollects how she loved the stories which make up this children's classic because they depicted a world 'in which everything was as it should be',[43] a world where 'heaven was full of heroes and martyrs, prisons were full of evil-doers, blood-spattered soldiers lay on the battlefields, parents and teachers were busy helping the poor and educating children. It was a world . . . in which I felt safe and protected'.[44] Despite responding to this with enthusiasm Ginzburg also felt, even as a child, that this perfect world had 'some secret flaw in it, some hidden, essential mistake',[45] and as a mature adult is now aware that 'It belongs to a time when false things were written about honesty, sacrifice, honour and courage',[46] qualities which, however, 'had existed or still did so, but at one remove'.[47] The strong sense of nostalgia which these words imply, together with an equally strong desire for stability, order, and established principle, is forcefully expressed in the conclusion to the essay: 'Today honesty, honour and sacrifice seem so far from us, so foreign to our world, that we cannot say anything about them; and, as we now have a horror of lies, we say nothing at all. Thus we wait in total silence, until we can find words to describe the things we love.'[48] This anguished withdrawal from the hustle and bustle of life, a kind of suspended

149

animation, is appropriate to those of Ginzburg's generation but is impossible for young people, who, equally conscious of the collapse of traditional myths and values, react by rejecting all links with the past in favour of total disengagement; thus they live from moment to moment without responsibilities or commitments in order to avoid having to confront the basic solitude which is central to every human being, the reality of death, which awaits us all, and the need to do something worthwhile with one's life. In *Collective Life*, written at about the same time, Ginzburg further stresses how sexual promiscuity, drug abuse, and the fashion for communal living are clearly an attempt to exorcise the 'emptiness and lack of faith'[49] characteristic of modern times and deepened by the awareness we all now have of the extent of pain and suffering in the world. In this context the hippy life-style is a desperate attempt to prolong indefinitely the period of adolescence, 'the age in which a person wakes to the pleasures of adult life, yet is spared the commitments of adults . . . the age in which faults are forgiven',[50] an attitude which extends to the world of the creative artist, where 'solitary thought is not considered at all important' and a 'false concept of the useful and the useless' has become the norm.[51] If in such circumstances Ginzburg could thus state quite unambiguously that 'my own time inspires me with nothing but hatred and boredom'[52] she also realised with characteristic perceptiveness that a blanket rejection of the world around us, an attitude typical of so many of her age group, was simply foolish in that 'Rejecting the present, isolating oneself in regrets for a past that is dead, means refusing to think',[53] an attitude clearly unworthy of a rational human being.

Deeply disturbed by these conflicting feelings and unsure as to whether she was still capable of creative writing Ginzburg chose for the main protagonist of *Dear Michael* not the young man whose name gives the book its title, but, instead, his mother Adriana, a woman who though somewhat younger than herself[54] is clearly the projection of her own doubts and uncertainties and whose subtly changing relationship with her son is indicative of the author's attempts to establish some sort of positive rapport with the younger generation. Though not alone in her country villa Adriana has no-one with whom she can communicate other than superficially; long separated from her husband, who is now dying, she shares the house with her sister-in-law Matilde, 'a fat old maid with a mannish haircut' (p. 9) with whom she has nothing in common, and a couple of teenage daughters who are far too young to understand her problems, while her two older daughters, Viola and Angelica, are married and live in town with their respective husbands. Conscious that the only member of the family her husband is on good terms with is Michael, a young tearaway who has left home to live in a basement flat in town and lead his own life,[55] Adriana writes him the first of many letters which make up this book, begging him to visit his father, and, in the process, reproaching him for his disorganised life-style. Too fixed in her ways to understand Michael's desire for independence Adriana has no hesitation in describing his behaviour as crazy,[56] indulging in tedious maternal comments about dirty washing and how damp and dark are her son's living quarters; at the same time, however, the seriousness of her husband's illness leads her to some more significant reflections on their past life and her own state of mind, something inconceivable in direct communication face to face but quite logical in a situation in which contact is possible only through a medium which encourages deeper analysis of one's feelings and calls for greater clarity of thought.[57] Already in this first letter Adriana emerges as a woman who is anxious to defend the traditional values of family life but is finding it more and more difficult to hold her own in a world whose terms of reference are no longer those she has grown up with, as a person whose reaction to an increasing feeling of estrangement is to withdraw into her shell and take refuge in self-pity; thus despite her criticism of Michael's life-style, at variance with the conventional norms of middle-class behaviour, she is herself unable to respond positively to something as basic as the birth of a child, aware that instead of reacting with traditional enthusiasm she now feels oppressed by its presence, aware that 'One has seen too many of these children' (ibid.). In the same way her desire to spend a stimulating morning watching the snow fall outside the window while she reads Pascal's *Pensées* is undermined by a sudden attack of depression: 'all of a sudden she felt a loathing for that snow-clotted landscape . . . she rested her head on one hand and with the other caressed her feet and ankles . . . and so she spent the morning' (p. 10).

Michael's sudden decision to flee the country for obscure political reasons which are never clarified, thereby ensuring that his mother can only communicate with him by writing,[58] further concentrates her mind. This is clear from her second letter, in which a long and tedious paragraph once more dedicated to dirty washing and warm clothing is suddenly interrupted by a perceptive comment on what is really important in the present situation – the reason for her son's abrupt departure: 'Don't think that I do not realise that your departure was a flight. I am not a fool. I ask you to write to me immediately and explain clearly from what or from whom you wanted to run . . . I always have a terrible fear that you could end up with the Tupamaros' (pp. 25–6). This move away from domestic trivia to what truly matters in absolute terms is, however, short-lived, and Adriana passes immediately to discussing the practical problems connected with her son's flight and the objects he has left in his basement; she writes with an intensity of feeling that leaves no room for other considerations, ending her letter by scolding Michael for not having knocked up a rabbit hutch before leaving for London. At the same time she is, almost despite herself, aware of the absurdity of such comments, pointing out in another flash of consciousness that 'Undoubtedly you will consider it stupid to be fond of a stove' and that 'You will say . . . there's no end to my worries about you' (p. 26). Ten days later, following her husband's death in hospital, Adriana sends Michael a very different letter in which domestic considerations are hardly touched on in favour of an extended re-evocation of her chequered relationship with his father, whose disappearance from her life has, despite everything, been a great shock, and whose affection for their son she now realises 'focused on a person he had invented and who didn't resemble you at all' (p. 41). In a desperate attempt to cope with her feelings in this moment of crisis she unburdens herself totally, recalling how during the first period of their separation 'I had built up such a hatred of your father that I thought of going into the house . . . with a pistol and shooting him' (pp. 43–4), a confession totally at variance with her previous maternal role, as she herself immediately realises, conscious that she is now no longer able to discharge this adequately, or, even, to believe it has any objective value: 'Perhaps a mother should not tell a son these things because they are not very edifying and educational. But nobody knows what a good upbringing is any more or if there really is such a thing' (p. 44).

Adriana's intense need to find some sort of relief for her emotions is a blessing in disguise in that it encourages her to use her letters to Michael as a form of therapy, something which automatically excludes the patronising tone of her earlier communications, establishing instead a straightforward rapport between two adults meeting on equal terms who can be mutually self-supporting. In this context her consciousness that Michael's past history as a child from a broken home cannot entirely explain his subsequent development indicates an awareness on her part that there may ultimately be little to choose between his own experience and the conventional norms her generation have adhered to in bringing up their families;

her ability now to express this realisation openly, previously buried beneath feelings of guilt and self-loathing,[59] is in effect the beginning of her transformation from unhappy and uncomprehending mother to thinking woman anxious to understand the world around her. At this point in the narrative her feelings also clearly recall those of the author in *Collective Life*, repelled by the life-style of the younger generation and the moral climate of her day, which she does not understand, nostalgic for the confident certainties of her youth[60] and yet conscious of a moral obligation to come to terms with reality as it exists here and now. In Adriana's case this process, while ultimately therapeutic, is also inevitably both painful and lengthy, involving an extended period in which her improved communication with Michael is balanced by moments of acute depression and emotional apathy. An interminable speech of the utmost triviality, in which the maid Cloti describes her relationship with a previous employer and his two sisters, is forced on her as soon as she has finished this first meaningful letter to her son; this further increases the strain she is under and provokes feelings of impotent rage which only gradually subside into crushing melancholy, feelings reinforced when she recalls the cowardly behaviour of her lover Philip, who has not only abandoned her in order to marry a much younger woman but had insisted on being accompanied by her daughter Angelica when he broke this news, frightened of Adriana's possible reactions. We already know from a meeting between Angelica and her father in Chapter 4 that this had been in the offing for some little time unbeknown to Adriana, who has 'the mind of a teen-age girl in spite of her forty-four years' (p. 35),[61] and even allowing for some exaggeration as a result of her estranged husband's bitterness it seems clear that Adriana's difficulties in establishing satisfying human relationships are an inherent part of her personality, springing from a basic naivety which she shares with many other women in Ginzburg's writing and which has led to a general incompatibility of spirit symbolic of the author's own position at this time.

The reserves of strength which had allowed Adriana to withstand the shock of Philip's betrayal[62] have now been exhausted and replaced by an equally extreme degree of vulnerability, something she conceals from her son but which he none the less learns from Angelica, who is also writing to him. By this time Michael has left London for Sussex, where he has found work as a butler and general factotum to a Professor of Linguistics, and it is clear from his mother's next letter that she is anxious to develop further the closer bond forming between them, now no longer limited to an obsessive concern with Michael's health and domestic arrangements. A fleeting reference to his need for boots useful for walking in the local woods is, we deduce, a hang-over from a recent telephone conversation, and is immediately followed by the expression of a more serious hope that despite being so far away her son is at peace and happy, while she has been advised by their mutual friend Oswald to leave him alone to get on with his duties. In this context Adriana's simple unfussy request 'to know when you expect to return' (p. 72) is a model of discretion, quickly passed over in favour of an amusing account of her squalid Christmas dinner and how absurd it is to suggest Oswald is in love with her, an apparently trivial remark which is none the less indicative of the more adult approach she is now cultivating in these letters. When two days later she writes to Michael once more to inform him of the details of his father's will her undisguised plea for him to 'come and look at these matters and decide what you want' (p. 76) is motivated by a genuine practical need affecting the whole family, and is qualified by two sentences which make it clear that her request now springs from a basic acceptance of her son's right to lead his own life: 'I can't decide for you. How can I, when I don't know where and how you want to live' (ibid.). Michael's reply, only the second time he has seen fit to make any response to his mother's frequent letters, is, like his first, a brief note prompted by purely practical considerations: the need to inform Adriana of a further move, this time from rural Sussex to the northern city of Leeds, where his new girlfriend has found work as an art teacher and will arrange for him to be hired by her school as an odd-job man; meanwhile he needs some money. Never particularly involved in his family's affairs Michael is now completely detached from what has happened since his departure, and tells Adriana quite openly that he has no desire to return to Rome and that his relatives can sort out the details of his father's will for themselves, a clear indication that he is on a completely different wavelength and likely to remain so. The news of his impending marriage just over one month later to a thirty-year-old American divorcée with two children, whom Michael himself describes as 'not pretty . . . Extremely thin. Covered in freckles' but who is also 'very intelligent' (p. 92), provides further confirmation, if any were needed, of his impetuous and foolhardy nature; more importantly, in this context, it completes the process of self-examination and growing self-awareness that has been taking place within his mother, now able to see Michael as a fully autonomous individual, capable – or so it seems – of taking on adult responsibilities, something which brings home to her with particularly intensity how shallow is their relationship: 'Sometimes I think . . . how little we have been together, you and I, and how little we know each other, how superficially we evaluate each other' (p. 96).

This news reaches Adriana while she is suffering from pleurisy, her first ever serious illness and, as such, an intimation of mortality she finds particularly disturbing; the combination of these two totally unexpected events reinforces her sense of vulnerability, ensuring that 'I am in a continuous state of fright and disbelief' (p. 95) and encouraging her to adopt an increasingly languid and resigned attitude to the business of living – as a result her good wishes to her son are especially melancholic. Her next letter, the seventh in sequence, maintains this elegiac tone in Adriana's description of her garden, which she realises she will never have enough energy or talent to cultivate and where in any case she will no longer plant roses, since these remind her of her former lover. Conscious that she is now addressing her remarks to a supposedly mature adult who has himself experienced sexual passion and marriage Adriana recalls at length her relationship with Philip and speculates on the reasons for its having ended unsatisfactorily, certain that such intimate matters can now be appreciated by her correspondent, who will be able to share her feelings and provide some kind of sympathy. Significantly she also mentions that, although she has been promised a phone very shortly and cannot wait to call her son, 'the thought of telephoning you upsets me' (p. 106), realising, whether consciously or not, that she can communicate with him in depth only through writing.

It is of course deeply ironical that Adriana's attainment of a meaningful level of discourse in her correspondence should be balanced by increasing feelings of fragility, both physical and spiritual, as she comes to terms with her mortality and the true nature of her emotional relationships. Her concluding comments stress her sense of vulnerability,[63] and prepare the way for what turns out to be her last letter to Michael, in which her disappointment at hearing he has cancelled a trip home to introduce his wife is expressed with a gentleness far removed from the shrewish tone of her first communications, while the instinctive pride she still feels in her domestic role is now for the first time seen as something objectively trivial and unimportant. Fully conscious at last that Michael has always inhabited a world of his own making, and not simply an extension of her own, Adriana sadly admits that she has no control over her son's actions; at the same time she is conscious of her new-found ability to communicate with someone who, although her own flesh and blood, must inevitably remain to some degree a stranger. The letter ends with a joyful evocation of their last meeting, when they had both felt happy at being together despite having wasted valuable time arguing about domestic trivialities.

Notwithstanding the pessimism still central to Adriana's existence[64] it seems clear she is now confident of being able to eschew mistakes made in the past and establish a new and fruitful rapport with Michael, who will surely come back one day.[65] But these hopes are cruelly dashed, first on hearing that Michael has left his new wife and abandoned Leeds for parts unknown, then, shortly afterwards, by the news of his death in a student demonstration in Belgium, during which he is mobbed by a group of Fascists and knifed. We never learn whether he received his mother's last letter, and it is supremely ironic that her separation from her son, which has stimulated and determined her growth to a greater maturity in human relationships, should be made permanent precisely when it has achieved its purpose, especially since at no time during this process has he seen fit to collaborate actively in Adriana's transformation, which he has thus brought about both indirectly and completely unaware. The book thus ends on a delicately balanced note of elegiac longing in which Adriana, now fully capable of bridging the gap between her own generation and contemporary youth, is none the less still quite unable to do so; if her achievement is in itself something positive, and thus essentially indicative of an optimistic element in Ginzburg's thinking at this time, Adriana's continued spiritual isolation, now relieved only by memories of her dead son, is also clearly indicative of the author's extreme diffidence when confronted by the increase in violence and social fragmentation characteristic of Italy in the early 1970s.[66]

A similar sense of ambiguity is clearly central to Ginzburg's portrait of Mara Castorelli, a girl Michael had known before leaving Rome and whose chequered relationships with all those around her are a source of much comic relief in this novel.[67] We first meet her in Chapter 2, when she is introduced as an acquaintance of Oswald, the family friend, summoned to help her move from a boarding-house to an empty flat she is borrowing. It becomes clear almost immediately that Mara, near-destitute and with a new-born baby to look after, is both infinitely deserving of sympathy and a menace to anyone foolish enough to respond to her needs. Totally irresponsible she has no hesitation in adapting reality to suit her purpose, eschewing the truth in favour of what people want to hear or what can be turned to her advantage, borrowing money and possessions she has no intention of returning, and generally exploiting every human contact with an unyielding intensity that rapidly ensures both friends and lovers cannot wait to see the back of her. Potentially a tragic figure and in many ways similar to Michael in her impetuous and irrational behaviour Mara remains an essentially comic character precisely because of the absurd contradiction between, on the one hand, her desperate need for human solidarity and the basic necessities of life, and on the other the ability with which she invariably alienates all those around her by insatiable demands on their time and shameless appropriation of their goods and chattels. Typically her treatment of Oswald during this first meeting, in which querulous complaints about her misfortune alternate with offensive remarks about his family, becomes positively farcical when on hearing that he does not want to make love to her she tells him to '"Go to hell"' and then bursts into tears, begging him to prepare the baby's milk and adding '"For Christ's sake, help me!"' (p. 23).

Oswald's infinite reserves of patience, quite beyond the norm, are not shared by the other people Mara comes into contact with as the novel progresses. His attempt to find her a job as a live-in maid with his shop assistant and her elderly mother is – predictably – a disaster, since '"She was no help in the house. In fact, my mother ended up cooking for her"', and quickly ends after Mara has not only created chaos in the household but also taken to waking up both women in the middle of the night '"to help her change the baby. She said it depressed her to do it alone . . . the more people around the better"' (p. 57). Having thus precluded a possible solution to her immediate needs, a pattern destined to be repeated *ad infinitum*, Mara returns to her absent friend's flat, where she lives on hand-outs from Oswald and from Adriana, who has agreed to help on the grounds that Michael was, on his own admission, one of her casual lovers and might thus be the father of her baby. When Oswald's estranged wife Ada subsequently finds her a job as secretary to her lover Fabio, a publisher, Mara – again predictably – rapidly seduces him, and turns up on his doorstep shortly thereafter on learning she can no longer stay in her friend's apartment; a brief period of harmony is followed, as always, by the rapid disintegration of this relationship when Fabio realises Mara is too vulgar and uninhibited to appear with him in public. Meanwhile she has turned his luxurious penthouse into an extended nursery for her vociferous child, and Fabio makes his increasing annoyance so plain that one day she takes advantage of his absence at work to pack and leave, heading for a small seaside town on the west coast where she has some reluctant relatives. Her total inability to grasp that she has once again been the sole cause of her misfortune is a further source of comic effect in her fiercely resentful description of herself in a letter to Michael as 'cute, pretty, young, nice, and I have such a pretty baby. I do him [Fabio] the favor of staying in his house and spending his money which is of no use to him' (p. 111). Fabio's subsequent letter thanking her for having left him and telling her quite plainly that 'I could not stand you any more' (p. 117) causes not the slightest ripple in her self-assurance.[68]

Coolly received by her relatives Mara decides to resume contact with Lillia, a woman she had befriended in the Roman boarding-house; having discovered she has moved to Sicily with her husband Mara writes to ask if she may visit them, making sure she leaves for Trapani before they have a chance to reply. Grudgingly accepted by this couple, who also have a small child, Mara settles into a new routine as housemaid and baby-minder, initially quite content to spend her mornings doing domestic chores and in the afternoons taking the children to the local park, where 'I talk with everyone I meet and I tell lies' (p. 134). She soon grows discontented, however, since 'I don't like being a servant, and I guess nobody likes it' (p. 135), especially since Trapani is a dreary place with nothing to do in the evening and 'Here there aren't any men who appeal to me' (p. 137). Prostrated by the news of Michael's death, something which ironically makes her presence even more of a burden for Lillia and her husband, she finally exhausts their patience entirely, first by clumsily smashing a complete set of dinner-plates, and then, more seriously, by being discovered one Sunday afternoon in her hosts' bed with Lillia's brother-in-law when they return unexpectedly from a trip to Catania. Ejected on the spot she spends the night at a friend's house before phoning Oswald, who, ever receptive to her needs, finds her a job as a companion to his rich elderly uncle in Varese, 'quite nice, maybe queer . . . deaf as a post so he doesn't hear the baby cry at night' (p. 149). Once more safe and sound, at least for the moment, Mara relaxes in this prosperous environment where she is in effect a lady of leisure, her only worry the thought that Ada, clearly less concerned for her welfare, may send a butler to replace her.

This is the last we see of Mara, who is clearly first and foremost a typical representative of disaffected youth, totally disorganised, cheerfully promiscuous, and naively convinced there will always be someone to provide food and lodging at their own expense and be a soft touch for funds.[69] Her unquenchable spirit of survival and her ability to bounce back unscathed after every disaster recall the character of Giuliana in *Ti ho sposato per allegria*, but the context here is a much grimmer one in that no permanent solution is provided for Mara's problems, while the shock of Michael's death, the first and only event to impinge seriously on her throughout the novel, does ultimately make her realise at least in part how fragile and exposed is the life she leads; thus in her last letter, to Angelica, she ends her whimsical account of past events with the very different revelation that 'I never used to be afraid, but now at a certain point a sort of terror grabs me and I feel my throat tighten. I remember Michael and I begin to think that I too will die' (p. 150), something which perhaps indicates the first glimmerings of maturity. If the unvarying contrast between Mara's desperate situation and her destructive behaviour is the mainspring for humour in this book, as already indicated, she also serves to communicate the author's awareness that while the rootless and aimless generation which she personi-fies[70] may be the source of much anguish and disturbance for those living a more traditional and ordered existence this occurs not because of any innate malice or wickedness in young people but simply because of their total freedom and deliberate rejection of any kind of conventional responsibility; their motivation is for the most part instinctive and thus indicative of a basic good nature. On the one occasion Mara decides to formulate a plan of campaign – her relationship with Fabio, whose wealth she covets – she is rapidly overcome by feelings of melancholy on realising how much more intelligent he is, and is unable to act rationally because 'I was madly in love with him and he didn't give a damn about me' (p. 113). Aware that her casual attitude to sex is a source of scandal she revealingly tells Michael in one of her letters that 'you know very well . . . I am not a tart . . . just a girl and that's all' (p. 108), a phrase which makes it clear her promiscuity is totally disinterested; hovering on the edge of destitution she never once neglects her child or considers abandoning it, since 'the thing I like best is to have babies' (p. 99), thereby demonstrating that despite her crazy life-style she has a strong maternal instinct. In this context her shame-less exploitation of people and things is clearly no more than a struggle for survival made more difficult by her refusal to conform to society's rules, a refusal which has a certain fascination for those whose life-style is more conventional and who recognise their own carefully controlled anarchic impulses in her supremely disordered existence.[71] Mara's essentially serious function in this novel over and above her more immediate role of comic character is thus clearly to provide more evidence of the gulf that separates people of her age from those of Adriana's generation, a gulf which is especially noticeable in the context of family relationships; Ginzburg's claim three years earlier that old age begins at the precise moment one gives birth to children[72] is thus further emphasised in the contrast between Mara's utter rootlessness, both literal and metaphorical, and Adriana's inability to move from her entrenched position, at least at first. When she does at last succeed in breaking the mould her new-found ability to communicate with her son is perhaps indicative – despite the irony of the book's conclusion – of a more hopeful approach to the problems of the generation gap when compared with Ginzburg's statement in that same essay that 'there could never be any kind of reciprocity between us and our children . . . never any kind of equality, never any friendship',[73] possibly because, as she was to write in another essay only two months later, a parent's relationship with a child is inevitably a 'dark and visceral love . . . that has nothing to do with reason and judgement . . . buried in the depths of the spirit.'[74]

If the general impression created by *Dear Michael* is thus in some ways positive, and reminiscent of earlier days when Ginzburg had seen such relationships as developing in a climate where 'feelings, instincts and thoughts can flourish',[75] the fact remains that the young man's death effectively puts paid to any practical realisation of these hopes, and that the book ends with a supremely melancholic letter by Oswald to Angelica from Michael's empty house in Leeds, while Angelica herself, in a misguided but well-intentioned desire to save her widowed mother further anguish, deliberately avoids any meaningful dialogue with Adriana, ensuring that 'her replies are always marked by a cold calm' (p. 126) and thus recreating the atmosphere of 'gray, good-natured, and useless words' (p. 128) which had characterised Adriana's last meeting with her son. Sadness and resignation are thus ultimately what predominates in this novel, and clearly represent the author's belief that although there is still room for hope in human relationships the reality that confronts us is, for the most part, totally lacking in any redeeming features. In *Maledetta domenica*, an essay published in 1972 and thus clearly written at the same time as *Dear Michael*, Ginzburg speaks quite uncompromisingly of 'the total absence of happiness in the human condition at this point in time',[76] adding that 'in a world devoid of happiness the only satisfaction one can hope for is a mature understanding of one's condition, free from any illusions';[77] while in

160

another essay written a year later she states even more pessimistically that 'we believe the world has never known such widespread and indeed universal unhappiness as we do today'.[78] This all-consuming pessimism shows no sign of diminishing in the numerous other essays written during this period, all clearly composed in a state of deep depression; thus in *Il traforo* (1971) she writes that the world of her youth, characterised by 'pride, euphoria, and self-assurance', has 'completely collapsed',[79] while in *L'unico libro di Elizabeth Smart*, published a month later, she describes those of her generation as being totally isolated and 'unable to communicate their anguish to a living soul';[80] in *Un governo invisibile* (1972) she likewise concludes some lengthy reflections on the disappointing nature of political activism by stating that 'the future has suddenly crumbled before our very eyes . . . although we all want a better life we can no longer believe it will materialise in the future',[81] and in *Goffredo Parise*, the following year, describes how this author's work perfectly represents a world in which 'the present is hostile, with no room to breathe or to move, and . . . he feels he cannot believe in the future',[82] stressing the 'immense melancholy' which is central to Parise's writing.[83] The idea of death as something not only inevitable but also imminent, hinted at in the last line of this essay[84] and clearly a logical conclusion to Ginzburg's train of thought, is fully developed in the essay entitled *Vita immaginaria* one year later,[85] preceded by further pessimistic considerations along the same lines which confirm the author's bleak and joyless vision of human existence:

> There was a moment in our lives when we realised we would never again know happiness, that fate could bring us all manner of things except happiness, now for ever excluded . . . when in our old age we try to remember what it was like to be happy we remember that . . . it was a time when silence and immobility made us creative instead of bringing us face to face with our deficiencies and our regrets . . . our thoughts now focus increasingly on what is inexorable . . . which leads us to an ever-increasing familiarity with the reality of death.[86]

It is hardly surprising that in these circumstances Ginzburg should have waited a further three years before publishing anything in book form and that when she did so it should consist of two long short stories which are undoubtedly the most pessimistic elements in her output.[87] *Borghesia* was first published in instalments in *Corriere della sera* in the summer of 1977 and subsequently reprinted together with *Family* in the autumn of that same year in a slim volume whose title reproduces that of the second novella; it is an intensely sad tale whose protagonist, a middle-aged widow called Ilaria Boschivo, is clearly Ginzburg's *alter ego*, a woman unable to relate to the changes that have taken place in the world around her, confused by the behaviour of the younger generation, and conscious of the fact that despite being surrounded by other human beings she is nevertheless very much alone. Lacking any outlet for her emotions and with nothing to fill up her empty days Ilaria is overjoyed when someone makes her a present of a cat, on which she lavishes all the affection she is no longer able to confer on her daughter Aurora, a teenage bride who lives in the flat next door with her husband Aldo, a young drop-out with no prospects and happy to live off Ilaria's brother-in-law Pietro, a wealthy antique dealer. Mother and daughter have been cool and distant towards each other since Ilaria's son died from meningitis seven years previously at a time when her husband was in hospital with a nervous breakdown, a combination of misfortunes which, instead of bringing them closer together, has led them 'not to talk about painful things' so that 'prudence became a habitual part of their relationship' and 'Every syllable was weighed carefully so as to sound light and cheerful' (p. 76). This attitude is clearly reminiscent of the unsatisfactory rapport between Angelica and Adriana in *Dear Michael*, here made worse by the fact that Aurora's placid manner conceals a certain animosity towards her mother, a feeling she has carried over from her childhood when her father's unsuccessful attempts to resume a normal life after his illness had made Ilaria feel 'her daughter was developing a deep resentment against them both, thinking them stupid and unhappy and hating them for their unhappiness' (ibid.). When Ilaria's cat is accidentally crushed by Pietro while he is moving furniture it is Aurora who informs her mother of what has happened, and she does so with a brutal directness which reminds Ilaria that 'her daughter derived acute pleasure from bringing her bad news' (p. 75) and inevitably adds to her distress.

Ilaria's intense grief at the death of her cat, apparently far in excess of what might normally be expected in such a situation, becomes more understandable when seen in relation to the general greyness of her life, a life in which, as she now understands, 'even poor sorts of pain are acute and merciless, and quickly take their place in that immense, vague area of general unhappiness' (p. 76). The animal's death is also clearly a reminder of Ilaria's own mortality, and its disappearance especially agonising when she realises how it has been the only living creature within her immediate circle

162

to show her any affection and communicate with her in any meaningful way. She acquires a replacement, who is given the name of
Fur, and with whom she develops a similarly close relationship; but
he too is killed, by falling off a roof during a struggle with a rival, and
is succeeded in turn by Lulla, a she-kitten who rapidly grows to
maturity and produces a litter of five babies, events which are a
constant reminder to Ilaria of the inexorable passage of time and
cause her to reflect how 'every time you saw [a cat] walk silently at
your feet, the burdensome memory of everything that had happened
to you went by with it' (p. 97). In the last we see of her, after she has
been taken ill and gone into hospital, where she is diagnosed as
suffering from cancer of the lung, she tells her friend Rirì that
'whenever she looked at Lulla, it made her think about dying', and,
in a significant phrase confirming the reader's earlier deductions,
that 'she had started to think about dying from the moment Rirì had
sent her that first little cat in a shoe-box' (p. 109).

Ilaria's death at the end of this story is a fitting conclusion to a life
in which relationships within the family circle have been supremely
unsatisfactory. The love she feels for her daughter despite their
reciprocal lack of warmth is merely another source of pain; Aurora's
separation from Aldo to live with a young man she has met while on
holiday fills her with grief, causing her to burst into tears. She sheds
more tears later on when she intuitively realises this new relationship has disintegrated and Aurora is desperately unhappy, but she
none the less cannot bring herself to broach the subject at their last
meeting, when she is on her death-bed, and is only able to repeat the
usual banalities that have passed for dialogue between them over the
years. Her relationship with her brother-in-law is no better; their
close proximity over a period of time has in no way produced any
feelings of intimacy between them, so that they never discuss
important matters affecting the way they live their lives. Pietro's
affair with a nineteen-year-old girl is thus deliberately passed over in
silence, despite the fact that it has destroyed his peace of mind, until
'At last, one evening, he told her he was getting married' (p. 83),
adding that 'he was almost certainly making a grave mistake' (pp.
83–4). This moment of truth, in which Ilaria discreetly expresses
her concern at the absurdity of such a decision, soon passes, and is
never referred to again; when Pietro's marriage begins to fall apart
after only a few months all three of them continue 'to make polite
conversation about light-hearted cold topics' (p. 100) while things
go from bad to worse, and after his wife has run off with Aldo they go
on behaving as if nothing serious had happened, since '[they] had

never been able to talk to each other very much, and they were still unable to do so' (p. 105). Ilaria's awareness that 'she had got out of the habit of telling people what she thought some time ago' (p. 102) recalls Caterina's decision to avoid talking seriously to her brother at the end of *Valentino*, being clearly likewise a source of anguish and frustration; and if this civilised coolness ensures a certain superficial calm which has enabled Ilaria to live her own life from day to day without being directly involved in other people's problems, thereby avoiding the overpowering anxiety and the patronising domesticity so typical of other maternal figures in Ginzburg's earlier work, her independence, both practical and spiritual, is a lonely conquest, ultimately foreign to her nature, and one which we realise she would gladly exchange for a relationship providing the kind of fulfilment she obtains in surrogate form from her domestic pets. Unlike Adriana in *Dear Michael* Ilaria at no time transcends the limits of her world, unable till the last to communicate meaningfully with anyone while being infinitely more aware of the need to do so; at the same time it is clear that in their separate ways both women are not simply conscious of their maternal role but also aware that communication can and should take place on other levels, in different contexts, as a basic requirement in human nature.

Given Ginzburg's increased pessimism during this period it is hardly surprising to find that Ilaria's fate is notably grimmer than Adriana's. We leave Michael's mother not only alive and physically in good health but also comforted in her bereavement by the knowledge she has acquired and drawing some relief from her memory of their last meeting; here, on the other hand, the protagonist dies a grim death alone in hospital, unable to derive any consolation from evoking times past, since 'Words became so loaded with memories as the years went by, and because of that, they became full of weariness and pain' (p. 109). Aurora is no better off, her self-assurance affording no protection against the inevitable collapse of her relationships, both unstructured and supremely unpractical, typical of a generation determined to act on impulse and live for the moment. Her comments early on that 'The essential thing in life . . . was to refuse unhappiness with clenched teeth' and that 'There were three things in life you should always refuse to take: hypocrisy, resignation and unhappiness' (p. 86) are touching in their naivety, and recall Mara's insensitive spontaneity throughout *Dear Michael*; here too, however, we are presented with a much grimmer picture which lacks the humour of the earlier work and creates an infinitely starker picture of rootlessness and the bleaker aspects of an undisciplined life-style. At her mother's death-bed Aurora realises that 'it was impossible to shield yourself from those three things . . . They were too strong and too cunning for mere humans', and is painfully aware that her detached attitude towards her mother over the years now precludes her speaking about her problems, conscious – too late – that 'unhappiness was not only a very complicated thing to talk about, it was humiliating too' (p. 110). In keeping with the general tone of this work there is similarly no hope that the letters which occasionally replace the useless small talk in the family circle when one of its members is temporarily elsewhere may improve communication, as these are purely functional, lacking any deeper significance,[88] and confirming the desolation that is virtually unrelieved throughout this tale. Pietro's wife Domitilla, a fringe character despite the damage she causes, confirms Ginzburg's hopeless view of the younger gener-ation in the author's description of her as 'one of those girls who always keep their lips pressed tightly together and never look you in the eyes' (pp. 78–9), possessed of 'a cold, indifferent, silent sort of youth', and, as Pietro himself acknowledges, someone who ' "doesn't really love anything except herself" ' (p. 84). The only sign that Ginzburg's sense of humour had not completely vanished at this time is provided by her picture of the maid Ombretta, a lazy creature more concerned with improving her appearance than doing the housework, quietly promiscuous while constantly proclaiming her respectability, and invariably falling ill whenever she is threatened with dismissal; she is, however, a minor character oc-cupying relatively little space in the story.[89]

Family, which opens this volume despite having been written three months later, confirms a tendency already apparent in *Dear Michael* and further developed in *Borghesia*, namely a broadening of ap-proach which has gradually led Ginzburg to extend her deep compassion for female misfortune to members of the opposite sex, now seen as potentially just as vulnerable and thus equally deserv-ing of sympathy. If one recalls that the characters at the centre of her early work are also male – the wretched Maurizio of *Un'assenza* and the pathetic Walter of *Casa al mare* – this may appear at first sight to be a kind of regression; it soon becomes clear, however, that the protagonist of *Family*, Carmine Donati, though equally unhappy and misunderstood, is in no way abnormal in his emotions. He is thus seen with very different eyes as symbolising the inevitability of human suffering, now no longer the exclusive province of the weaker sex, traditionally victims of a male-dominated society, but – sadly

– affecting the whole of humanity.[90] The female characters in this story occupy largely subordinate roles, but are none the less indicative of Ginzburg's continued awareness that human relationships, whether successful or not, are what dominate our lives and condition our behaviour; this is particularly noticeable in Carmine's wife Ninetta, a mindless beauty only interested in high-class socialising and who, conscious of her ravishing appearance, 'offered her smile as if it were a precious jewel' (p. 14), thereby proclaiming what she sees as an innate superiority over all those around her. This confidence in her natural distinction is dealt a rude blow when she falls in love with an unprincipled journalist whom they both consider 'a total imbecile' but who none the less inveigles Ninetta into a shameful rapport she is unable to break off, despite being convinced that 'adultery was a sad, degrading thing' which causes her to exchange her radiant expression for 'a humble, tremulous, pained little smile' (p. 36). The affair ends when the journalist decides 'it was hurting his wife too much' (p. 43), and Ginzburg skilfully dissolves the sympathy which we inevitably feel for Ninetta in her subsequent depression by informing us that what causes her most anguish is not so much the separation in itself but the fact that her lover has abandoned her peerless excellence to return to 'a short, fat woman with a prominent chest, scrawny legs like a chicken, and a faded bun' (p. 45) – thereby stressing Ninetta's essential superficiality and confirming that, as another character states earlier on, she is 'as stupid as a pear' (p. 10). If her main function is to emphasise the emotional isolation of her husband she also clearly serves to indicate the author's belief that we are frequently slaves to our passions, and, in this way, extends the range of her pessimism to the point where it becomes little short of fatalistic.

A similar feeling of inevitability emanates from Ivana, the other woman in Carmine's life, whom he meets for the first time ten years after they had separated following the death of their child and the subsequent break-up of their relationship. Now thirty-seven and thus on the brink of middle age Ivana is still scratching a living as a free-lance translator, always short of money and with a young daughter, Angelica, born after a brief affair with a student she had met while working in a dead-end job in England. Protected from the worst effects of poverty by her parents, after their return to Rome following the student's removal to a mental hospital, Ivana avoids actual destitution but is never able to become self-sufficient economically, while her emotional life appears similarly destined to be simply a source of pain and suffering. She is happy to meet up with

166

Carmine, with whom she develops a platonic relationship infinitely more satisfying than their previous tortured rapport as lovers, but she remains unable to find fulfilment with her long-term partner, a doctor who lives in a village in Umbria and who, though less violent than the English student (who used to beat her mercilessly) is equally disturbed in that 'he suffered from long periods of depression that lasted for months at a time, and he did not always want to see her' (p. 20). His suicide early on in the narrative removes Ivana's one remaining link with this area of experience, plunging her in turn into a deep depression which only gradually disperses and is destined to return with the death of Carmine, an event she clearly foresees after he falls ill and is taken to hospital where, like Ilaria in *Borghesia*, he subsequently dies of cancer, thereby depriving her of her one mature source of affection. Her solitude at the end of this tale is made more poignant by the re-emergence of Ginzburg's awareness of the generation gap, now seen as extending beyond first youth into the middle years, where, if anything, incompatibility becomes more marked; in politics there is now no common ground between Ivana and her parents, who have grown increasingly reactionary with old age. As she ruefully comments to Carmine on his death-bed, '"My parents criticized the way we lived, and ate and spent our money . . . nothing was right for them. But it's the same now that I'm living on my own. I still can't do a thing right"' (p. 66). Carmine's parents, though very different from Ivana's, are equally cut off from their offspring; elderly peasants who have never progressed beyond the simple things of life they are unable to understand the atmosphere of emotional estrangement in their son's house during a visit that takes place after Ninetta's affair with the journalist, and simply add to the general strain under which the couple are labouring, so that 'He loved them, but he could just have strangled them . . . adored and detested their wrinkled faces' (p. 52). It is none the less Carmine's mother, together with both Ninetta and Ivana, who watch over his last moments, three women who have each had a profound influence on him in their separate ways but who inhabit three totally different worlds and have nothing else in common, a further example of the author's ironic pessimism.

This general incompatibility is deepened still further by Ginzburg's inclusion of a fourth female character: Olga, the 27-year-old daughter of a wealthy musician, who, despite her prosperous middle-class background and her advancing years, is pleased to affect a hippy life-style, living from hand to mouth and rejecting anything which implies responsibility or commitment. Her casual attitude to life and her availability for new experiences are inevitably a source of deep attraction for Carmine, an unhappily married man of forty trapped in a conventional mould and unsure whether he is still capable of creative work, but their relationship, which initially gives Carmine a new lease of life, is necessarily short-lived and rapidly deteriorates when, like Lorenzo in *The Advertisement*, he attempts to inject some sort of order into his lover's life, heedless of the fact that she is pathologically incapable of any such thing. If the situation is reminiscent of this earlier work the characters are, however, very different: Carmine, a successful architect with artistic pretensions, has very little in common with Lorenzo the dispersive playboy, while there is likewise no indication that Olga's rootless frivolity and sexual permissiveness might proceed, as in Teresa's case, from an unhappy childhood and a frustrated need for affection; they recall instead the unsuccesful attempts made by Silvana in *La segretaria* to detach herself completely from any emotional involvement and live life entirely for herself. Olga, a less sensitive person, has clearly achieved this aim, and has no qualms about abandoning Carmine for a younger lover when she becomes bored with his moralising;[91] similarly she has no difficulty in breaking off all contact with Ivana and Angelica, whose house she had virtually taken over after first meeting them while on holiday and who had naively imagined she was animated by feelings of genuine friendship. When their paths cross by chance some time later Olga's neutral greeting – the one word ' "Hi" ' – shocks Angelica, who recalls how ' "She was always at our house . . . and now she hardly says hello" ' (p. 59), a reaction which clearly represents Ginzburg's own despairing incomprehension of the manners and life-style of the younger generation. Needless to say Olga at no time visits Carmine after he goes into hospital.[92]

If this story is, in general terms, no less pessimistic than *Borghesia* – both deal with characters who are almost continuously unhappy and with the dismal death of the protagonist – *Family* also shows a welcome increase in the author's sense of humour, now no longer restricted to a minor character as in the previous tale, but clearly evident (albeit in a minor key) throughout the narrative, in a style which recalls her earlier work. In the original Italian it is at its most noticeable in the character of Matteo Tramonti, a gentle teenage drop-out with a speech defect whose essential goodness of spirit provides an interesting and reassuring contrast to the soulless negativism of Olga and whose comments, reproduced phonetically, are unfortunately less comic in English translation. In addition there are frequent instances of the absurd juxtapositions which Ginzburg has always found diverting, such as the bemused reactions of Carmine's rural parents when confronted with a carefully nurtured pet rabbit in his flat in town, or the naive good-will of Ivana's neighbour Isa, who washes up for her after Ivana has been informed of her lover's suicide so that 'Ivana could go without having to worry about the dishes' (p. 24). In retrospect it is clear that despite everything the second tale in this slim volume is indicative of a renewal of Ginzburg's vital spirits, which, while in no way affecting her basic conviction that life is essentially an unpleasant and disappointing experience, also leaves room for an appreciation of the positive aspects of human existence, one of which is undoubtedly the ability to laugh at our more absurd manifestations, thereby making the whole thing that much more bearable. It seems clear that in the seven years that were to elapse before her next novel, *The City and the House* (published in 1984), she succeeded in fully re-establishing a more balanced relationship with the world around her, eventually focusing once more on a male protagonist whose varied relationships with other characters of both sexes, all of whom find it virtually impossible to achieve fulfilment, confirm Ginzburg's desire to extend her sympathy across sexual barriers to encompass the whole of humanity, and whose failings and inconsistencies are documented with a sharply humorous eye once more fully capable of appreciating how frequently things serious and comic combine in people's lives. In the intermediate period she likewise appears to have published few essays, and it is doubtless no coincidence that her inspiration during this time seems to have been the work of other creative artists; at its most simple a range of short articles commenting on television programmes and published in *Corriere della sera*, on a higher plane her work in various archives and libraries, eventually brought to fruition in the lengthy and untypical *Manzoni Family*. The development in Ginzburg's treatment of male characters, first fully evident in *Family* and now totally consolidated in her last novel, will be the subject of the final chapter, where *The City and the House* will be examined in detail.

Notes

1. Simonelli, 'Intervista-confessione', p. 51.
2. *Never Must You Ask Me*, pp. 31–3.
3. Ibid., p. 32.
4. See *Human Relationships* in *The Little Virtues*, pp. 75–95; and the essay entitled *The Little Virtues* in ibid., pp. 98–9.
5. *Old Age* in *Never Must You Ask Me*, p. 33; Isabel Quigly translates *indecifrabile* as 'unreadable'.
6. *I figli adulti* in *Vita immaginaria*, p. 204.
7. Ibid., p. 206.
8. See *Human Relationships* in *The Little Virtues*, p. 95.
9. *Le donne* in *Vita immaginaria*, p. 124.
10. Ibid., p. 125.
11. Ibid., p. 221.
12. See her review of *Mai devi domandarmi*, in *Forum Italicum*, vol. V, no. 3 (1970), p. 474.
13. L. Tornabuoni, 'I suoi elzeviri: Omaggio a Natalia', *La Stampa*, 5 Dec. 1970, p. 3.
14. Lidia's reactions on hearing of Ginzburg's return to Rome from Turin is to exclaim: '"She will send them out in rags . . . she will send them out without buttons. Out at the seat!"', p. 173.
15. *The Child Who Saw Bears* in *Never Must You Ask Me*, p. 114.
16. See Lidia's comment in *Family Sayings*, p. 155: '"I know you support the Soviets. You are all for the austere life. I want to see the children properly dressed."'
17. *Vita immaginaria*, p. 129.
18. *Never Must You Ask Me*, pp. 66–9.
19. Ibid., p. 66.
20. See also her comment in *Le donne* in *Vita immaginaria*, p. 129: 'At the end of a day spent with the children the old women feel exhausted as if after a long battle', a direct echo of the protagonist's statement in *The Dry Heart*, p. 115 (already quoted in Chapter 2), implying that by identifying ever more closely with a traditional maternal role Ginzburg had lost the ability to see beyond this sphere, in contrast with her statement in *My Vocation*; see Chapter 2, note 30.
21. His wife's comment that 'he's a man who doesn't really like women', p. 27, would seem to imply that he is in reality a repressed homosexual.
22. Anne-Marie O'Healy comments in *A Woman Writer*, p. 143, that this section of the play 'belongs to the clearly identifiable tradition of the comedy of manners', while also stressing that the work 'gives a realistic and candid portrait of a certain segment of society' which is 'clearly less than flattering', p. 145.
23. This is never more apparent than when she postpones committing suicide in order to get herself invited to lunch by an elderly gentleman she meets on a bridge crossing the Tiber.
24. At one point she claims that as a result of her ambiguous relationship with the neurotic Manolo 'I had learned to think, I had become a different person', p. 23, but in reality this affair merely widens her

range of accessible subjects without encouraging her to pursue any of them in depth.

25. This distinction between Pietro's assurance and Giuliana's uncertainty is completely lost on Pierre Marcabru, who in his review of a Paris production, there entitled *Adriana Monti*, in 'Mariage réussi', *Le Point*, no. 733, 6 Oct. 1986, p. 27, writes 'they are linked by an equal inability to understand their destiny or take possession of it'; more accurate is the comment by Gianna Panofsky in 'Il teatro di NG come testo di lingua straniera', *Italica*, vol. 47, no. 4 (1970), p. 448: 'the female protagonist, empty-headed and scatter-brained, redeems herself by acting as a counterweight to the unbearable heaviness of boring mindless respectability, thereby creating a new kind of matrimonial model of opposites.'

26. Giuliana leaves home not only to seek her fortune but also 'because I couldn't stand the sight of . . . those newspapers any longer', p. 20.

27. Baldini, 'Questo mondo non mi piace', p. 135.

28. Toscani, 'Incontro con NG', p. 211.

29. Lennie, *Posso presentarle?*, p. 73.

30. Giuliana's is further described as 'timorous, diffident, bitter . . . with trembling hands, glancing around her with frightened eyes like a hare on the run', p. 49.

31. At one stage he attempts to improve her mind by giving her a reading list, but 'everything I read, it was like water off a duck's back. I forgot everything the minute I'd read it – perhaps because I could never stop thinking about him', p. 16, an attitude especially irritating for a man with intellectual pretensions.

32. Teresa sees this dependence as a natural consequence of her love for her husband; in Act One she tells Elena 'He dominated me, and he dominated me because I loved him', *L'inserzione*, p. 92; Henry Reed translates differently.

33. These considerations were lost on Harold Hobson, who wrote in 'Flower-powerhouse', '*Sunday Times*', 29 Sep. 1968, p. 59, that '*The Advertisement* is about as fresh and challenging as a story from a forty-year-old issue of some magazine like *Woman's Own*'; Alan Blyth likewise in 'New Cast of Lovers', *The Times*, 20 Nov. 1968, p. 9, describes the play as 'superficial'. These negative judgements were not shared by the international commission which awarded the play the Marzotto Prize in 1968; one of its members, Martin Esslin, subsequently stressed in 'Approaches to Reality', pp. x–xi, how 'it is constructed with its complex interaction of different levels that mutually put each other into ironical relief . . . There is an affinity between the work of Pinter and *The Advertisement* . . . [it] is a tragicomedy and the tragicomic is the dominant mood of our age.'

34. Barbara comments in Act One that 'My granny never even taught me to wash my face. It's a miracle if I learned to wash my face when I wake up in the morning' (p. 143).

35. See Anne-Marie O'Healy's comments in *A Woman Writer*, where she describes this play as reflecting 'the decadent traits of a social class in decline' (p. 161), and the characters as 'members of the traditional bourgeoisie who have . . . dispensed with the trappings of the life-style

171

of their parents, but have found nothing to replace these and search distractedly for objects to fill the void in their existence' (p. 162).

36. When reproached by Sofia for her irresponsibility Titina at first claims that she is reluctant to go against the Church's ruling on contraception, but subsequently admits that her main reason is the fear of growing a moustache, thus revealing that she is ultimately as immature as her feckless husband.

37. She is clearly an extension of Barbara in *Fragola e panna*, described by Anne-Marie O'Healy in *A Woman Writer*, p. 154, as having 'a peculiar resilience which comes from having numbed certain regions of her mind to pain, embarrassment and hurt, but who is nonetheless haunted by a deep-seated anguish', a description in reality more appropriate to Silvana.

38. All this is made more poignant by a hint in the text that at one point she has engineered her husband's absence in order to go to bed with Gianni.

39. See *The Little Virtues* in the collection of that name, pp. 109–10.

40. Anne-Marie O'Healy in *A Woman Writer*, p. 176, stresses how the dialogue between husband and wife is 'full of ironies, concealments, misunderstandings, distracted answers and momentary tangents . . . it conveys a mood of anguish, alienation and existential perplexity.'

41. The wig of the title is a present, dating from the first years of their marriage, which Massimo has thrown out of the window into a rain puddle, an apparently lunatic gesture which is in reality deeply revealing of his feelings.

42. S. Brata, book review, *The Times*, 30 Jan. 1975, p. 9; see also Ginzburg's own description of the novel as 'a story about confusion and dissension' in Baldini, 'Questo mondo non mi piace', p. 135.

43. *Mai devi domandarmi*, p. 137; Isabel Quigly translates differently.

44. *Never Must You Ask Me*, p. 98.

45. Ibid.

46. Ibid., p. 99.

47. *Mai devi domandarmi*, pp. 138–9; Isabel Quigly translates differently.

48. *Never Must You Ask Me*, p. 99.

49. Ibid., p. 102.

50. Ibid.; Isabel Quigly translates *fatica* as 'weariness'.

51. Ibid., p. 101.

52. Ibid., p. 99.

53. Ibid., p. 100.

54. We are told in Chapter 1 that she is 43, while in 1973 Ginzburg was 57.

55. H. Stuart Hughes comments in *Prisoners of Hope. The Silver Age of the Italian Jews 1924–1974* (Harvard University Press, Cambridge, Mass. and London, 1983), p. 149: '*Dear Michael* depicted a family in full dissolution: far from sharing a private language, the voices of its members, apathetic and selfish, barely reached one another.'

56. Sheila Cudahy translates *balordo* as 'scatterbrain', p. 6.

57. This important distinction is unperceived by Valentine Cunningham in 'Griding Mistress', *New Statesman*, vol. 89, no. 2293, 28 Feb. 1975, p. 284, where he stresses the 'elements of effective non-communicat-

iveness' in the letters; more accurate is Carlo Bo's description of them in 'La cenere nelle vene' in *Interventi nella narrativa contemporanea 1973–5* (Matteo, Treviso, 1976), p. 17, as 'cries of frustration and mortified despair'.

58. Her first letter, written while he is still in Rome, springs from the fact that 'I am still without a telephone', (p. 7), following her move to the villa ten days previously.

59. She significantly states in this same letter 'I often felt and still feel that I dislike the person I am' (p. 44).

60. See the last paragraph of *The Son of Man* in *The Little Virtues*, p. 52, which she concludes by stating 'we're happy to have become mature adults'; Dick Davis translates differently.

61. This is an error of calculation on her husband's part, corrected by Angelica.

62. We are told on p. 50 that 'She was solid as an oak'.

63. 'To think I was strong as a horse once. I have been through too much. I am frail now' (p. 106).

64. In the same letter she states that 'Over the years I have become meek and resigned' (p. 127).

65. The author's comment, in an interview with Mariangela Melato and Sandra Bonsanti published by the latter in *Epoca*, XXVI, no. 1313, 10 Dec. 1975, p. 85, entitled 'La Ginzburg parla del suo romanzo "Caro Michele" ora portato sullo schermo con Mariangela Melato: "C'era una volta la famiglia"', that '"His mother does not understand Michael at all and understands nothing because she thinks only of herself"' must be interpreted in this context; Adriana still cannot indeed understand her son but now knows how to remedy this, while her concentration on her own problems has not been mere self-indulgence but a voyage of discovery in the field of human relationships.

66. She clearly identifies with Adriana, as is apparent from her comment in ibid., pp. 84–5: '"I love this mother . . . I have a great affection for her . . . We are all sorry for each other these days, being sorry for each other is a full-time occupation."'

67. Olga Lombardi's comment in 'NG', p. 7624, that 'there is no room for humour in this book' is quite incomprehensible.

68. See also Michael's comment in a letter to his sister Angelica: 'I couldn't stand her for long because after she had listened to me she would dump all her problems in my lap and she would stick to me like toffee and never leave me in peace' (p. 119).

69. Rosetta Piclardi describes her in a telling phrase in 'Forms and Figures in the Novels of NG', *World Literature Today*, vol. 53, pt. 4 (1979), p. 587, as 'a flower child Italian style'.

70. See Ada's remarks to Oswald in Chapter 8 when discussing Michael's departure for England: '"The world today is full of boys who drift aimlessly from one place to another. One can't imagine how they will grow up. It seems as if they won't ever have to grow old; as if they will stay as they are with no home, no family, no working hours, nothing. Just a couple of rags"' (p. 55).

71. See Angelica's comment in a letter to Mara: ' . . . you are an aimless drifter, a lonely foolish girl. However . . . there is something of the

173

drifter and the fool in all of us and to that extent we can put ourselves in your place and understand you' (p. 142).

72. See *I figli adulti* in *Vita immaginaria*, p. 204.
73. Ibid., p. 206.
74. *On Believing and Not Believing in God* in *Never Must You Ask Me*, p. 150.
75. *The Little Virtues* in the collection of that name, p. 98.
76. *Vita immaginaria*, p. 47. The title refers to the Italian version of John Schlesinger's film *Sunday Bloody Sunday*.
77. Ibid., p. 50.
78. *Infelici nella città bella e orrenda* in ibid., p. 202.
79. Ibid., p. 141.
80. Ibid., p. 39; see also the statement in *Bergman*, written during this same year and quoted in Chapter 1 note 159.
81. *Vita immaginaria*, p. 173.
82. Ibid., p. 68.
83. Ibid., p. 72.
84. She speaks of Parise contemplating a fragile world with 'a farewell glance', ibid.
85. Ibid., pp. 209–28.
86. Ibid., pp. 223 and 226–7. See also *Sussurri e grida* (1973), where she defines Ingmar Bergman's main theme as 'the idea of death' (ibid., p. 73), stressing how in such a context happiness can only exist 'within a limited framework' of 'uncomprehending childish innocence' (p. 79); the title refers to the film billed in English as *Cries and Whispers*; also *Il vizio assurdo*, in which she describes the world we live in as 'one in which people are prepared to put up with and tolerate any sort of outrage' (ibid., p. 89); the title refers to a play by Davide Lajolo and Diego Fabbri on the figure of Cesare Pavese.
87. Isabel Quigly in 'The Low in Spirit' stresses how Ginzburg's characters are 'doomed to an everlasting melancholy . . . a sort of low-spiritedness, a sense of fatality'.
88. They are described as 'a few lines scribbled on a page' (p. 103); 'a few hastily scribbled lines' (p. 104); 'a few hastily scribbled but affectionate lines' (p. 106).
89. The same is true of Ilaria's friend Rirì, who appears from time to time and is throughout kind and affectionate, but no happier than the protagonist, being saddled with an elderly husband and four children, who ruthlessly exploit her; while her seven-year-old affair with Pietro, once 'an amazing source of consolation' (p. 80), has now ended, leaving her emotionally high and dry.
90. A more accurate comparison is with Paolo, Barbara's husband in *Fragola e panna*, who reacts to his wife's infidelity with a nervous breakdown.
91. She chillingly informs him that 'she never had long-lasting relationships anyway' (p. 51).
92. Claudio Marabini in 'Due gemme di Natalia', *Il Resto del Carlino*, 29 Dec. 1977, p. 7, stresses how in this volume the younger generation are 'without principles or rules for living, and wander aimlessly in a kind of limbo . . . not only is there no longer any concept of social class but humanity itself, seen as a spiritual entity, offers little hope for its survival.'

5 Men or Mice? Winners and Losers in the Battle of the Sexes

> that monstrous inexplicable race who are of a different
> sex from us and who possess a terrible ability to do
> everything good and everything evil to us, who have a
> terrible secret power over us . . .[1]

Although Ginzburg is not normally classified as a feminist writer
alongside such typical representatives of the genre as Marilyn
French or the younger Germaine Greer her most obvious talent and
thus her main claim to fame is clearly an undoubted ability to
communicate the complex subtleties of female sensibility through
the portrayal of fictional characters whose context is almost invariably one of submission or exploitation, whether active or passive, in a society where women are still more often than not relegated
to positions of inferiority and where masculine values are correspondingly seen as naturally and necessarily predominant. If Ginzburg's intuitive rejection of this assumption and her resulting
sympathy and compassion for the female of the species is thus the
basic stimulus for most of her writing, as already indicated, she has
always been equally aware that although the dice are heavily loaded
in men's favour the so-called stronger sex are in essence just as
vulnerable as their female counterparts; further, that their superiority is frequently determined by the sacrifice, willing or otherwise, of
a woman whose aims and desires are viewed solely in relation to
those of her nearest and dearest and ruthlessly subordinated to
men's unquestioned need to maintain their position, a process
especially insidious because usually gradual and imperceptible over
an extended period rather than sudden and brutal. Alongside these
apparently superior characters, whose natural dominance is more
apparent than real and whose affection more a liability than an
advantage, Ginzburg also shows us men possessed of a genuine
sensitivity and anxious to do the best for those around them, but
who are unable to affirm themselves in an environment where
success is essentially reserved for the more cynical or more corrupt

175

members of society; or men who are basically honest but who lack power or are too weak to assert themselves or change things for the better, their good nature paradoxically sometimes detrimental to themselves or to others. Last of all we find rare instances of men who appear to know their limitations and organise their lives accordingly, men in control of their passions and able to evolve a life-style which ensures their emotional survival while at the same time allowing them to provide counsel and assistance to their partners; in short men who appear to deserve the status that society automatically assigns to their sex.

Masculine inadequacy is indeed the central theme of Ginzburg's first '"adult"' work, the short story *Un'assenza*, written in 1933. Deliberately inverting traditional sexual stereotypes at a time when they were significantly more rigid than in our own day she here examines a loveless marriage of convenience in which the dominant figure is clearly Maurizio's wife Anna, an ambitious woman anxious to establish a position in polite society and openly dismissive of her placid good-natured husband, who is possessed of enough wealth to make work unnecessary and whom she consequently despises. Maurizio's general passivity and lack of emotional drive, traditionally a female characteristic,[2] has allowed him to dawdle through life unthinkingly, and he is only made aware of the essential aridity of his existence when his wife leaves him for a trip to San Remo (where he suspects she is meeting a lover) and in the void created by her absence he realises for the first time that her presence is quite indifferent to him, that their small son is merely a nuisance, and that he is cut off completely from the world of 'normal' people, whose inferior life-style disgusts him. In a fleeting moment of truth he contemplates killing himself, only to draw back at the chilling thought of mud at the bottom of the river. In a supremely ironic finale Ginzburg shows him seeking refuge in that most typical of masculine stereotypes in Latin society: a visit to the local brothel, where, however, he arrives bored and joyless, unable even to summon up basic lust, a fitting conclusion to an apparently simple story which in effect seriously questions basic assumptions about human behaviour. The message is further emphasised by Ginzburg's concentration throughout on the pathetic Maurizio, his self-assured wife only appearing indirectly as he reflects on the inadequacy of their relationship.

Ginzburg's story *Giulietta*, written one year later, focuses on a very different kind of male. Aldo is an ex-rustic who has moved to the city and become a doctor, acquiring more sophisticated habits and now

176

living with a girl, the Giulietta of the title, something he has carefully kept from his family back home. When his younger brother Ferruccio decides to follow in his footsteps and moves to town in his turn to attend grammar school he naturally expects to be put up by Aldo, who is thus obliged to reveal his relationship with the young woman; and if it is easy to appreciate his embarrassment at explaining this to someone who is little more than a child and who must now also conceal what is clearly – in view of the period and the brothers' background – a shameful secret, Aldo's reactions to this crisis are clearly contemptible. Too shy to explain the situation to Ferruccio on the way home his confusion at seeing how easily his brother and his mistress make friends quickly turns to frustration and anger at his own inability to make things clear, and is equally quickly revealed as springing from a basic deviousness of character. Initially tempted to flee the apartment and leave the two young people to their own devices he reluctantly returns home after having gone out to buy cigarettes, only to lose his temper at table when Ferruccio naively suggests they all spend Sunday with the family, feeling 'suffocated by a mixture of sadness and spite' (p. 56); conscious that his brother is blameless he inevitably directs the full brunt of his feelings on Giulietta, whom he observes 'with hostility' as they prepare for bed after he has at last explained things to Ferruccio. The story ends chillingly with Aldo's sudden awareness that her expression resembles that of her mother, 'an old hag in a rest home' (p. 57), while she touchingly asks him if he is angry with her. If Maurizio is basically reconciled to his lot at the end of *Un'assenza* and destined to continue drifting through life unscathed Aldo is clearly insufficiently strong to cope with *his* problem, which has already affected his feelings for Giulietta and will almost certainly lead to pain and suffering for all three characters concerned.

Casa al mare, three years later in 1937, is more complex, employing the device of a male narrator who is also one of the protagonists. Summoned by his old friend Walter from his home in the city to a small seaside town the writer is charged with resolving a domestic crisis involving Walter's relationship with his wife Vilma, a neurotic woman unable to communicate with her husband and infatuated with a middle-aged musician named Vrasti. Initially disturbed at the thought of becoming involved in someone else's affairs he is none the less anxious to be of assistance, and despite the fact that no counselling of any kind takes place soon begins to experience feelings of fulfilment which gradually acquire a specific focus as he allows himself to fall under Vilma's spell, first unconsciously and then, on

177

realising what is happening, with increasing inevitability as he attempts to delude himself into thinking that all is well. When he finally makes up his mind to depart Vilma reacts with a tearful scene that predictably degenerates into a passionate embrace, and when he leaves next morning, filled with 'sorrow and disgust' at what has happened, he is conscious that 'I had resolved nothing, and had indeed made things worse, possibly ruining them for ever' (p. 380). If the narrator's total lack of will-power clearly marks him out as a perfect example of masculine indecision his friend Walter is equally inconclusive, hiding his inability to make contact with his wife or offer her any assistance under a mask of cold indifference to all that surrounds him, even after learning of his friend's betrayal, to which he reacts with 'a gesture of impotence' (p. 381). The third man in this short tale, Vrasti, is no better, an unkempt and incompetent piano-player who regularly drinks to excess and babbles incoherently in his cups, a more obvious example of the fundamental powerlessness affecting both the other male protagonists and which ensures that Vilma's neurosis continues unchecked. In the last paragraph we learn that following the death of her child she left her husband to live with the musician, confirming the narrator's suspicions that his incompetence has helped to destroy this marriage.

Equally obvious, albeit not at first, is the powerlessness afflicting the husband of the female narrator in Ginzburg's next short story, *Mio marito* (1941), a woman who gradually realises that her marriage to a doctor practising in a depressed southern village is no more than a futile attempt on his part to overcome a sexual obsession with a local peasant girl. The husband's gradual disintegration is skilfully traced in no little detail; away from the village he is 'extraordinarily self-confident' with 'an air of seriousness which was both measured and determined' (p. 383), but this superficial image vanishes after his return home with his new bride, to whom he soon confesses the truth about their marriage, informing her that the mere sight of his peasant mistress '"awakens something irresistible within me"' (p. 387). This is a moment of truth which, while apparently strengthening the bond between husband and wife, in reality drives a wedge between them, producing 'a certain strain in our dealings with each other' (p. 389) which extends to their relationship with the two children she bears him in the following years. When one day she catches sight of him on his way to meet Mariuccia in the woods she realises that 'He had learned how to lie to me and no longer suffered because of it. My presence in his house had made things worse for him' (p. 391), at which point he admits he feels no love for her, especially since Mariuccia is now pregnant. Conscious, however, that he has failed his wife by marrying her under false pretences he is gradually overcome by shame and increasingly withdraws into silence and solitude, neglecting his appearance, refusing food, and spending sleepless nights alone in his study. When Mariuccia dies in childbirth he is unable to face life without her and shoots himself.

Ginzburg's evident sympathy for the unfortunate women in these last three stories is given full rein in *The Road to the City*, where the female narrator Delia occupies a central position and the various male characters who influence her behaviour and ultimately determine her destiny are seen as background figures; this thereby reverses the pattern of her earlier work while at the same time providing further examples of masculine incompetence or inadequacy. Delia's father, nominally head of the house, is quite unable to face up to his obligations, as already hinted in Chapter 2, preferring to 'take his hat down from the rack and go out' (p. 12) whenever a row develops, attacking his daughter when she becomes pregnant, and, subsequently overcome by shame, looking 'permanently hurt and sad' when 'all the strength required for getting angry or shouting or beating anyone up seemed to have gone out of him' (p. 56). Her brother Giovanni, a young man with no ties and anxious to enjoy life, allows himself to become involved with Antonietta, who is well past her prime,[3] whom he is unable to shake off, and with whom he refuses to live for fear of being pressurised into marriage, while his parents insist he turn all his salary over to them once he has found a steady job. Her sister's husband, 'an oldish man with eyeglasses and a beard' (p. 10), is no better than her father, perpetually apprehensive about what he reads in the newspapers and uninterested in his wife, both partners having illicit relationships outside the family home. Alongside these essentially marginal characters Ginzburg devotes no little space to Delia's cousin Nini, a sensitive youth whose shy nature is totally out of place in these squalid rural surroundings and who is clearly marked out as one of life's victims. Unable to confess his love for Delia Nini attempts at length to make her realise his feelings, but she is too empty-headed to understand him and it is only after the arrangements for her shotgun marriage have been finalised that he finds the strength to speak to her directly, by which time it is of course too late. Nini is presented throughout as an untypical if not eccentric individual – he reads books and is conscious of having a basic intelligence which could be developed – unable to overcome the loneliness his different nature condemns him to and whose one chance of emotional fulfilment he is unable to grasp while there is still time; aware that Delia's marriage precludes any possibility of an emotional relationship between them he abandons any hope of happiness and turns to drink, deliberately encouraging a tendency he has hitherto kept under control and which now appears as the most effective way of putting an end to his suffering.[4] Among these supremely inconclusive characters the one positive male figure is Delia's husband Giulio, initially portrayed as a thoughtless playboy reluctantly forced into marriage but in due course developing what appears to be a genuine affection for his young wife, something which will afford her some kind of security for the future.

The essential bleakness of all these stories is clearly in keeping with Ginzburg's basic pessimism in her approach to human relationships, and would appear to leave little room for any evidence of humour, the other basic characteristic of much of her writing. While this is undoubtedly true of *Casa al mare* and *Mio marito*, both of which examine extreme situations where humour would be quite out of place,[5] it is none the less clear from the very first of these tales that Ginzburg has always been aware of the absurdity of much human behaviour and in possession of a fine sense of irony which she has no hesitation in deploying where appropriate. Thus in *Un'assenza* the shallowness of Maurizio's character is effectively stressed by having him realise that Anna's preference for tea as opposed to cocoa, his own first choice of beverage, is a clear sign of their incompatibility, while his essentially submissive role in their relationship is emphasised by the phrase 'mentally asking his wife's pardon as he did so', which occurs on three separate occasions in situations of increasing importance, ranging from his neglect to remove his shoes before stretching out on the couch (p. 370) to his ringing the bell outside the brothel at the end (p. 374). In *Giulietta* there is similarly considerable scope for ironic writing in the contrast between Ferruccio's naive enthusiasm and Aldo's anguished awareness of the ambiguous situation created by his brother's arrival. In *The Road to the City*, a much longer story, Ginzburg was at last able to develop this particular strain, especially appropriate to rural characters whose lack of sophistication leads them to act in ways that seem comic to the literate reader; thus when Delia's mother-in-law visits her in hospital after the birth of her child and brings her a box of dates as a present Delia scoffs the lot as soon as she is left alone and then 'put the box away, thinking it might be good to keep gloves in' (p. 59). Earlier on when she is exiled to her aunt's house in an even more primitive village to conceal the shame of her condition she discovers that although the community is 'pervaded by the smell of manure and unwashed babies squatting on the stairs . . . no electric light in the houses, and all the water came from a public fountain' (p. 38) the inhabitants have a highly developed sense of social propriety, to such an extent that when in a state of advanced pregnancy she goes for a walk with Nini, who has come to visit her, she compromises the reputation of her aunt's daughter.

In 1945, one month after the official German surrender, the cultural review *Mercurio* published a short story by Ginzburg entitled *Passaggio di tedeschi a Erra*, which describes in chilling detail how the initial euphoria occasioned by the 1943 armistice in a small rural community gives way to apprehension as the countryside swarms with occupying German forces and the villagers gradually realise that for them the war is not yet over after all. When one of the local rustics shoots a drunken soldier disaster is inevitable, and seven inhabitants are executed as a reprisal, including – by mistake – the only person who can speak German and who has throughout acted as interpreter, a striking example of black humour sharper than anything so far produced by the author. With the benefit of hindsight this tale can be seen as a prelude to *All Our Yesterdays* seven years later, but is clearly in the first instance dictated by the possibility of speaking freely after so long about the harrowing events Ginzburg had lived through, and, as such, outside the normal range of inspirational subjects. At the same time we may note that the slaughter of the villagers is the direct result of yet another example of masculine thoughtlessness: Antonino Trabanda's long-standing desire to kill a German, 'something he thought about ceaselessly; it was an obsession that never left him' (p. 40), an action which while apparently brave and virile is in reality stupid and catastrophic in its results.

Two years later in 1947 Ginzburg published *The Dry Heart*, in which the lack of understanding between the unnamed protagonist and her husband Alberto is clearly the mirror image of that which exists between Nini and Delia in *The Road to the City*, as here it is the woman who embraces the role of misunderstood victim while the man is happy to indulge himself at her expense. Alberto is in no sense a vile seducer and has no malice within him; he is, however, totally immature, something which is soon revealed as much worse. Quite incapable of any kind of long-term commitment, whether emotional, professional, or artistic, he drifts aimlessly from one interest to another, his private means making it unnecessary for him to work and ensuring he remain an eternal adolescent, unable to

181

penetrate beneath the surface of life.[6] Fully aware of this – indeed he describes himself as being 'like a cork bobbing on the surface of the sea, pleasantly cradled by the waves but unable to know what there was at the bottom' (p. 83) – Alberto at no time makes any effort to transcend what should have been a normal stage in his development but which he has instead adopted as his adult personality. This inevitably makes him a strongly negative character whose consistent inability to understand his partner's needs is the immediate cause of her unhappiness and eventual destruction; and yet he too, like his wife, is in reality a victim of the family, in his case an ancient widowed mother with whom he still lives despite being in his forties, and who has dominated his life completely, likewise precluding any capacity to form satisfactory sexual relationships. Though never appearing directly Alberto's mother is frequently mentioned in ways which make it clear that she has an oppressive influence on him which is little short of tyrannical and conditions every aspect of his life; when she dies unexpectedly his initial grief is soon followed by '"a sudden feeling of relief"' (p. 141), inevitably succeeded in turn by the realisation that he is now alone in the world. Thus when shortly afterwards the narrator is moved to confess her love for him he is quickly able to overcome momentary panic and take advantage of the situation to tell her that 'Since his mother had died the house was very lonely and the days when he didn't see me were empty and cold' (p. 88), a revealing phrase whose implications she does not grasp, so that 'When Alberto asked me to marry him I said yes' (p. 89).

If this information undoubtedly provides greater depth to the novel by making the reader realise how Alberto's thoughtless egoism is, at least in part, the inevitable result of his conditioning, it in no way lessens his effect on the narrator, who soon realises she is essentially acting as a surrogate mother with an additional sexual dimension whose benefits in no way prevent her husband from continuing with an unsatisfactory extra-marital affair which has been dragging on for years. The shock of this discovery and its implications inevitably affect her feelings for her husband, which cool progressively as she understands that he is no more willing to allow her into his life than before their marriage, evading all attempts at communication other than on the most trivial level while leaving her at irregular intervals to go off on trips with his mistress. In this context Alberto's encouragement to his wife to 'cure myself of the habit of thinking about things so hard' is both ironic and appalling in its insensitivity, and it is logical that in the same breath he should announce that 'The main thing for a woman was to have a baby', then adding 'and for a man too' (p. 94), a claim which reveals the full extent of his duplicity; for he is well aware that the task of caring for a new-born child will be sufficiently demanding to keep his wife fully occupied, thereby allowing him to regain the freedom he had enjoyed before getting married and ensuring that during the time he does spend with her she will be too busy to pester him. His plan works, the narrator's resentment gradually dissolving to the point where husband and wife resume sexual relations, abandoned at an earlier stage after one of Alberto's adulterous excursions, thus allowing him to have the best of both worlds; when, however, she catches sight of him one day in town arm in arm with his mistress she feels devastated, like the wife in *Mio marito*. As they decide to separate he callously informs her that, like the doctor in the short story, he had married believing '"it would go smoothly and then I could forget her"', now realising that '"I just can't live with you any longer"' (p. 119). Their subsequent reconciliation following their child's death from meningitis destroys the narrator's one chance of freedom and independence; it re-establishes a relationship in which she is dependent on her husband, who inevitably reverts little by little to his old ways as she comes to terms with her loss, his tender affection gradually giving way to impatience and an increasingly obvious desire to spend as little time as possible with his wife, who realises 'there was no use counting on him for anything' (p. 141). Incorrigibly deceitful once his domestic circumstances are back to normal he is too insensitive to appreciate that his partner has been changed by her experiences, acquiring a new determination which eventually leads her to shoot him when he refuses to admit that he is preparing to spend some more time with his mistress, an action seemingly identical with Antonino Trabanda's foolish gesture in *Passaggio di tedeschi a Erra* but in reality having a totally different significance; superficially identifiable as an act of weakness gener-ated by neurotic frustration, it is rather a logical – if delayed – reaction to the countless humiliations the narrator has endured in the five years they have known each other and during which Alberto has been completely incapable of establishing an adult rapport with a woman now at last driven beyond the limits of endurance. If, as suggested earlier, Nini's death in *The Road to the City* is in effect a form of suicide, it is tempting to suggest that this assassination can likewise be seen more accurately as the execution of an individual whose hopeless duplicity and monstrous egoism have caused such extensive damage as to make him unworthy to continue living; it is to the author's credit that such a contemptible character should have been given a background which, while in no way justifying his behaviour, goes some way to explaining it, placing him in the wider context of family relationships and their destructive effect on the personality.

In complete contrast to Alberto is his childhood associate Augusto, a marginal character and one-time unsuccessful rival for his mistress's favours, whose lonely existence is in reality far more fulfilling than that of his supposedly more fortunate colleague, complete with wife and lover; though initially distraught as a result of Alberto's good fortune he wisely decides that '"it wasn't worth while losing my head over anybody, and I began to study and write a book about the Polish wars of secession"' (p. 123), which is in turn followed by 'his new book on the origins of Christianity' (p. 130). Consistently unhappy in love, as is clear from his tormented relationship with Francesca, Augusto finds ample compensation in his research, which eventually occupies almost all his energy, so that he has little time left for Alberto's inconclusive literary efforts. The narrator realises he is able to survive and make something of himself because he has grasped that life has more than one dimension;[7] he is clearly the first example in Ginzburg's writing of that small band of men who are sufficiently clear-headed to order their lives intelligently and whom the reader can esteem and admire.

There is no trace of any such person in the author's next two compositions: the short story *La madre* (1948) and the novel *Valentino* three years later, where male characters are once more seen as either incompetent or destructive. The absence of any understanding between the young widow of the first work and the male members of her family, either too young or too old to appreciate her needs, has already been touched on in Chapter 2, together with the elusive figure of her lover Max, an archetypal scoundrel who has no hesitation in abandoning his mistress once he has tired of her, heedless of the disastrous effect this will have on her emotions. In *Valentino* this theme of callous exploitation is developed more fully in the character of the protagonist, a pathological scrounger who cunningly uses and abuses all those with whom he comes into contact, starting with his immediate family and gradually extending his range into other areas, invariably drawing on a limitless supply of human affection and creature comforts which ensure that he can spend his days in dispersive idleness. The fundamental contradiction between Valentino's true nature and the unrealistic expectations of those around him is first evident in the attitude of his father, who believes the lad is 'destined to become a man of consequence . . . a famous doctor' who will 'attend medical congresses in the great capitals and discover new drugs and new diseases', quite oblivious of the fact that Valentino 'spent his time playing with a kitten or making toys for the caretaker's children . . . Or he would don his skiing outfit and admire himself in the mirror' (pp. 9–10), a narcissistic tendency later revealed as having more disturbing implications. Initially happy to amuse himself with pretty teenage girls, whose shyness he can easily take advantage of, Valentino's unexpected engagement to the older and decidedly unattractive but very wealthy Maddalena shows quite unambiguously where his true interests lie, and the horrified reactions of his family, able for the first time to appreciate his deviousness, have no power to modify what is in effect a skilful plan of campaign. Once installed in his wife's luxurious villa Valentino virtually abandons all contact with his relatives, heedless of the fact that they are still struggling to make ends meet while he 'didn't give a snap of his fingers but was always buying himself new clothes' (p. 22), and it is some time before Maddalena realises she has married a feckless playboy with whom she has nothing in common. When he is thrown out after the suicide of her cousin Kit and the subsequent discovery of his homosexual affair he simply moves in with his sister, who is now living alone after the death of both their parents and who still has some feeling for him despite everything. Once more assured of the care and attention of a willing victim Valentino sinks back into idleness, his morning spent 'reading magazines or doing crossword puzzles' (p. 48), his afternoons in mysterious trips to town which he does not discuss with his sister and whose significance is not difficult to imagine.

Alongside this supreme example of destructive self-centredness[8] Ginzburg provides two contrasting male figures: Valentino's father and Kit, his lover, both victims of their emotional involvement with that ruthless individual. The former, traumatised by the late realisation that he has completely misjudged his son, is presented as a man totally lacking in authority, constantly humiliated by his wife, who 'always interrupted his speeches, leaving him choking on a half-finished sentence' (p. 13), and whose eloquent but inadequate reaction to Valentino's marriage – he throws away his pipe in disgust on seeing his son flaunting a gold lighter he has received from Maddalena – is typical of someone who has never been able to hold his own in an adult environment. His happy memories of days gone by when as an elementary school-teacher 'he could talk as much as he wanted' (p. 15) recall Valentino's skilful manipulation of his teenage sweethearts, and it is clear that both men are essentially inferior specimens of humanity, Valentino having skilfully learned to compensate for his deficiencies by exploiting his charm, while his father, who we are told 'never said anything sensible' (ibid.), has remained an ineffectual failure. Unable to tolerate his son's shameful behaviour he becomes increasingly depressed, growing ever more alienated from those around him, repeatedly asserting that he is not long for this world; and, indeed, he does die soon thereafter, his final letter to Valentino perceptively stating that 'there was indeed no necessity for him to become a man of consequence, it would be enough if he became a man at all, because at present he was merely a child' (p. 22). This view of Valentino as a victim of arrested development recalls Ginzburg's presentation of Alberto in *The Dry Heart*, but it is clear that she has now refined this type of character, making him more cunning and so ensuring that the reader has no sympathy whatever for someone who is not only able to solve all his problems while remaining unscathed but who does so by effectively destroying the three people closest to him – father, wife, and lover; someone who, as his sister is well aware at the end, 'has always taken from others with never a thought of giving anything in return' (p. 49), and thus a typical representative of her largest and most negative category of male figures. Kit, apparently as degenerate as Valentino in his preference for a life of pleasure-seeking idleness, is on the contrary possessed of a strong sense of honour which obliges him to break off his engagement to his lover's sister, who is unaware of his true nature, and to tell her quite bluntly he is ' "a failure and a layabout" ' (p. 29), elsewhere describing himself even more brutally as ' "no better than a floorcloth" ',[9] an equally typical example of the well-intentioned but inconclusive male whose efforts to do good only make things worse for himself and those around him.

All Our Yesterdays, published one year later in 1952, remains Ginzburg's most ambitious novel, focusing on a broad spectrum of characters in deeply contrasting environments. As Europe is gradually torn apart by the Second World War the reader becomes increasingly aware that while the young Anna is attempting to resolve an intensely personal crisis, which inevitably takes precedence over all other considerations, the young men who surround her, whether in her own family or in the house across the street, and who are obsessed with the fate of Western civilisation, all represent different aspects of inadequacy which make them worthy representatives of the ineffectual male; while her youthful lover, totally self-centred and impervious to anything which does not concern him directly, is clearly a prime example of destructive irresponsibility in the most traditional of masculine contexts. The theme of masculine inadequacy is indeed stressed from the very first chapter in the figure of Anna's father, a life-long Socialist who, shortly before his death, destroys his unpublished memoirs full of 'fiery attacks upon the Fascists and the King' (p. 9) which have occupied him for years and which he now realises are quite useless. He is a loquacious but passive individual who has never acted on his principles and whose total lack of discretion has ensured he has no friends in his old age, during which he vents his impotent spleen on his children by consistently taunting them verbally and forcing them to spend long summer months in a sleepy country village where they are bored to tears. His opposite number in the house across the street is even less assertive, an elderly gentleman who at one time had founded a soap factory which is still going strong but who is now deaf and in his second childhood, heedless of his younger wife's infidelities and suffering from an ulcer which eventually kills him.

It is perhaps inevitable that the lack of an impressive paternal figure should have a negative effect on the male offspring of both these families, all left to their own devices and appropriately dismissive of the mindless female figures who are nominally in charge of them. Least reprehensible is Anna's brother Giustino, initially a schoolboy too wrapped up in his childish interests to be aware of what he is living through, subsequently an adolescent at grips with the problems of puberty and thus equally detached from the realities of the world around him. When, however, he falls in love with Marisa, alone and unprotected following her husband's arrest and exile, he is too honest to take advantage of the situation, and resolves it by joining up as soon as he has passed his last examination, something which has the added benefit of getting him away from Signora Maria's obsessive mothering. If this decision lends him a certain romantic charm it is also true, as one of the others harshly reminds him, that he is contributing to the Fascist war effort, and his fanciful claims that 'he had simply wanted to know what sort of a thing war was' and 'what difference did it make, one person firing more or less' (p. 199) confirm he has remained somewhat naive in his approach to the basic principles of life. Especially revealing is his statement virtually in the same breath that 'he wanted to be like other people, he wanted to be neither better off nor worse off than others' (pp. 198–9), and it is clearly this basic conformity of spirit, carried over from his childhood and first youth, rather than any genuine political consciousness, that subsequently leads him to join the partisans. When the war is over he has difficulty in adapting to the more organised routine of peace time and feels unable to enter into a relationship with Marisa despite the fact that she has by now separated from her husband; he is nostalgic for the adventurous life he had led as a guerrilla and reluctant to accept that 'there were no more trains to blow up and he must finish his course at the University and then look for a job to keep himself going' (p. 295). Giustino's attitude, if understandable in such a young man, is ultimately incompatible with reality, and suggests he may well remain an unhappy individual, caught in an emotional time warp and condemned, like his father, to fruitless inactivity, especially since 'he had no desire to take up with any woman' (ibid.), though there is some hope implied in his willingness to admit that his behaviour is stupid.

Less starry-eyed but infinitely more disturbing is Marisa's husband Danilo, a young man whose father is a commercial traveller spending long periods away from home and who is thus similarly lacking a strong paternal influence. He is first seen in the grip of an adolescent infatuation for Concettina, which, however, he soon transcends to become a political activist; impatient with the interminable theorising of his friends Emanuele and Ippolito, who collect foreign pamphlets banned by the Fascist authorities but otherwise do nothing, Danilo leaves for the big city, where he hopes to engage in subversive activities, but is soon arrested and imprisoned, experiencing directly the harsh reality of life on the wrong side of the law. When he is released he has become a different person, older and more mature, aware that he has wasted much of his past life and anxious to begin a new existence; this is symbolised by his marriage to Marisa, a working-class girl who 'would not be frightened on the day when they put him in prison again, but would just go on with her work' (p. 69), and whom the reader realises he does not actually love in any real sense of the word. Back home and under observation as a known dissident Danilo is unable to engage in any further activities, venting his frustration on the well-intentioned but essentially passive feelings of his friends, quarrelling with Anna's seducer, whose empty-headed egoism he cannot tolerate, and, inevitably, being rearrested and sent into exile as soon as Italy declares war. When he is released after the armistice in 1943 he naturally returns to militant activity under the German occupation, becoming a partisan and establishing a close relationship with Giustino, now his companion in guerrilla warfare; if, however, like Giustino, he subsequently finds it difficult to adjust to normality it is because *he* adapts only too well to the new climate of political opportunism, attending rallies and delivering carefully crafted speeches which are 'almost too fine . . . almost too well composed', having become 'someone [Giustino] did not know, someone who was not in any way his friend', now speaking with words very different from 'the ones he and Danilo used to say to each other at night when they were going to blow up trains' (p. 294). By now he has separated from Marisa, having formed another attachment during his days as a partisan, and is apparently quite content to let his wife eke out an impoverished existence while he makes his way in the political arena with a new sophistication totally foreign to his old environment. Always a realist, his unbending criticism of his ineffectual colleagues during their early days is eventually revealed as the positive side of a ruthless nature quite prepared to abandon friends and relatives for a career which, though clearly based on genuine political feelings, he has no hesitation in giving pride of place to in his life once this becomes feasible.

In complete contrast to Danilo Concettina's husband Emilio is also an opportunist but through laziness and mental apathy rather than conviction or cunning, and clearly a far more suitable person for Anna's sister in his limited intelligence. Perceptively described by her brother Ippolito as 'fresh and healthy as a young calf in a meadow' (p. 81) Emilio is under no illusions about his intellectual potential or political consciousness, freely admitting he is 'stupid . . . easy to please and quite satisfied' (p. 82), impressed by those who choose the stony path of ideological dissent but lacking the energy even to contemplate following them along it when it is so much easier to put on a black shirt and march up and down in the main square at regular intervals. Apparently harmless and quite touching in his simplistic attitude to life and life's problems he, like Danilo, is later revealed as having more disturbing characteristics which similarly mature during the time he spends in hiding, first from the Germans and then later from the partisans, emerging 'pale and puffy' (p. 293), his childish trust in people and things replaced by a fierce avariciousness which he shares with his wife and which betrays a basic dissatisfaction with life. In the last we see of him with Concettina and their child they are portrayed as 'a miserable couple' who 'spent their whole time together wrangling and putting brilliantine on the boy's hair' (ibid.), and it seems clear that the author's intention is to show how those who passively and unthinkingly accept political oppression and adapt to it conceal a fundamental moral weakness beneath what may under normal circumstances appear to be an easy-going and attractive nature. Emilio's limited intelligence prevents him from deriving any benefit from the broad-minded attitude of his father, a prosperous businessman who, despite being in good odour with the authorities, is able to see beyond their stultifying propaganda and is aware that 'even amongst revolutionaries there were fine people, it seemed strange but there were fine people to be found everywhere' (pp. 78–9); he thereby reveals a perceptiveness quite beyond his son, whose mindless conformity to the trappings of the Fascist regime shows him to be a distinctly inferior specimen.

More obviously dubious, and indeed little short of contemptible, is Emilio's opposite number Franz, the sometime lover of the elderly gentleman's younger wife in the house across the street and in due course husband to her daughter Amalia. A Polish Jew and therefore increasingly at risk, first from the easy-going Fascist authorities, who are quite prepared to turn a blind eye to his existence in return for bribes, and later, far more threateningly, from the occupying German forces, Franz cannot fail to arouse our sympathy, and it is interesting to see how Ginzburg skilfully balances this by showing him to be not only a person whose life is in danger through no fault of his own but also someone who lives off his wits and is, in effect, an adventurer eager to exploit the credulous and the naive, especially if wealthy. He first appears in Chapter 3 as a deserving refugee his married lover has picked up in Monte Carlo on learning that 'he was the son of a German baron and had escaped from Germany because of the Nazis, because his father . . . still believed in the monarchy' (p. 31), a tall story which has immediately aroused the suspicions of Emanuele, the young man of the family, whose instinctive distrust of Franz is little by little revealed as being fully justified. Possessed of no little charm Franz contrives to make Amalia fall in love with him, and is only too happy to drop her mother and marry her when her father dies and she inherits the greater part of his wealth, believing he is now set up for life; when, however, the Germans invade Poland he sends Emanuele a pathetic letter in which he confesses the truth about his nationality and speculates tearfully on the possible fate of his parents, in danger because his mother is part Jewish, and playing on the young man's sensitivity to request some money as he and his new wife are running short. This incident, whose true significance only becomes apparent later, when Franz confesses the full truth about his origins, is a perfect example of his deviousness; it reflects his technique of turning a genuine crisis, itself deserving of compassion, into a source of material gain, while at the same time keeping his options open by only revealing part of the truth. It is only when he is overcome by panic as the Germans are increasingly victorious that he blurts out one night he is 'completely Jewish and it was well known what the Germans were doing to the Jews, if the Germans came down into Italy the only thing for him to do would be to put a bullet through his head'; here too Ginzburg is quick to cool the reader's instinctive feelings of pity by mentioning in the same paragraph that Franz has repeatedly put off going to America and certain safety because 'he liked Italy too much' (p. 111), a deliberately sentimental statement designed to conceal his desire to live off his wife as long as possible and ensuring the reader share Emanuele's attitude of being 'sorry for Franz and at the same time irritated with him' (p. 105).

When he foolishly becomes involved with a lady chemist whose husband works as a magistrate's clerk, thereby provoking a scandal in the local community, his wife abandons him to go and spend some time with her mother on Lake Maggiore;[10] he correctly thinks it prudent similarly to leave the area and go south, eventually fetching up at Cenzo Rena's village, where, typically enough, he attempts – unsuccessfully – to move into Cenzo's house. Totally incapable of adapting to the primitive environment of San Costanzo he quickly makes a thorough nuisance of himself with absurdly unrealistic requests; he soon alienates Cenzo, who tellingly describes him as 'this silly little man in tennis shorts' (p. 227) while forcing himself none the less to be kind to someone who 'was a Jew and might end up in one of those sealed trains' (p. 228). When San Costanzo is overrun by the Germans Franz is understandably horrified, but here too Ginzburg makes it clear that his reactions go beyond a normal desire to stay alive, overflowing into a naked panic which makes him refuse all nourishment while he cowers under the blankets in a friendly peasant's spare bed. This constant desire to stress the more unattractive aspects of his character, already given full rein in his contemptuous treatment of a Turkish refugee with whom he shares the local inn and who 'never stopped saying how disgusting Franz was' (p. 243), reaches its climax in the author's decision to show how his absurd refusal to accept a degree of hardship and discomfort in such circumstances is, albeit indirectly, the cause of his death and that of Cenzo Rena; spirited away to a small village higher up in the mountains where there are no Germans and he can remain safe and sound until the war is over Franz foolishly returns to San Costanzo after a month, no longer able to tolerate 'long days spent alone . . .

in that black, cramped kitchen that filled with smoke' (p. 255) in the care of an old peasant woman. When Cenzo's ignorant servant foolishly informs an apparently benevolent German soldier that they are hiding a Jew in the cellar along with a deserter from the Italian army, thereby provoking a confrontation in which the soldier is killed, the subsequent arrest and condemnation of ten villagers as a reprisal is resolved by Cenzo Rena, who claims he is responsible for what has happened and allows himself to be shot in their place; at this point Franz appears to redeem himself, seized by a sudden awareness that 'he had lived pretty stupidly' (p. 281) and deciding to accompany Cenzo to give himself up, making sure the Germans recognise him so that he too is immediately arrested. This is perhaps his way of making amends for his wretched life through a gratuitous virile sacrifice, but even this gesture is not without some degree of ambiguity as he also claims 'it no longer mattered to him whether he died or lived' (ibid.), and the suspicion remains that he may simply have decided he can no longer stand the strain of living as a hunted man, something which would make his surrender to the Germans not a heroic act, but, instead, a supreme example of cowardice; Cenzo's repeated description of him as a 'bloody fool' (p. 283) as they both make their way to the German headquarters reinforces this uncertainty, which is never resolved.

If Franz thus remains to the end an ambiguous figure Anna's seducer Giuma is throughout crystal-clear in his unswerving egoism and ruthless insensitivity. During their first meeting as children he ignores her totally, preferring to work on his scrapbook until obliged by his sister Amalia to help her look at an encyclopaedia, at which point he merely turns the pages, having nothing to say to her; and if this is apparently unremarkable behaviour in a shy child suddenly confronted with an unfamiliar situation it is also clearly, in retrospect, deeply indicative of his character. The brutalising games he subsequently inflicts on her, already described in Chapter 2, and which she is incapable of resisting, are equally clearly a prelude to her later sexual submissiveness and well described by Emanuele as the work of a scoundrel,[11] while his interminable accounts of athletic prowess and his list of fascinating friends are all pure invention and denote another disturbing characteristic. When they meet again as adolescents he has become a raging snob, contemptuous of everything and everyone around him, constantly comparing the unsophisticated environment of their small town with the glories of Switzerland, where he has attended college, and systematically alienating his new school-friends through his pretentious behaviour, which they soon identify as an ineffectual cloak for a basic inadequacy in both school-work and human relationships, so that 'everyone in the class had begun to hate him' (p. 66), and Anna is 'seized by a suspicion that in reality Giuma knew no more . . . than she did . . . that he had to pretend in order to feel powerful and proud' (p. 92).

At one point Giuma's isolation from his peers is momentarily broken when he forms a brief friendship with Danilo, something which exhilarates him so much that this new contact virtually extinguishes all other interests and he can speak of nothing else. Inevitably the relationship soon founders as Danilo becomes increasingly aware of Giuma's boundless superficiality and total lack of political awareness, eventually throwing him out of his house and telling him 'never to show his face there again if he was going to talk like that' (p. 99); at this point, once more alone and rejected by everyone except Anna, Giuma predictably proclaims his ex-friend a primitive provincial living in smelly rooms he no longer cares to visit, later demonstrating the full extent of his mindlessness by stating quite openly that 'he didn't care in the least about Norway' (p. 106) and that 'he was pleased if the Germans were advancing a little, so that he might enjoy the faces of Emanuele and the others' (p. 108). By this time he has once more turned his attention to Anna, whose emotions he selfishly toys with, kissing her with increasing passion while at the same time informing her one day that he is perhaps going to fall in love with a girl in white velvet trousers he has met on one of his skiing trips; when she understandably bursts into tears his only worry is that she should not make an exhibition of herself in public. His reaction to Anna's pregnancy reveals the full extent of his childishness; not only is he flabbergasted at something he has clearly never contemplated but he makes it clear that the thousand lire he gives her for an abortion represents an immense sacrifice on his part, as he had wanted to spend them on a motor-boat, '"the only thing I want . . . but for the time being I must give up that idea"' (p. 126). This serves to confirm Anna's realisation that while what has happened has brought her a new maturity he has remained 'a little boy, with his heat-flushed face and his rumpled hair' (p. 117) whose departure to spend the summer months at Stresa with his family, leaving Anna to solve her problem on her own, is a fitting conclusion to his consistently irresponsible behaviour. When Anna meets him again by chance during a brief trip from San Costanzo to Turin after the birth of their baby he appears to have changed radically, informing her that he is now an impoverished student who realises the absurdity of his past life and feels guilty because 'he knew he had been very cruel to her' (p. 213), even claiming he now believes in revolution, but despite this promising new image he avoids all mention of their child and is clearly no nearer facing up to his responsibilities. The suspicion that his improvement is more apparent than real is confirmed when he last appears, at the end of the novel, once more elegantly dressed and accompanied by a snobbish wife with intellectual pretensions who looks down on all his relatives and friends, while he blithely announces that it only took him a few days to dispel strong feelings of guilt at having gone to Switzerland rather than join the partisans during the German occupation. Confronted by his daughter he blushes and laughs but makes no attempt to recognise her, preferring to run after his wife, who has foolishly gone off in a huff, and confirming he has remained essentially unchanged, forever evasive and inconclusive.

Giuma's elder brother Emanuele, in many ways his exact opposite in terms of character, none the less has in common with him a basic conformity of spirit, the difference being that while Giuma represents the traditionally frivolous and irresponsible attitude of rich children, happy to live off their parents' wealth, Emanuele is at all times conscious that as his father's elder son and heir it is his duty to take over the soap factory and ensure its survival, something which initially weighs heavily upon him but which he ultimately accepts, gradually resigning himself to what he has always known is inevitable. As a disaffected teenager he has no hesitation in lamenting his fate and inveighing against it,[12] preferring to join Anna's elder brother Ippolito in conspiratorial discussions about anti-Fascist activity which, as already mentioned, never passes beyond the planning stage, and he is deeply embarrassed when Cenzo Rena pours scorn on their passive idealism, describing them as 'two little provincial intellectuals' (p. 54) who have 'created around themselves . . . a complete dream-world' (p. 56); however, this does not prevent him from starting work in the factory soon afterwards, where his equally naive and totally impractical projects for improving working conditions are invariably rejected by the managing director, who tells him quite bluntly that he is too young to understand these things, thereby incurring his hatred. As time passes, however, and he acquires more knowledge he becomes increasingly involved in the factory, his interests gradually shifting away from political idealism to more pressing practical considerations, and it is not long before he feels obliged to announce, albeit with some hesitation, that he feels unable to use any of the firm's capital to help the families of political prisoners, eventually reaching the stage where he vigorously defends the once-hated manager against foolish criticism from Franz, a clear sign that the complexities of industrial production are now what most concern him.

If this change in Emanuele's conscious behaviour and life-style is undoubtedly a kind of compromise which makes him, at least to some extent, a part of the establishment as a minor industrialist it in no way affects his basic opposition to Fascism, which remains unaltered. He is thus unsparing in his criticism of Concettina's marriage to the Fascist Emilio and intolerant of Ippolito's inability to prevent it, now able to criticise his old friend's passivity by bewailing the fate of 'poor Italy that had to depend on types like Ippolito for the revolution' (p. 77). When France falls he loses all interest in his job and becomes apathetic, spending long hours asleep and agreeing to leave town to spend the summer with his family in Stresa because now 'he . . . no longer thought about anything' (p. 122). Unlike Ippolito, however, he never entirely abandons hope that things will eventually improve, his old idealism remaining alive even after Italy's declaration of war, when he proclaims that 'the Germans might take Paris and London too, into the bargain, and yet it would not be all over' (p. 136); when the tide does at last begin to turn he regains his enthusiasm, happy that 'It was not like the time of the fall of France . . . when he used to spend his days sleeping so as not to hear any more about it' (p. 175). By this time, however, he has once more buckled down to his job in the factory, and his complaints are no longer about the tediousness of his work but, significantly, about the poor quality of the raw materials he has to make do with, while the concern he shows for the peasants of San Costanzo during a visit to Anna and Cenzo Rena likewise springs not from any humanitarian interest as such but rather from a desire to discover how things are organised in the village in relation to 'grain and wine and pigs and Government land' (p. 181); it is clear that he has gradually developed a bureaucratic mentality no doubt highly appropriate to a factory owner but which appears to have obscured or diluted his more spontaneous regard for people's emotions and states of mind, a quality previously much in evidence in the attention he paid his mother after her elderly husband's death, the care he lavished on the love-sick Amalia during the early stages of her passion for Franz, and his attempts to console Concettina after her graduation thesis had been rejected. But once again Emanuele shows how his basic instincts are, despite everything, unchanged, blushing and apologising when reproached by Cenzo Rena for his enthusiasm at the increasing defeats suffered by the Italian army when this inevitably means 'poor innocent people dying in Africa and in Greece' (p. 175) and an increase in the number of dead and missing from San Costanzo; in the same way his subsequent refusal to evacuate in order to escape from the bombing, 'saying that he could not leave the soap factory' (p. 222), is a conscious decision to do what is expected of him as a public figure, but he does not stand on his dignity when it comes to tending the wounded and retrieving the dead after a direct hit on one of the residential quarters of the town.

When Mussolini is defenestrated in July 1943 Emanuele sees that there are more important claims on his energies than running a factory at a time when the country needs to be put back in working order; accordingly he leaves for Rome, where he is at last able to realise his old political idealism in a practical context, helping Danilo and other anti-Fascists now at liberty and anxious to make up for lost time. The signing of the armistice six weeks later and the subsequent occupation by the German forces only sharpens his resolve and he goes underground, printing and circulating a dissident newspaper and now at last running the kind of risks he and Ippolito had naively believed they were exposed to some years before. This is his finest hour, a time in which he can follow the more adventurous and disinterested side of his character, living in constant danger and drawing inspiration from the uncertainty and precariousness which are now part and parcel of his everyday existence. When the war is finally over and these incentives are removed he realises, with no little bitterness, that there is no longer any need for his skills, which are quite inappropriate to normal peace-time journalism in which 'You had to sit and grind away at a desk without either danger or fear', while the end of a clear-cut political context in which everyone knows which side they are on inevitably produces 'a lot of ignoble words' impossible to avoid or recast 'because there was a hurry to get out the newspaper for which people were waiting' (p. 298). Aware that instead of contributing to the struggle for freedom he is now spending all his time writing inferior articles, or, worse, attending board meetings, Emanuele decides to abandon his new profession and return home, where he will perforce go back to running the 'bloody awful soap factory'[13] and once more become a conventional business man with conventional values. He too thus remains, like Franz (albeit for very different reasons), an ambiguous figure, his brief moment of successful affirmation unable to override a basic passivity which conditions his behaviour both before the war, when his good intentions are unsupported by any radical action, and after peace has returned, when he lacks the courage to adapt to a new environment, preferring the familiar security of factory ownership, however humdrum and boring, to being actively involved in a new society in the making; at the same time it is clear his decision to return to his roots in 1945 is both an honest acknowledgement of his own limitations and an equally honest acceptance of his original duty to follow in his father's footsteps, making it difficult for the reader to sit in judgement on him.

Emanuele's friend Ippolito is in every sense a much weaker individual, equally passive but lacking Emanuele's basic optimism, indeed soon revealing himself as possessed of an essentially depressive nature which prevents him from asserting himself in any way and eventually drives him to suicide. His first appearance in Chapter 1 as an obliging son ever willing to minister to his father's needs is immediately qualified by Concettina's dismissive description of him as having 'the soul of a slave . . . and camomile in his veins instead of blood . . . with no girls whom he liked and no desire for anything' (p. 15); he is clearly an extension of Maurizio in *Un'assenza*, who is similarly described[14] but whose depression is only momentary. Like Maurizio Ippolito seems quite unable to give vent to any emotion, even remaining 'still and silent, his face thin and white as usual' (p. 20) at his father's death-bed; and if his subsequent friendship with Emanuele and their increasing interest in political conspiracy turns him briefly from a robot into a human being anxious to find something positive in his life this is only, as Franco Riva has perceptively stated, 'so long as their relationship with the outside world remains in the realms of fantasy',[15] and his new-found enthusiasm for subversive theorising is ultimately of no more significance than has been his father's useless dedication to writing his memoirs.

The arrival of Cenzo Rena and his merciless criticism of the young men's passive idealism, already mentioned, recreates the kind of servile relationship that had previously existed between Ippolito and his father, as we read that 'he had found someone else who took pleasure in tormenting him, and it seemed to be his fate that people should torment him' (p. 56), thereby making him especially receptive to Rena's gloomy prognostications of 'a war with poison gases and cholera germs' (p. 55) in which the whole of humanity will be destroyed. Deeply influenced by Rena's strong personality but unaffected by his buoyancy of spirit Ippolito grows more and more pessimistic, and with the benefit of hindsight it is clear that when the Germans invade Poland he is already beyond hope, proclaiming that 'it no longer mattered to know whether there would be an end to Fascism or not. Because in Poland people were dying' (p. 64). As time passes he becomes increasingly moody and withdrawn, refusing food and neglecting his appearance, like the doctor in *Mio marito*, and spending his nights walking agitatedly round his room, smoking incessantly and unable to sleep, ever more obsessed by what he sees as the inevitable destruction of everything positive in the world around him. When he claims some time later that the thought of what is happening in the concentration camps makes him want to stop living it is clearly only a question of time before he carries out a threat whose significance is unperceived by friends and relatives, all too busy with their own problems, and who fail totally to grasp that the fall of France, which prostrates Ippolito completely, giving him a 'death-like face' (p. 122) is a further shock to his psyche. A hysterical outburst in which he predicts that the future will consist of 'Germans with tanks and aeroplanes, masters of the whole earth' (p. 125) comes immediately before the news of Italy's declaration of war, the final blow, and the next day he shoots himself.

Ippolito is clearly a weak individual, a servile masochist who cannot help always focusing on things negative, whether real or imagined, unfit for the pressures of adult life in war-time. It is equally clear, however, that his weakness is in no way a symptom of cowardice but rather springs from his awareness that, if triumphant, Fascism and Nazism will bring about the collapse of Western civilisation, and a belief, more easily understandable then than now, that this triumph is inevitable. Seen in this light his suicide is no longer a contemptible act of faint-heartedness, recalling instead those Jews in Germany who killed themselves when Hitler assumed power rather than await public humiliation and a worse fate at the hands of the state. It is Ippolito's good nature and love of his fellow men, first evident in his constant willingness to comply with his father's wishes, however absurd, and later repeatedly emphasised in his agonised evocation of bombed cities, homeless families, and tortured prisoners, which finally destroys him, and which is stressed in his last contact with his relatives, whom he treats with unexpected gentleness and affection during the final evening he spends with them; it is doubtless this also which leads him to shoot himself in a public park rather than in his room, thereby ensuring that his family is not implicated in the official investigations which he knows will follow. Unlike the other characters in this novel (other than Giuma) Ippolito shows no radical change in temperament, nor does he undergo any experiences which directly affect him personally, instead gradually deteriorating as he takes stock of world events and interprets them as heralding general disaster. When dealing with him Ginzburg accordingly adopts a narrative style which consistently stresses his apartness from the others, repeatedly emphasising significant details such as his twisted smile, his erratic behaviour, and, as time passes, his increasingly disturbed appearance and manner. The amount of space devoted to a character who disappears half-way through the book and the care with which she charts his gradual disintegration are clearly indicative of the sympathy she feels for him, and it is doubtless not without significance that the manner of his death is identical with that of Ginzburg's maternal uncle Silvio, who, we learn from *Family Sayings*, 'killed himself when he was thirty, blowing his brains out one night in the Milan public gardens' (p. 22).

Cenzo Rena, possibly the most impressive of all Ginzburg's male characters, is in complete contrast to all those mentioned so far. A mixture of rugged good sense and optimistic idealism he is essentially a free agent, aware that man has within him the potential to realise his destiny but can do so only by rejecting the conventional limitations placed on him by a narrow-minded society such as Italy, which he contemptuously dismisses as 'just a flea, and Mussolini a flea's droppings' (p. 54). An astute businessman who has amassed considerable wealth he has no interest in formal elegance or polite society, wearing casual clothes, eating and drinking when the fancy takes him, and pouring scorn on the inhibitions which govern other people's lives, happy to spend his time travelling round the world in between periods spent living in a tumbledown villa in the depressed south. His arrival at the family's country house is like a breath of fresh air which sweeps through the whole village, disturbing and invigorating, and when he leaves as suddenly as he has arrived, following a drunken brawl at a local dance, they are all relieved to be able to sink back into their old routine, no longer constantly reminded of how blinkered is their life-style. Beneath his flamboyance and anarchic behaviour, which make him appear no more than an egocentric individualist, Rena possesses a strong social conscience, something which only emerges fully in the second half of the book but which is already implicit in the letter he writes to the village doctor after his departure reproaching him for allowing the local chemist to run out of snake-bite serum. As becomes clear later his deep-rooted opposition to the Fascist regime springs not from political idealism in the strict sense but from an instinctive and deeply felt response to the human needs of his fellow creatures, whom he sees throughout as individuals rather than as representatives of this or that ideological strain; it is plainly this aspect of his character which prompts his offer of marriage to Anna when she is pregnant and, after weeks of neglect by all and sundry, feels that 'at last there was someone who was listening to her' (p. 143).

Rena's immediate grasp of the situation, and his awareness that Anna's problems are not simply limited to resolving the question of her illegitimate child, not only saves her from conventional dishonour in the short term, but also ensures that her existence thereafter is infinitely closer to the realities of life as she accompanies him to his southern village and sees for herself the condition of the local peasantry. Her husband's impatience with romantic idealism, already evident in his earlier claim that 'when fate announced itself with a loud fanfare of trumpets you always had to be a little on your guard' (p. 151), is confirmed in his attitude to the peasants, whom he defends against bureaucratic inefficiency and neglect on a day-to-day basis, deliberately postponing until a more favourable time some radical ideas for improved social structures which are clearly impossible to realise while the Fascists are in power; meanwhile it is more important to de-louse the local children by shaving their heads, and to pressurise the chemist to ensure he stocks snake-bite serum. Ever ready to perceive human needs beneath social or political trappings he has no hesitation in lending the local police-sergeant money, despite the fact that this man represents a regime he abhors, and a quarrel which later develops between them in no way prevents him from providing a further loan when the sergeant's wife falls ill and has to go into hospital for an operation; in the same way while totally opposed to the Axis war he is none the less deeply sympathetic to 'the poor devils sent off to Russia from a great many villages like San Costanzo, poor devils who had cold feet and were firing neither for nor against anybody' (p. 200). At no time, however, does his humanity blind him to the fact that the village people are also ignorant and stubborn, continuing to feed their children on almond paste although they know this brings on dysentery, and, inevitably in such a small community, consumed with hatred and envy, constantly accusing each other in anonymous letters to the police-sergeant; it is indeed precisely this mindless malice which eventually leads to the arrest of four Jews who have sought refuge among the peasants only to be denounced by an unknown enemy in what Rena furiously describes as 'a rotten village . . . full of spies' (p. 253).

Rena's unflagging energy and passionate desire to alleviate suffering and do good wherever possible ensure that he is never inactive in an environment where every new day brings forth a new problem provoked by poverty or bureaucratic incompetence. Totally committed to his vocation he is also conscious that too great an involvement with other people's affairs is a threat to one's own safety, and that there is great danger in giving way to compassion, especially since 'all men made you sorry for them if you looked at them closely' (p. 217) – a feeling which even extends to the occupying German soldiers, also ultimately 'poor unfortunates whom it was not really worth while killing' (p. 271). It is of course compassion for the ten hostages about to face the firing squad which eventually leads to his own death, as already indicated, in a dramatic sequence which provides grim proof of a truth Ginzburg was to stress more than once in her later work, here formulated for the first time; and it in no way reduces the value of Rena's sacrifice to suggest that it may also be motivated by feelings of remorse for his gradual withdrawal from positive action as the war intensifies, as Allied bombing of Italian cities increases, and more and more refugees arrive in San Costanzo, 'carrying mattresses and babies . . . Italy was now pouring mattresses out of her ravaged houses' (p. 236). Gradually overcome by depression and feelings of anguish at the thought that 'possibly in a short time the whole earth would go to ruin in one immense crash' (p. 226) and conscious that the problems confronting the village community, now a microcosm of the whole country, are beyond his control, he becomes apathetic, gloomy, and ill-natured; he is unable to contemplate the thought that he and his family may also become refugees, and, while deeply ashamed of his unwillingness to take in some of the homeless, is unable to bring himself to do so, reflecting helplessly that 'shame was the thing that spoilt human beings, probably without shame human beings would have been a little less nasty' (p. 236). The fall of Fascism appears to restore his confidence and rekindle his energy but his recovery is short-lived as almost immediately he falls ill with typhus; when he is eventually cured, after spending some time in hospital, 'he seemed to have become much older, and quieter and lazier' (pp. 257–8), aware that, now over fifty and a convalescent, he can no longer boldly defy the world and impose his will on others. As his strength returns he becomes more active again, on several occasions convincing the German soldiers not to round up young men and deport them for forced labour; but he is no longer capable of organising militant opposition, realising that 'he would be very much afraid, afraid throughout the whole of his body, and he felt his hands all limp' (p. 271), a feeling he is henceforth unable to dispel and which disturbs both the army deserter he is hiding, who 'had lost some of his esteem for Cenzo Rena' (p. 270), and his wife Anna, who goes so far as to accuse him of cowardice. Though realising that such comments proceed from their inability to grasp the pointlessness of any active resistance to the powerful occupying forces Rena is also conscious that he has indeed become a changed man and is clearly disheartened at the loss of his old vigour and optimism, now replaced by a weariness afflicting both body and spirit. In this context his decision to take responsibility for the death of the German soldier can be seen as an act of courage which is not only of infinite value in itself, since it saves the lives of ten innocent people, but also, in a more personal sense, restores his self-respect, amply compensating for his recent passivity and, by transcending anything he has done in the past, forming a noble conclusion to a life essentially devoted to self-affirmation and the defence of his fellow men.

Seen in close-up throughout the second half of the book Cenzo Rena is clearly in one sense the most important character in this novel, a man with numerous qualities whom we are encouraged to admire and respect but who is also skilfully presented as essentially human and thus also possessed of certain defects which ensure he remains throughout totally credible. Impatient with narrow-mindedness or naive idealism he frequently acts and speaks exactly as he feels, thereby causing scandal in polite society, as in the episode of the drunken brawl; or alienating people's affections, as with Anna's father, who renounces his friendship, and with Ippolito, whom he humiliates unnecessarily; while his refusal to suffer fools gladly leads him to be especially unpleasant to Franz, whose threatened Jewishness is ironically the only thing that ensures Rena can bring himself to tolerate him. Rena's vulnerability as a human being is first evident in his inability to banish the feelings of despair that gradually overcome him as the country is brought to its knees, and when he subsequently falls ill with typhus he experiences what is later revealed as an accurate presentiment of death in 'a spot in his back that trembled and pulsated . . . a spot which was quite cold and trembling' (p. 245), a feeling which returns when he decides to give himself up and which gradually extends to the whole of his back as he waits for the firing squad. When he is finally led out to be shot it is with 'his back all feeble and cold, and his knees trembling and jerking and a cold sweat upon him' (p. 284). His last gesture is to cover his face with his hands, an intensely human portrait in complete contrast to the conventional heroics normally associated with such situations and typical of the loving care which the author has lavished on this character, a man by no means perfect but whose qualities and talents outweigh his faults and failings.

This long novel – all of three hundred pages in the English translation – provides ample scope not only for a wealth of intimate detail in relation to the personalities of the characters involved, more fully developed than any so far, but also numerous opportunities for Ginzburg to indulge her sense of humour, pin-pointing both the frequent absurdities implicit in the naive conduct of the younger people of both sexes and the comic behaviour of adults, who are supposedly old enough to know better but frequently no more able to distinguish fact from fantasy and who live in their own private world. As the context in which the characters find themselves becomes increasingly grim humour and irony are maintained, and indeed at times increased, by Ginzburg's consistent use of the device (already employed in *I bambini* and *La madre*) of narrating events through the eyes of a specific individual or group of individuals whose personality is crucial to their interpretation, thereby both creating an appropriate atmosphere and providing information in terms of plot and characterisation. Thus in Chapter 2, in which the young Anna meets Giuma for the first time, the reader is informed that the family dog, of whom she is frightened, was not in the garden that day 'because he had been sent off to some friends in order to get married';[16] elsewhere Emanuele's contempt for Franz is well conveyed by the news that following a course of injections imposed on him by his wife 'Franz's behind was as full of holes as a nutmeg-grater' (p. 105); more gruesomely the simplicity of the villagers of San Costanzo is effectively rendered by the author's statement that 'No one could understand why the Germans should have burnt down the stable with the cows and the people inside, but perhaps it was only because they had some petrol to throw away' (p. 285). If this technique has its limitations and can sometimes become slightly tiresome when applied systematically over an extended period it has the undoubted advantage of reinstating a crucial element in Ginzburg's writing, largely absent from the chilling inevitability of events in *Valentino*, and of course, totally inappropriate to the sparse brevity of *Passaggio di tedeschi a Erra*, while being necessarily restricted for most of *The Dry Heart* to situations involving the narrator before her marriage.[17]

Ginzburg's next novel, the much shorter *Sagittarius* (1975), contains only one male character of any importance: Dr Chaim Wesser,
a Polish refugee, victim of racial persecution in his homeland, who is
none the less still capable of practising his profession and thereby
ensuring an adequate if essentially modest income from the small
Italian community where he has made his home. Wesser's greatest
drawback is his distinctly unprepossessing appearance – the narrator's mother claims sharply that 'even after a bath he still smelt
un-fresh, still had that peculiar odour of mustiness and decay',
adding that he has 'Ugly hands with broken, chewed nails and hair
all over them' (p. 58) – which complements physical drawbacks all
too obvious in a later less prejudiced description of him as a man
nearing forty who 'carried himself badly and walked awkwardly,
with one shoulder higher than the other and shuffling his feet'
(p. 68). As the narrative progresses it gradually transpires that despite
this supremely unattractive image Wesser is a highly efficient doctor, a
great favourite with the local children, who run up to greet him
whenever they see him passing in the street, and, in addition, extremely learned, 'speaking sixteen languages, knowing a great deal
about music and having read all the philosophers' (p. 71): in short a
worthy individual whose talents, though limited by fate and ill-fortune,
nevertheless bear fruit in this (admittedly restricted) context.

Voices in the Evening, written in 1961 and published the following
year, is, in contrast, a novel of standard length which, while focusing
principally on the female narrator and her oppressive mother, also
provides detailed portraits of five male characters whose respective
development and unhappy destiny unfailingly mark them out as
representing different aspects of masculine inadequacy.[18] Most
striking is Tommasino, the youngest son of Balotta, the factory
owner, whose inability to withstand the pressures put on him by
Matilde once he has become formally engaged to her daughter is a
supreme example of spiritual and emotional impotence which inevitably determines the unhappiness of both partners, both equally
lacking in any independence of spirit which might enable their
relationship to survive. Conditioned by their middle-class upbringing to accept unthinkingly a social norm which decrees that they
stay attached to their roots they have both, in effect, remained as
children within an environment in which every aspect of their life is
mapped out for them in advance. If this is more easily understandable in Elsa, whose sex inevitably predisposes her to a more passive
acceptance of traditional female roles, it is less comprehensible in
Tommasino; he has no desire to broaden his horizon and create a life

of his own, ignoring the greater freedom automatically assigned to him as a male and preferring to maintain his links with the village community, even returning home regularly at weekends when his university studies oblige him temporarily to live elsewhere. It is clear from his life-style that the centre of his attention has never seriously varied since adolescence, and thus quite logical that long years of emotional and intellectual apathy have left him incapable of creating an adult sexual relationship, while he is also sufficiently intelligent to realise that he could not be satisfied with a public bond based on domestic trivia and lack of communication. Protected by his wealth he has no need to work and is thus no more productive in his professional capacity as an executive at the factory, which he visits every day only to spend long hours doodling on the blotter in his luxurious office, and, like the youthful Emanuele before him, imagining complicated projects which will improve production but which never reach the drawing-board. Ultimately aware that within him there is ' "no real vitality" ' (p. 159), so that ' "I feel a shudder of disgust when I should assert myself" ' (p. 160), he realises that his energies have been permanently sapped by life in the village, which ' "has a weight of lead, with all its dead . . . it just gets me down" ' (p. 161); as a result it would be pointless to marry Elsa and emigrate to Canada, since ' "we should not be able to create anything new . . . It would be exactly the same as being here" ' (p. 162).[19]

Less obviously conditioned by his environment in the long term, Tommasino's older brother Vincenzino is also to a large extent a victim of the norms which regulate social behaviour in this restricted society. In his youth a scruffy intellectual with artistic pretensions he is permanently at loggerheads with his father, who cannot understand the boy's supremely impractical interests and disorganised life-style, something which ensures he spends most of his military service confined to barracks and makes it almost impossible for him to complete his university studies. Despatched thereafter to America to broaden his outlook and learn English he returns in due course a changed man who has now 'learned to wash himself, and to stand more upright and to speak more loudly' (p. 59), full of exciting new ideas about factory management and determined to pull his weight in the family business. His exposure to psychoanalytic theories while in the New World have shown him he has a father complex, but despite his awareness of this he allows himself to be drawn into marriage with Cate, a local beauty whom he does not love, because 'He had . . . thought in some tortuous way that a marriage like that would please his father' (p. 71): an obvious recipe for disaster. When later she is unfaithful to him, first sporadically and then with increasing frequency, he cannot bring himself to reproach her and pretends not to notice, unable to contemplate the endless discussions and recriminations which would inevitably follow. If he subsequently explains the refusal to face up to his responsibilities in terms of more psychoanalysis – a pathological horror of cruelty deriving from his having seen a dog stoned to death when he was a child – this in no way justifies his deliberate inactivity while Cate is drifting away from him, ostensibly 'in order that she should not be wounded and suffer' (p. 102); but paradoxically this thereby ensures the breakdown of his marriage, which in turn determines his wife's commitment to a promiscuous life-style that ultimately brings her only bitterness. Their progressive estrangement and eventual separation, together with Vincenzino's earlier disastrous engagement to a Brazilian girl he had met at a seaside resort and which he breaks off in the nick of time, convinces him that he has no aptitude for emotional relationships, and he lives alone, despite having developed 'a cool rather weary manner of authority that appealed to the women' (p. 95), working hard at the factory and writing books in his spare time. Although successful both professionally and culturally he remains a lonely man, his only close companion his brother Tommasino, eventually dying after a car crash during one of his regular trips to Rome to visit his children – perhaps another indication of the perils of remaining close to one's roots.

Mario, Balotta's second oldest son, is, as already mentioned, the only one of his children to achieve any degree of emotional fulfilment through his marriage to the ambiguous Russian refugee Xenia, a blissfully happy relationship in which he cheerfully allows his wife to take charge of everything, thereby drawing from Vincenzino the perceptive comment that 'Mario had a mother-complex and felt protected by Xenia, who had an authoritarian temperament and ruled him and ordered him about' (p. 68). Narrowly escaping a formal engagement to an eminently suitable but in reality quite inappropriate local girl Mario daringly chooses an eccentric alternative to this conventional match, which resolves at a single stroke the nervous disorders which have been a regular feature of his youth and which he has hitherto attempted to keep at bay by obsessive socialising, aware that in actual fact he is unable to realise himself within the limited confines of the stifling village community. It is, however, significant that he is only to take this extraordinary step during a period spent away from home on a business trip to Munich, and it is clear that despite being fully conscious of his needs he lacks the necessary strength of purpose to affirm them within his family and his environment, while the happiness he enjoys with his wife is likewise dependent on his assuming an essentially submissive role which is clearly central to his personality.

Apparently very different but in reality no less limited are the elderly Balotta and his distant relative Purillo, both in their separate ways providing further examples of masculine inadequacy. Balotta, the very image of the self-made man who has transformed a squalid workshop into a prosperous factory which has raised the standard of living of the whole community, realises as he grows older that by devoting all his energy to this task he has neglected everything else in life, becoming increasingly 'melancholy and sullen' (p. 22) and announcing he no longer wishes to live. An old-time Socialist who never abandons his principles he is inevitably persecuted by the Fascists when they seize power, and has to go into hiding when his very life is threatened; at this point he realises he has no resources to fall back on, a feeling which intensifies after his wife dies and his children are scattered, Mario and Vincenzino called up by the army and Raffaella with the partisans, while Gemmina escapes to Switzerland and Tommasino, too young to be directly involved, is in boarding-school. Lacking anything to occupy his mind he becomes increasingly withdrawn and confused, and when he returns to the village after the war has ended and discovers that his house has been ransacked, his garden devastated, and his factory made useless after the retreating Germans have made off with most of the plant, he bursts into tears, aware that he is now too old and frail to start again. The mayor's invitation to deliver a speech from the town hall balcony to celebrate the Allied liberation is too much for Balotta, who is still in a state of shock, and he develops a fever which leads to his death the following night.

Possessed of a natural flair for business Balotta is a perfect example of capitalist enterprise who has no difficulty in reconciling his talents in this sphere with his Socialist principles, lacking as he does any social pretensions and never happier than when chatting on the shop floor after a day's work. Unswerving in his beliefs he retains till the very end a totally unselfconscious rapport with his subordinates, as is evident from the scene where he embraces a chauffeur whom he recognises as the son of one of his workers, and is thus in many ways an admirable individual whose integrity the reader cannot but admire. It is equally clear, however, that he is totally unreceptive to anything outside the narrow sphere of his business interests, whose limitations he only becomes aware of as he

207

grows older and finds his health deteriorating, realising at last when forced to leave the village that his successful record in this area has been at the expense of his spiritual development. Inevitably Balotta's narrow-mindedness makes it impossible for him to understand his children; he reacts to their individuality by describing them as fools unable to manage the factory, which is handed over instead to Purillo, mercilessly ridiculing the intellectual Vincenzino when he first becomes engaged to someone outside the village, and becoming virtually apoplectic at the news of Mario's marriage. His attitude to his elder daughter Gemmina is equally blinkered in that he cannot reconcile himself to the fact that she is not a pretty empty-headed girl but an intelligent woman with a strong business sense who happens to be rather unattractive in appearance; he is thus ultimately revealed as a man only apparently in control of his life and his feelings, in reality imperfectly realised in terms of overall development and maturity, a phenomenon destined to repeat itself in a different form in his son Vincenzino.

Equally limited but happy notwithstanding is Purillo, a shiftless fellow with a chameleon-like personality ensuring he is always ready to conform to whatever social context he finds himself in. Mindful of the political situation 'When Fascism came Purillo became a Fascist' (p. 23), thereby moving Balotta to compare him contemptuously to '"a gold-fly settling on a pile of shit"'.[20] It is supremely ironic that his subsequent misfortunes should spring directly from the one good action we see him performing during the whole of his lifetime: the forcible removal of the old man and his wife to a safe hiding-place, thereby saving their lives when the *squadristi* (Fascist strong-arm squads) are after Balotta's blood, a gesture which, while revealing an unexpected humanity beneath the selfish exterior, also exposes the insubstantial nature of his political beliefs and leads to his being himself persecuted, first by the Fascists (who rightly conclude that he has betrayed them) and later by the partisans, anxious to eliminate someone whose behaviour has in every other way marked him out as a supporter of the regime. Forced to seek refuge in Switzerland Purillo cautiously returns to the village after the war, thereby revealing his liking for a restricted environment in preference to a newer and more stimulating life elsewhere, loudly denouncing his previous political allegiance, now very much *non grata*, and repeatedly stressing the importance of his one good deed. Gradually he creeps back into circulation, working once more at the factory and devoting his spare time to physical fitness and the pursuit of pretty peasant girls, two activities which emphasise his essential shallowness; this is further confirmed in his subsequent marriage to Raffaella, the ex-partisan who, although now disenchanted with the post-war political scene, has never renounced her left-wing views. It is typical of Purillo's unaltered ability to adapt to any situation that he should see nothing improper in such a marriage, despite still believing that '"Mussolini was the right man . . . If he had not sided with the Germans things would have gone very differently"' (p. 98). In the last we see of Purillo he is enthusiastically playing tennis with the factory manager's son, a clear indication that he is now once more fully integrated into the community, where all his simple needs are satisfied and his financial position assured through his marriage, while Tommasino reflects that unlike himself Purillo is stupid but has '"plenty of vitality, or rather . . . he behaves as if he had, and he gets the results he wants"' (p. 161) as he now enjoys the harmless pleasures of peace time with the same enthusiasm he had once applied to his activities as a blackshirt, ever happy to focus on the glossy surface of things while ignoring the emotional and intellectual bleakness that lies beneath. Blithely unaware of how limited he is in his range of interests he affects a free and easy life-style which is determined by a basic shallowness only marginally relieved by his one untypical gesture of human solidarity, ultimately insufficient to earn him the reader's unqualified esteem.

Family Sayings, the autobiographical work published two years later in 1963, is, as already indicated, a lengthy evocation of Ginzburg's life from her earliest childhood to her second marriage, an extended period during which her contacts with a wide range of male figures, initially from within her immediate family circle and subsequently on her own behalf outside it, inevitably provided her with a wealth of interesting and amusing episodes for which this book is rightly famous. As is only to be expected her attitude to these individuals, reproduced directly from real-life experience and thus distinct from characters in the normal sense of the term, is radically different from her usual approach to human personalities in her writing, here less disciplined and more dispersive or anecdotal in that her aim is essentially to recapture moments from the past rather than to construct a progressive sequence of facts and events which determine a character's nature and advance a plot. This makes for a deliberately fragmentary approach which encourages the reader to see the various episodes which make up this book as a series of vignettes to be enjoyed for their own sake irrespective of any relevance they may have to the author's fiction.

One exception to this general pattern is Ginzburg's father Giuseppe Levi, whose influence, inevitably far greater than that exercised by any other male during her childhood and first youth, is here revealed through a series of incidents which in their cumulative effect provide a highly detailed portrait whose characteristics have clearly served as a springboard for some of the author's creations in her earlier writing. A distinguished scholar, accustomed to laying down the law in his laboratory at the University, he is unable or unwilling to grasp that the rigorous discipline essential to the efficient running of an academic department is unsuitable for family life, and constantly gives vent to his irritation whenever his wife or one of his children says or does something of which he disapproves – a frequent occurrence. Possessed of strong views on a variety of subjects he dismisses modern painting as 'Messes and slops' (p. 9),[21] imposes strict etiquette at table, and is convinced that most of his fellow men are fools. At weekends he forces his family to go on climbing trips, controlling every item of clothing, deciding which provisions are and are not suitable, and exploding with anger if anyone suggests anything different. Despite this oppressive behaviour it is quite clear that Levi is at all times animated by the best possible intentions, and the deep contrast between his tyrannical conduct and his undoubted concern for his family's well-being is a source of much comic effect, especially in the early stages when the children are too young to resist him or circumvent his absurd demands. As they grow older and begin to form emotional attachments his fears for their moral integrity increase accordingly, whatever the circumstances, so that 'the nightmare of our father's outbursts of fury . . . for the pettiest reasons' (p. 36) are replaced by even more furious protests if his children, now fully autonomous, are planning to get married; by this time, however, they have learned to take evasive action, so that although 'On each occasion he forbade the marriage' he is powerless to prevent it, and 'we all married just the same' (p. 62).

An archetypal absent-minded professor, Levi is quite incapable of appreciating attitudes and actions which do not correspond to his own or are outside his intense but narrow field of vision, something which makes him appear unduly naive for his years. For example, having left Turin after his dismissal under the Racial Laws to work in a research laboratory in Belgium, from which he is subsequently forced to flee before the invading German forces, he has no hesitation in revealing his identity to an enemy patrol when the ambulance in which he is travelling is stopped, and it is only the incredible ignorance of the soldiers, who 'did not trouble themselves about his name, which was unmistakeably Jewish' (p. 134), that saves him from immediate arrest and deportation; when he is later evacuated to Ivrea and provided with false papers after the armistice he is likewise regularly unable to remember his alias, repeatedly giving his real name when asked and then hurriedly correcting himself. He survives the occupation only by moving to Florence, where he is unknown, after friends inform him he has been recognised and is in imminent danger. When the war is over and the family once more back in Turin he is unchanged by his experiences, still giving vent to his irritation at table, criticising his wife's interest in ' "never-ending rubbish" ' (p. 158), and unable to believe, against all the evidence, that his sons are not wasting their time in dead-end jobs. When he is asked to add his name to a list of candidates for the left-wing Popular Front he nonchalantly agrees, and, on hearing that he is required to address a political meeting, delivers a lecture on the importance of scientific research which totally mystifies his audience, especially bewildered to hear their representative state that in this field the Americans are ahead of the Russians, and who respond with wild applause when Levi incidentally mentions his habit of referring to Mussolini as 'a country bumpkin',[22] something which he in turn finds it difficult to understand. Totally at ease in a world of his own where he is in complete control Levi is correspondingly very much an innocent abroad as soon as he steps outside his laboratory, and can thus be seen as a perfect representative of the well-intentioned but socially and emotionally incompetent male, clearly the inspiration for old Balotta in *Voices in the Evening* – but with the all-important difference that Levi's interminable scoldings and unending criticisms of his wife and children at no time seriously alienate those around him, aware as they are that these tiresome manifestations are a sign of his undoubted affection, while his life-long devotion to an activity far more spiritually rewarding than industrial production ensures he is never in any doubt as to the importance and usefulness of his vocation.[23]

Ginzburg's eight plays, published between 1965 and 1971, all concentrate on problems affecting the female of the species, as already indicated; male characters are mostly seen in relation to the women whose lives they influence and whose fate they determine despite being almost without exception weak individuals, unable to fulfil their commitments adequately, and responsible whether directly or indirectly for their partner's unhappiness. Her first play *Ti ho sposato per allegria* presents the most striking example of this phenomenon in Manolo (who never appears on stage), whose tortured relationship with the protagonist Giuliana eventually leaves her pregnant and penniless after an extended period during which she has tried to dissolve his manic depression and neurotic frigidity, eventually succeeding only too well in her attempts to arouse his instincts. In complete contrast her husband Pietro, the only positive male in the whole of Ginzburg's theatre, appears as a level-headed and mature individual who, as the title of the play implies, is delighted to marry a scatter-brained and unreliable woman guaranteed to relieve the tedium of his respectable middle-class environment by providing entertainment every time she opens her mouth. Beneath the apparent frivolousness of this amusing juxtaposition of opposites Ginzburg also pin-points a concept first outlined more seriously in *All Our Yesterdays* and now developed more fully in comic vein: the dangers implicit in allowing one's behaviour to be influenced by feelings of compassion, something which invariably leads to extreme situations in which the last state is worse than the first. Thus although hurriedly agreeing, as he makes a late exit in Act One, that he has married his wife out of pity, Pietro later vigorously denies this, pointing out that 'if a man were to marry every woman he feels pity for he'd be in a fine state, as he'd end up running a harem' (p. 44), a statement he further qualifies by telling Giuliana quite bluntly that 'I would never have married a woman who cast a passionate spell over me; I want to live with a woman who makes me laugh' (p. 49), while his earlier claim that before meeting Giuliana he had contemplated marriage at least eighteen times before withdrawing from commitment at the last moment is a clear indication of his maxim that one should approach this important relationship with one's mind in working order and one's senses under control.

In *The Advertisement*, completed four months later, Teresa's husband Lorenzo emerges as a very different man, an overgrown adolescent whose intelligence and intellectual potential are vitiated by an inability to concentrate on work and a basic immaturity which leads to manic buying of antique furniture and old masters, which he then neglects, preferring to roar around in fast cars and on motor-cycles. While Pietro in the earlier play clearly represents someone most male readers would be happy to identify with Lorenzo in contrast is the personification of negative traits, including emotional involvements with unsuitable partners; if, however, as already indicated in Chapter 4, he is in one sense the root cause of his wife's misfortunes, this is not due to maliciousness or deliberate insensitivity but is clearly the result of a sheltered and wealthy upbringing which has encouraged him to pursue an idle life where work is a pastime rather than a necessity and sexual relations a form of self-indulgence whose deeper implications he has never stopped to consider. When Teresa succeeds in making him understand that she has found his casual affair with her deeply humiliating he is moved to make amends for his behaviour, first by accepting to live with her on a long-term basis, and, subsequently, by consenting to marriage, thereby revealing a basic good nature which is, however, unsupported by any consistency of purpose and which thus inevitably proves disastrous. His admission in Act Two that he was essentially motivated by feelings of compassion shows he has fallen into the very trap Pietro has been careful to avoid in *Ti ho sposato per allegria*, taking on commitments which he is then unable to fulfil and which deep down he knows are incompatible with his dispersive nature.[24] Unlike Pietro he does not find it amusing to be married to a woman who is the apotheosis of domestic incompetence and whose inability to pursue successfully any activity, whether intellectual or practical, reminds him constantly of how he has wasted his own creative talents as a pure physicist on hare-brained projects which never come to any conclusion. When he realises that 'we're only happy with people who aren't like us at all; we're only happy with our opposites' (p. 31) the damage has already been done and husband and wife have separated acrimoniously, but it seems unlikely that Lorenzo has learned from his mistakes – witness his relationship with Elena, in her own way just as inconclusive as Teresa, with whom it transpires he fell in love at first sight, and at the end of the play he is, if not unscathed, at least both alive and free and able to continue an aimless existence in which he will doubtless go on wreaking emotional havoc wherever he goes.

In *Fragola e panna* (1966) Ginzburg once more presents two contrasting male characters, one of whom never appears in the flesh but whose influence is fundamental to the plot and conditions the behaviour of the younger protagonist Barbara: her husband Paolo. A simple youth unable to foresee the consequences of his actions he foolishly impregnates his teenage girlfriend, whom he then agrees to marry despite parental opposition, thus both confirming the genuineness of his feelings and displaying a sense of duty, two characteristics destined to be his undoing in that he is subsequently quite unable to stand the strain of his wife's continued infidelity after she has solemnly promised to stop seeing her middle-aged lover Cesare.

Eventually he suffers a nervous breakdown which reveals the full extent of his inadequacy and destroys any chance of his resolving his marital problems. He becomes increasingly violent towards Barbara while being quite unable to take any action in relation to her lover, before whom he bursts into tears and then faints after trying to beard him in his chambers. Cesare's description of him as 'a puppy with damp hair who wouldn't hurt a fly' (p. 156), while effectively pin-pointing Paolo's pathetic defencelessness as a wronged husband, also indicates the author's sympathy for someone who has made up for his initial thoughtlessness and does not deserve the suffering his wife inflicts on him; unlike Vincenzino in *Voices in the Evening*, who deliberately and foolishly allows his wife to drift away from him, Paolo is clearly a man struggling desperately to prevent the collapse of his marriage while lacking sufficient strength or personality to compete with his rival in a situation which recalls that of the female narrator in *Mio marito* twenty-five years previously. In this sense he is clearly the first of Ginzburg's male characters to be cast in the role of undeserving victim, an example of how the vulnerability traditionally associated with the weaker sex can also be found among those supposedly made of sterner stuff. At the same time Ginzburg skilfully shows how, once Barbara has become infatuated with Cesare, his sophistication and his maturity inevitably make her realise that in comparison her husband is 'a silly little man . . . and the flat was poky and ugly and dirty' (p. 137), thereby emphasising Paolo's undoubted limitations, limitations which in no way justify his violence towards Barbara and yet ensure that this becomes an inevitable reaction to a situation he cannot resolve. Cesare meanwhile, as indicated in the previous chapter, is clearly delineated as an archetypal chauvinist, totally blind to anything outside his own gratification, running out on his young mistresses as soon as he grows tired of them, and systematically neglecting his wife, whom he has confined to a gilded cage while he loses no opportunity to indulge his freedom, a contemptible individual whose weakness of character, less immediately pathetic than Paolo's, is also infinitely more reprehensible.[25]

Ginzburg employs a similar technique in *La segretaria* (1967), in which Edoardo, a free-lance literary agent whose fortunes determine those of the other characters, likewise never appears despite being frequently mentioned and discussed. An intellectual overflowing with ideas Edoardo is at the same time totally lacking in organisational skills and pathologically lazy, spending his days idling in bed and his nights wandering aimlessly round town discussing politics and literature with a group of provincial hangers-on, while gradually drinking himself to death as his increasingly hare-brained plans for joining the Roman literati or handling best-sellers are consistently dashed. Like Paolo in *Fragola e panna* Edoardo is both pathetic and irritating; pathetic in that, as Enrico the doctor diagnoses, he is 'a desperately unhappy man' who is 'deliberately tearing his life to shreds' (p. 191) and systematically reducing his intellect and his emotions to 'dust and ashes' (p. 192), in effect realising a death wish;[26] irritating in that he is himself his own worst enemy, his misfortunes being the direct result of his foolish refusal to acknowledge that artistic ventures and commercial enterprises can only bear fruit when supported by a disciplined life-style, given that publishers are businessmen unwilling to make do indefinitely with vague promises or third-rate crime novels whose inadequacies are only revealed after translation into Italian. Permanently out of pocket he is inevitably unable to pay the lovesick Sofia for the work she none the less continues to turn over to him. When Silvana, supposedly hired as a secretary but in reality Edoardo's young mistress whom he needs to keep out of sight, attempts suicide during a momentary fit of depression and thereby exposes her relationship with her lover, his wife Isabellita promptly leaves him, a gesture which brings him face to face with the full extent of his wretchedness as he realises that he lacks any real feeling for either of these women and is no more capable of emotional fulfilment than he is of getting rich or making a name for himself. His own suicide, a logical reaction to this confirmation of all-round inadequacy, is both a fitting conclusion to his life and a final blow to his friends, who are all deeply shocked by the news. It is typical of Ginzburg's fine sense of irony that she should show this faceless individual virtually controlling all the other characters in the play, his supreme ineptitude being paradoxically what shapes their lives, while the two men who participate directly in the action are, each in their separate ways, total nonentities lacking both Edoardo's intelligence and his charm: Enrico, the doctor, a passive and insensitive person incapable of bringing any spiritual relief to his patients,[27] and Nino, the nominal head of the household, happy to neglect all his obligations, whether domestic, professional, or creative, in favour of an obsessional love for his horse, whose death he compares to the death of his father.[28]

A year later in *Paese di mare* Ginzburg presents an interesting variation on this same theme in the character of Alvise, a once-promising intellectual now turned factory-owner following his marriage to a rich sportswoman and clearly no longer the idealistic student of his first youth. Totally unable to understand or adapt to commercial pressures Alvise has seen his factory go from bad to worse in the last ten years and is now on the verge of bankruptcy, while his marriage to the lovely but mindless Bianca has similarly deteriorated to the point where they quarrel constantly over her promiscuity and drug addiction. If Alvise's inability to realise his original potential is essentially different from Edoardo's, his failure deriving not from laziness or lack of discipline but from a betrayal of his vocation, its effect on the protagonists of this play is even more decisive than in *La segretaria*, since it is the myth of Alvise's wealth and emotional stability which has drawn Marco and Debora to the small seaside town of the title in what is gradually revealed as one more ineffectual attempt on Marco's part to put down some roots, find and keep a steady job, and come to terms with the fact that he is not an unrecognised literary genius. Now nearly thirty Marco is conscious that 'We don't have any money . . . we don't have anything, nowhere to live, no friends, not even a town somewhere to go back to' (pp. 69–70), but is none the less incapable of facing up to reality; he is convinced, despite the lack of any supporting evidence, that his old friend will provide him with a well-paid job leaving him plenty of free time for academic research, while Debora and Bianca will rapidly become bosom friends and spend their days shopping and socialising with people in high places. Unable to realise that he is living in a dream world, despite Debora's frequent attempts to bring him down to earth,[29] and unable to reconcile a naive desire for total freedom with the need to ensure a minimal degree of economic stability for himself and his wife Marco has clearly remained an adolescent in spirit, an individual who, as Debora claims at one point, is 'full of hot air', allowing himself to 'get drunk on words' (p. 67) while never achieving anything in practice; and his nostalgic evocation of bygone student days with Alvise when 'We spent all our time talking incessantly' (p. 69) confirms that like other male characters before him he suffers from arrested development, an eternal optimist destined for eternal disappointment when reality does not match his expectations. The news of Bianca's suicide, followed by a message from Alvise that he is too distraught even to see them, eventually convinces Marco that it is time to move on yet again; if the reader is undoubtedly touched by his anguished appeal as he prepares to leave: 'Oh God, I must learn how to choose a place to live in and stay there', his confession in the same breath that 'I can't manage to stay put anywhere for long. I don't think I could have settled here even if I'd managed to find a job' (p. 101) clearly

216

implies he is never going to reach maturity.

Equally retarded, though in a very different way, is Alvise's friend Gianni, a young man too listless to break away from the drowsy atmosphere of the small seaside resort, where he scratches a living growing orchids in a large house once beautiful but now falling to pieces and consequently of no interest to prospective buyers. Unable to relate to his mother, whose yearly visits he dreads, Gianni is likewise unable to form satisfactory sexual relationships as he is terrified at the idea of any permanent attachment, proclaiming that 'women who become clinging are unbearable because you don't know how to get rid of them' (p. 87), a comment which reveals the full extent of his immaturity. His short-lived affair with Bianca and his brief coupling with Debora, implied rather than stated, are typical of his inconclusive personality, while his final comment that the human heart is 'invincible because it always lives in expectation of the unknown' (p. 102) confirms him as another dreamer destined to grow old without ever realising his potential and thus a fitting friend for the pathetic Alvise.

La porta sbagliata, written the same year six months later, is a more complex play in which the two most important male characters, Cencio and Stefano, are shown as totally incompatible while sharing a common bond with the neurotic Angelica, who has married each of them in turn. Supremely inefficient in the domestic sphere the intellectual Stefano is quite incapable of deputising for his wife in this area, his mind fixed instead on the need to complete his book on Thomas Mann, a task which will clearly remain completely beyond him while he is continually distracted by the practical problems of running a household and perpetually disturbed by Angelica's lunatic behaviour – two unremitting pressures which have contributed to a bad case of writer's block, thereby increasing his agitation. Unable to assert himself in the world of human relationships Stefano is shamelessly exploited by all those with whom he comes into contact: his wife, who shamelessly manipulates him by feigning anorexia nervosa, her mother, whose frequent and lengthy phone calls eat up a large part of his valuable time, and his friends Giorgio and Tecla, who appear to have taken root in his living-room together with Raniero, an unknown acquaintance who has attached himself to them the previous evening and shows no sign of wanting to leave. Accurately described by Giorgio as 'a victim . . . a martyr' (p. 127) Stefano is naturally powerless when confronted by Cencio, whose house they are all occupying, and who has suddenly decided to reclaim it in order to move in with his new wife; and if this crisis is objectively something over which he has no control his basic weakness is further emphasised in his inability to prevent Cencio from adding insult to injury by appropriating one of his ties and calmly walking off with it round his neck, an incident so grotesquely humiliating that it drives his staid middle-class mother to use strong language as he limply comments 'I'm not going to get possessive over a wretched tie' (p. 138). Aware from the beginning that his marriage to Angelica has been a grave error Stefano none the less has no regrets, having consciously chosen 'to make that mistake rather than live without her', believing that 'happiness is not the most important thing in the world' (p. 141), a comment which reveals him as a hopeless masochist who will never himself achieve anything positive, destined to remain at the mercy of his fellows. It is thus no surprise that at the end of the play he is still immersed in inconclusive apathy, no nearer finding alternative accommodation and happy to postpone any attempt to do so while the date of their eviction is still a month away.[30]

His friend Giorgio, apparently more dynamic and energetic, is, in reality, equally weak, though in a different context; intolerant of Angelica's neurotic posturings, whose spuriousness he sees through immediately, he has no hesitation in sternly rebuking her for her behaviour while being, like Stefano, totally dominated by a woman whose strong personality he is unable to resist: in his case his mother, whom he still lives with at the age of twenty-three and who pampers him obsessively while systematically denying him the means to develop his creative talents. Aware that his life in this gilded cage is slowly destroying his chances of ever becoming a writer Giorgio nevertheless cannot bring himself to leave home, despite telling Tecla that 'I've thought about it for years' (p. 113), afraid to take on the real world outside and conscious that while he remains safe and warm he will never have to discover whether he actually has any artistic potential. His peevish reactions to Tecla's description of him as 'a lap-dog' (ibid.) is a further confirmation of his basic inadequacy, and it is clear that his promise to move out next winter is quite meaningless.

This catalogue of dispersive and inefficient characters reaches its apotheosis in Cencio, Angelica's first husband. Like others before him he never appears on stage while being at the same time at the centre of other people's lives, a device which Ginzburg has now made more direct by showing this influence not in moral or emotional terms, as with Edoardo in *La segretaria* and Paolo in *Fragola e panna*, but in the supremely practical context of one of the most basic human needs: a roof over one's head. Totally blind to the needs of others Cencio has no compunction in evicting his supposedly ailing ex-wife and her new partner from his country villa, an apparently ruthless gesture which is soon revealed instead as an extreme example of a limitless insensitivity which conditions his every action and provides an impregnable defence against anything which might disturb his peace of mind. Incurably optimistic whatever the circumstances Cencio is blithely indifferent to the fact that everything he touches turns to dust, unperturbed by seeing his novels continually rejected by publishers and unaware that his constantly changing political views make him the very model of unreliability, while in his personal life friends contemptuously reject him and his sexual relationships invariably end in disaster. Untouched by all forms of hostility and humiliation Cencio strolls through life with a smile perpetually fixed on his face, a monumental failure convinced against all evidence that everything is for the best in the best of all possible worlds, and, as a result, effortlessly disarming all those around him, his boundless egoism ensuring that his victims are unable to resent someone whose child-like behaviour precludes what Stefano calls 'the great comfort of hatred' (p. 136), comparing him to 'an enormous . . . fish . . . swallowing up smaller fishes' (p. 140), while Giorgio later ironically describes him as 'the lord of the universe, the king of kings' (p. 147). When we last hear of him he has decided to abandon a Republican Party conference in Naples to fly to Jerusalem with Roger Vadim, who has offered him a small part in a biblical epic being shot in the Holy Land, and he has no qualms about similarly abandoning his pregnant mistress in hospital, where she will be looked after by Stefano and his family while he concentrates on playing the prophet Ezechiel in a colourful co-production doubtless destined to be savaged by the critics. If Cencio's unquenchable enthusiasm for life recalls that of Giuliana in *Ti ho sposato per allegria* his status as a male actively engaged in myriad activities ensures he does infinitely more damage to his fellows than a hapless country girl at large in the big city; encased in his own impenetrable self-assurance he is a unique figure in Ginzburg's work: a man whose inadequacy is absolute but who is untouched by it all, naively happy in his wretchedness and convinced of his own superiority.[31]

In Ginzburg's last two plays *Dialogo* (1970) and *La parrucca* (1971) she focuses on distracted female protagonists whose male partners, impoverished and insecure, are quite incapable of creating or maintaining any stability, whether emotional or practical, and are thus of no assistance to their disaffected spouses. The painter Massimo's pathological inability to reconcile a need for constant encouragement with the distressing awareness that his wife does not actually like his work, which is selling badly, is clearly what has brought about the gradual deterioration of their marriage in *La parrucca*, while the wife's lover, a penniless middle-aged writer with six children who are constantly under his feet as he tries to work, is clearly no better at organising his life or his emotional relationships. In *Dialogo*, likewise, it is Francesco's foolish refusal to accept a transfer to Brussels on the grounds that his wife Marta is reluctant to live abroad that has plunged them into penury and forced them to live in a cramped and squalid apartment which he contemptuously describes as 'a pigsty' (p. 24) and where he has no chance to work on his novel. If this appears at first to be no more than a misguided gesture prompted by conjugal affection his subsequent refusal to apply for teaching jobs, supposedly because this would interfere with his writing, clearly reveals him as essentially passive, no more capable than Marta of asserting himself, destined to remain unproductive (or at any rate unpublished) and consequently forever on the bread-line, his dreams of winning a literary prize and growing rich on the proceeds of foreign translations pathetically unrealistic in relation to a book that will never be finished. The news of his wife's infidelity and the realisation that her lover Michele's advice, on which he has so far relied, has clearly been less than disinterested, inevitably puts paid to any last shreds of will-power he might have possessed, and the play ends as he happily agrees to look after his rival's dog during Michele's absence, aware that although Marta's affair is over 'I can no longer give you anything; we're like two strangers under the same roof' (p. 47). Michele himself, though wealthy and professionally successful, is also clearly a weak character, happy to engage in a furtive affair with his friend's wife but too cowardly to break with her in person, preferring to send her a note and disappear from the scene along with his wife and sister while leaving Marta to sort out her marriage as best she can.

If the inadequacy of almost all the men in Ginzburg's plays is clearly in keeping with her increased pessimism typical of those years, and already examined in Chapter 4, it is pleasing to note that the more hopeful attitude apparent throughout Adriana's gradual maturation in *Dear Michael* (1973) also extends, albeit at a minimal level, to one of the male characters – the elusive Oswald, a quiet unassuming individual always willing to help those in need while at the same time contriving to remain somehow on the fringes of involvement in his relations with others. Separated from his wife Ada, whose unflagging energy he finds inhibiting and whose artistic expectations he cannot satisfy,[32] he none the less remains on good terms with her, paying her regular visits during which they talk amicably and exchange views on people and things in a civilised manner while agreeing that '"We couldn't live together. We are too different"' (p. 55). Evasive and desultory by nature he yet has no hesitation in responding to Mara's appeal for assistance in moving from her squalid boarding-house to an empty flat on the other side of town and lending her money for a pair of scales to weigh her new-born child, but has similarly no compunction in refusing to settle her debt to a fellow-boarder or telling her quite dispassionately that he does not find her sexually attractive, thereby ensuring he avoids becoming seriously involved in her problems while continuing thereafter to react positively whenever she needs help in a crisis. Touched by Adriana's distress at her son's unexpected flight to England he pays her regular visits during which 'He leafs through magazines and rarely speaks' (p. 73), his apparent insensitivity hiding a genuine concern which she gradually comes to appreciate, to the point where 'when he appears I am glad . . . I feel a curious sense of relief mixed with boredom' (pp. 73–4); he is clearly a man with hidden depths that Adriana perceives intuitively without ever penetrating beneath 'silences and vague answers' while always hoping he will 'suddenly open up and reveal his motives for living' (p. 127). Oswald's emotions, rigorously maintained within the bounds of social propriety, only manifest themselves in relation to Michael, whose departure has deprived him of a close friend and to whom he writes an affectionate letter on learning of the young man's forthcoming marriage. Its tone, surprisingly sentimental in one whose manner has so far been the very opposite of emotional, lends weight to the suggestion made at various points throughout the novel that Oswald is homosexual and that he and Michael have been lovers, a suspicion never clarified but further supported first by the intensity of Oswald's reactions at the news of Michael's death, and, more strikingly, by the elagiac tone of the letter to Angelica in which he describes a visit to Michael's abandoned house in Leeds and the 'strange and icy consolation' (p. 161) he has derived from 'a woolen undershirt that had been used as a dustcloth' (p. 160) and which is the only remaining sign of the young man's presence.

Ginzburg's decision to end the book with this gloomy letter, in which Oswald stresses the importance of memory, proclaiming that 'there is nothing . . . at present that can compare with the moments and places we experienced in the course of our lives' (p. 161), is plainly indicative of the cautious optimism typical of her mixed feelings during this period. It seems clear that while identifying principally with Michael's mother Adriana she also has close links with Oswald, a contemplative survivor deeply conscious of the complex nature of human relationships, whose strong feelings are kept in check by an equally strong need to remain on the fringe of other people's lives, and aware that while happiness does indeed exist it is largely restricted to the evocation of past moments recollected in melancholy, a concept which recalls the author's own comments almost thirty years previously in *Winter in the Abruzzi*, already quoted in Chapter 1.[33] In this connection it is tempting to suggest that Oswald's supposed homosexuality and its implications are further indicative of Ginzburg's increased sympathy for the male of the species in a conscious realisation that among the 'monstrous inexplicable race'[34] there are people whose problems can be just as difficult as those facing the weaker sex and whose emotional relationships just as fraught, Oswald being the only male character so far whose unconventional sexuality is not seen in a specifically negative light but in the wider context of his complex personality,[35] while his continued solitary existence as an eccentric but independent individual also places him in a different category from the rare specimens of positive manhood present in Ginzburg's earlier writing.[36]

If Oswald is thus something of a new development in Ginzburg's catalogue of male figures her fellow-feeling in no way extends to the other men in the novel, who are all poor specimens of humanity. Adriana's husband, an ageing painter whom she aptly describes as 'a weary old panther' (p. 5), boasts shamelessly about the quality of his work in a 'croaking voice . . . with the grating solitary sound of a broken record' (p. 33) and is perpetually at odds with the world around him, his marriage long disintegrated and his relationship with his ex-wife 'abject and despicable' (p. 45); while his boundless affection for Michael, the only positive thing about him, exists in a void in which there is no spiritual contact between father and son. His death while estranged from friends and relatives at his bedside when Michael is in exile abroad is deeply ironic, recalling Vincenzino's death in hospital in the presence of his old enemy Purillo instead of his brother Tommasino in *Voices in the Evening*. Adriana's lover Philip is no better, an inconclusive and spineless character whose essential inadequacy is immediately apparent in the way he looks around him 'with an expression of false determination and

222

authority' (p. 49) and whose cowardly behaviour when deciding on marriage to a younger woman has already been mentioned in Chapter 4. Equally pusillanimous is Fabio Colarosa, the wealthy publisher and short-lived lover of Mara Castorelli, an efficient businessman who however finds it impossible to make a clean break with his mistress when he can no longer stand her, preferring to alter his behaviour towards her so that 'you could hardly miss the point' (p. 116) and admitting, in the same letter, that 'You will think me a coward. The word fits me precisely. I feel sorry for you . . . with the gloomy pity of a coward' (p. 117). Michael himself, the character at the centre of the novel, is the very model of dispersiveness and unreliability, the carelessness of his life-style extending beyond a natural reluctance to concern himself with things domestic to more serious matters such as forgetting to dispose of a machine-gun hidden in his lodgings before leaving for England. Safe and sound in London he is incapable of making a new life for himself, first registering at an art college only to leave immediately to work as a butler in Sussex, a job which he then abandons with equal speed in order to follow a new girlfriend to Leeds, where he is happy to work as an odd-job man. His subsequent decision to marry a divorced thirty-year-old mother, whose intelligence he praises fervently, re-veals the full extent of his immaturity, further confirmed by his enthusiastic devotion to gardening, doing the housework, and bringing up his wife's two children, activities totally at variance with his essentially rootless nature. Michael's chameleon-like personality, most apparent in this retreat into a domesticity which is inevitably short-lived, also casts doubts on the seriousness of his political views (the reason for his flight to England in the first place), and it comes as no surprise to find him writing that 'I am still non-Communist. I am still nothing', a statement which is especially ironical when he also informs his sister in the same letter that his wife is 'one of the very few Communists here . . . I don't bother about politics; my wife does that and it is enough for me' (p. 102). When he once more establishes contact with left-wing activists in Belgium following the breakdown of his marriage there can be little doubt that this is not from any desire to reassume a role he had temporarily abandoned but simply because he is now at a loss for something to occupy his time; it is typical of Ginzburg's black humour that she should show his death in the student demonstration as the direct result of a decision which is essentially meaningless. Oswald's subsequent discovery that the marriage had lasted no more than eight days and had been prompted by Michael's desire to save his wife from alcoholism reveals a perfect example of the young man's willingness 'to be called upon to help others' while at the same time stressing his inadequacy as a human being, given that, as always, 'his generosity was useless because it was too brief' (p. 159). He is accurately described by his sister Viola as someone who '"never settles down . . . drifts from place to place, tries one thing and then another"' (p. 85), an aimless individual whose ambiguous relationship with Oswald she attributes to his being bisexual and this in turn as another aspect of his inability to focus consistently on any one aspect of life or human relationships.

As already indicated *Borghesia* and *Family*, the two long short stories published in book form four years later, are the most quintessentially pessimistic of Ginzburg's writings, while at the same time showing some signs in the latter of a renewal of confidence in the individual's capacity for emotional survival. If Ginzburg's main interest in *Borghesia* is concentrated on the protagonist Ilaria, whose inability to communicate with those around her is the root cause of her unhappiness, she also makes it clear that this defect is in no way an exclusively female characteristic; it extends to her brother-in-law Pietro, who, despite having a conventional masculine image – he is a successful antique dealer earning enough money to support not only Ilaria but also her daughter and son-in-law – is a timorous individual with 'a kind sensitive soul' under his gruff manner, pretending to be 'hard and strong' while 'inside he was as frail as a leaf' (p. 78). Unable to resist the free-wheeling teenager Domitilla, who fascinates him, he marries her despite knowing intuitively that this is a recipe for disaster; and he is incapable of acting positively when things start to go wrong, sitting motionless 'for hours on end, doing nothing, just smoking and stroking his chin and cheeks and hair', his literary activities also affected by his marital troubles so that 'he had come to a halt with his memoirs' (p. 100), a fruitless and self-defeating attitude in keeping with his consistent reluctance to discuss things with Ilaria at an earlier stage, when her counsel might have dissuaded him from his folly. Significantly on the one occasion he is sufficiently distressed to talk about his feelings he has already decided to enter into marriage, and, though agitated, is impervious to Ilaria's gentle suggestions for avoiding what they both suspect will only cause him more pain and suffering. Ilaria's son-in-law Aldo, a young drop-out with the mind of a child who has no qualms about living off his new family, is even more inconclusive, having no prospects and no plans, his interests limited to 'making a cabinet out of rotting old boxes and then painting it blue and sticking transfers on it' (p. 77), from which he graduates, temporarily, to making wooden puppets. Inevitably he drifts into an affair with Domitilla, who, when discovered, uses this as an excuse to make a definite break with Pietro and move with her new partner to the country, where her wealthy parents have bought a stud farm in which Aldo is happy to care for the horses, an eternal parasite whose ability to take advantage of any situation recalls the dubious talents of Valentino twenty-six years previously.

Despite the supremely depressing limitations of these two characters it seems clear the reader is intended to distinguish between Aldo's impressive but contemptible talent for ensuring he is never deprived of a meal ticket and Pietro's despairing inability to understand or control his emotional needs, a failure plainly more deserving of sympathy. Although it is not the first time that Ginzburg has focused on male figures in the grip of sexual passion this feature is now shown no longer in the near-pathological context of *Mio marito*, the youthful inhibition of *The Road to the City*, or the disgraceful duplicity of *The Dry Heart*, but, instead, in a middle-aged individual whose apparent maturity and social standing conceal an emotional naivety totally at variance with both his years and his status, both of which paradoxically ensure that he is ultimately able to survive a painful and humiliating experience without loss of dignity. In this he resembles Oswald in *Dear Michael* and it is doubtless no coincidence that as in the earlier novel Ginzburg should have chosen to conclude this tale by focusing on a male character whose loneliness cannot leave the reader indifferent, here seen by Ilaria's daughter when she drives away from her dead mother's apartment as an upright figure 'with his shabby purple jacket, his delicate grey head held high, and his dry, stern eyes' (p. 111), a combination of opposites which skilfully stresses both his wretchedness and his ultimate indestructibility.

Ginzburg's heightened awareness of the universal nature of human frustration and suffering reaches its climax in *Family*, written immediately after *Borghesia*, a story where the protagonist is a male architect of forty whose unhappy lot is as touching as that of any of the author's earlier female characters. Comfortably off and apparently happily married Carmine Donati is none the less dissatisfied with his life, both professionally and emotionally, conscious that although 'He earned good money at his work [he] had not achieved any of the goals he had set himself in his youth', a phrase suggesting he has abandoned youthful ideals in favour of a more conventional and more profitable approach to the demands of his vocation and reinforced by the subsequent statement that his study of suburban planning, on which he has been working for some time, 'seemed mediocre to him one moment, and fresh and original the next' (p. 11). His unexpected meeting with an ex-lover, Ivana, with whom he establishes an increasingly close though entirely platonic rapport, likewise makes him gradually aware that his marriage to the beautiful but mindless Ninetta is a sterile relationship in which the couple have nothing in common and thus nothing worthwhile to offer each other; it is thus not long before he realises that Ivana and her young friend Matteo Tramonti are 'the people with whom he felt best in the world', while in his contacts with his wife, his wife's friends, and his colleagues, 'he felt forced to adopt a stiff, complicated stance, and he felt himself become numb and cramped' (p. 27). Ninetta's affair with an unprincipled numbskull journalist, 'totally obsessed with whether the grimace that constantly contorted his lips was sufficiently wry and masculine' (p. 36),[37] none the less causes him much pain in forcing him to confront the failure of his marriage, thereby increasing the sense of disorientation he is already experiencing in his contact with the unbuttoned and free-wheeling lifestyle of his new friends; and when shortly afterwards he is struck down with pneumonia he realises during the long hours he spends in bed nursing his illness that 'he did not love her any more' (p. 42). Despite this Ninetta's subsequent distress at her lover's decision to end their squalid affair is a source of much concern to Carmine, but once she has come to terms with her situation and regained her composure he is conscious of being 'excruciatingly bored' (p. 45), inevitably thus drifting in his turn into a supremely inconclusive affair with the hippy Olga. As a middle-aged man still shackled by the conventions of his upbringing while also urgently seeking a new reason for living Carmine brings to this relationship a commitment and an impassioned intensity quite inappropriate to what Olga sees as merely one more sexual escapade as she drifts from place to place, secure in the knowledge that as the daughter of a wealthy musician she can drop back into middle-class society any time she chooses; it is not long before Carmine realises he is living in a fantasy world, his affair 'a frivolous superficial happening' (p. 49) rather than something which can transform his life and give it meaning. The overpowering happiness he initially experiences 'surging over him like a warm river' (p. 48) is replaced by equally intense feelings of depression which rouse him from sleep early in the morning, 'planting great forests and mountains over his outstretched body' and driving him to spend long hours working obsessively on his book as he can no longer bear to make contact with the world outside, a world full of 'contaminated places' (p. 54) where he and Olga have spent time together. Ginzburg's insistence on the extent of Carmine's feelings both before and after the collapse of this relationship is a clear indication of her sympathy for a human being undeservedly entangled in a set of circumstances totally incompatible with his age and temperament. There is clearly an obvious parallel with her own feelings of incompatibility *vis-à-vis* the contemporary world at this period in her life, when, as already indicated, her essays proclaim strong feelings of unhappiness mixed with a nostalgic evocation of the bright hopes of her youth, now dashed and seemingly illusory.

As Carmine gradually regains his emotional stability, a lengthy process during which he receives much moral support from Ivana and Matteo, he realises there is no hope of reconciliation with his wife, for whom he feels only 'a sort of melancholy, petty curiosity' (p. 56). Though still living under the same roof they now sleep in separate rooms and hardly speak to each other, aware that the next stage in their relationship must be a formal separation but unable to arrange this, first because of an instinctive reluctance to engage in further unpleasantness and then as a result of Carmine's illness, a viral infection which is subsequently diagnosed more accurately as 'malignant lymphogranuloma' (p. 66). His death in hospital, surrounded by friends and relatives, is described in elegiac detail as he gradually loses touch with reality, his last conscious experience an evocation of a moment during his infancy when he and his mother had been waiting to catch a train, surrounded by crowds of people and umbrellas in the pouring rain while 'mud was running between the tracks' (p. 68) in the middle of the night. This gentle and affectionate vision confirms the author's sympathy for this character, a man with his share of faults but whose defects have caused no pain to others and whose kindly disposition and open-mindedness have allowed him to experience genuine friendship during the last years of his life, thereby compensating to a large extent for his emotional failures and unrealised ambitions. Her decision to end once more by focusing closely on a male figure is further indicative of an increased willingness to extend her compassion for human suffering to both sexes; likewise Carmine's death is in itself in keeping with Ginzburg's acutely pessimistic feelings during this time and in this context a fitting counterpoint to the death earlier on of Ivana's long-term partner Amos Elia, a manic depressive whose suicide in a squalid provincial village brings to an abrupt end their supremely unsatisfactory relationship. Her teenage friend Matteo Tramonti, whose speech defect is a constant source of humour, as indicated earlier, is also at least in part a reflection of the author's dark view of life and life's problems; happy to live from hand to mouth while playing his guitar and socialising with young left-wing artists Matteo has no fixed abode and no plans for the future, his refusal to adopt a conventional life-style a potential source of conflict and distress as is his unabashed homosexuality, of no importance to his friends but likewise likely to add to his difficulties in any future attempts to drop back into society.

Ginzburg's latest work to date, *The City and the House* (1984), focuses once more on a male protagonist: Giuseppe, a journalist in the throes of the male menopause who decides to tear up his roots in Rome and move to Princeton, where he has a brother, Ferruccio, who will help him make a fresh start. 'Quirky and agoraphobic', as he is rightly described by Rita Signorelli-Pappas,[38] Giuseppe represents Ginzburg's new-found conviction that in the post-feminist society of this day and age men have lost their traditional preeminence and regressed to the point where now 'women appear stronger, more active than men',[39] able to assert themselves as never before and indeed developing a competitive spirit which Ginzburg sees as essentially counter-productive, since 'men are our comrades and thus very dear to us, so that I cannot conceive of them as enemies'.[40] On the brink of his fiftieth birthday Giuseppe is conscious that he has accomplished nothing worthwhile in life, neglecting his creative potential to the point where 'I'm tired of writing articles for newspapers' (p. 8) while having nothing to show for the years he has devoted to this activity, aware that if he is to make any radical changes to his life-style he cannot afford to delay much longer putting them into effect. The reader's first impression of Giuseppe as a man at last able to fulfil an honourable and praiseworthy vocation – an idyllic retirement in which he can devote himself to scholarship – soon proves illusory; for he is gradually revealed to be an inconclusive and awkward individual who has become increasingly solitary as he approaches middle age, set in his ways, and quite incapable of committing himself in any real sense to a fellow human being. Unable to communicate with his wife, whom he had foolishly married without realising 'how immensely stupid she was', or with his small son, who bored him 'because he was a child' (p. 11), he has separated from the first and lost touch with the second, dumped on an elderly relative and grown to manhood deprived of any close contact with his father, who can thus calmly inform Ferruccio in his first letter 'I won't miss my son because I never see him anyway'.[41] Meanwhile Giuseppe has enjoyed a long affair with Lucrezia, a married woman with five children, happy to maintain this relationship until she suggests moving in with her family, a prospect which terrifies him and to which he reacts with such evident horror that his mistress is immediately filled with deep contempt, deciding there and then to break with him. Lucrezia's husband Piero, whose friendship for Giuseppe has enabled him to accept his wife's infidelity while maintaining cordial relationships with his rival, none the less has no illusions about his true nature, defining him as someone who has 'many fine qualities but . . . lacked back-bone' (p. 22), reinforcing Lucrezia's more impassioned accusations of cowardice during their last meeting; Giuseppe's subsequent refusal to admit that he has fathered one of Lucrezia's children is clearly in keeping with his refusal to accept responsibility for his actions or acknowledge any moral obligations towards others, and confirms Ginzburg's own recognition that as a human being he is undoubtedly 'a failure'.[42]

If Giuseppe's inadequacies identify him quite plainly as one more ineffectual man in Ginzburg's gallery of futile male figures she is also on record as stating quite unambiguously that 'he is not to be condemned',[43] his inability to face up to his commitments a result not of malice or insensitivity, as with so many of her earlier characters, but, instead, of a kind of arrested emotional development which has prevented him from reaching maturity and thus rendered him incapable of adult behaviour. This failure she sees as symptomatic of the essential insecurity of contemporary life in Western society, where the traditional stability of close-knit families has been replaced by fragmentation and the isolation of the individual, supposedly more independent and self-sufficient, in reality lacking the means to assert himself when deprived of a familiar background once able to provide support or encouragement and now dispossessed of its original status and power. Previously seen as impinging on young people in the more traditional context of broken homes or parental short-sightedness this attitude is now shown as also affecting the lives of older generations, similarly cut adrift in the new permissive age and equally incapable of coping with situations and circumstances inconceivable in the more rigid society of their youth, where the power of conventional morality largely ensured that the strict rules governing personal relationships were followed unquestioningly. No longer themselves able or willing to exercise self-discipline these older characters are inevitably their own worst enemy; untroubled by problems of conscience or social disapproval they are also no longer inhibited by the need to conform to the expectation of their own elders, long since dead or exiled to the outer fringes of their lives where they have no direct relevance to their children's behaviour and are thus unable to influence it. In this context Giuseppe is clearly the end product of what Vittorio Spinazzola has called Ginzburg's interest in 'the crisis of the family, seen above all as a crisis of male authority in the male's role both as father and husband',[44] his desire to make a fresh start in America a desperate attempt to create some order and stability in what has so far been an emotionally rootless existence now to be succeeded, or so he hopes, by a more disciplined life in which he will once more enjoy the 'authoritative, slightly contemptuous and high-handed protection' (p. 35) of his elder brother, an established academic whom he plainly sees as a surrogate father.

It may seem ironical that after having devoted so much time to pin-pointing the negative aspects of traditional family life Ginzburg should now apparently be bemoaning its disappearance. It would, however, be inaccurate to interpret this latest development as a contradiction of her previous views; rather is it a lament for the fact that the disintegration of an established order whose defects she has long been aware of has simply left a void in which individuals of both sexes and all ages are no better off than before, indeed in some ways more likely to encounter frustration and unhappiness. In Ginzburg's view the absence in our time of a superior force whose directives one can attempt to subvert while not questioning the authority from which they emanate has exposed a basic human need for clear ethical parameters without which the individual feels deprived, and her uncompromising claim that 'nowadays we are all orphans'[45] is clearly indicative of the increased pessimism in keeping with her advancing years and already mentioned, a feeling here rendered by her characters' despairing endeavours 'to establish some emotional stability and some sense of family in a world which has been turned upside down'.[46]

Giuseppe's strivings to satisfy what Ginzburg has aptly described as 'a nostalgic craving for paternal influence'[47] are, however, only partially and temporarily successful. Ferruccio dies suddenly and unexpectedly almost as soon as Giuseppe has arrived in America, and after a decent interval he marries his widow Anne-Marie, a fiercely efficient biologist whom he clearly views in her turn as fulfilling the same protective function as his brother, only to see her also die of leukaemia some months later. Both surrogates fail to fulfil his need for stability: his contact with Ferruccio is strained and

230

awkward from the beginning, so that 'I have to go back years and years before I can rediscover a happy intimate relationship between us' (p. 74);[48] in the same way he soon realises that he has nothing in common with Anne-Marie other than their sorrow at Ferruccio's death, and that he has once more foolishly contracted marriage without understanding his partner's true nature, a dedicated scientist engrossed in her research being just as inappropriate as his immensely stupid first wife, long since dead. In this context his brief infatuation and short-lived affair with the neurotic Chantal, Anne-Marie's daughter by a previous marriage, is one more instance of his pathetic inability to control his emotions or behave intelligently in sexual matters. Meanwhile Lucrezia has fallen desperately in love with Ignazio Fegiz, a picture-restorer she has met through a family friend and who appears to share her all-consuming passion, so much so that in due course she leaves her husband in order to begin a new life with him, happy to find she is pregnant by her lover and looking forward to the birth of a sixth child whom she imagines joining the rest of her family, now ensconced in a cramped flat in Rome. Lucrezia's naive hope that Fegiz will leave his long-term partner Ippolita to move in with her gradually fades as their relationship cools, and the increasingly long periods he spends away from her eventually convince her that, as she uncompromisingly states in one of her letters to Giuseppe, 'I've got myself in a real fucking mess' (p. 134), her marriage now destroyed and her future uncertain. The death of her child a few hours after its birth is a further blow which brings her to the edge of nervous collapse, and when shortly afterwards Fegiz finds the courage to break with her she is aware that her emotional life is now definitely over as she has become 'ugly and old. My hair is falling out. I've got wrinkles' (p. 158). Though convinced that reconciliation with her husband is impossible she is none the less deeply shocked to learn that he has become involved with 'a young, confused girl . . . not always sincere' (p. 194) who has taken over his life and whom he wants to marry, a situation clearly modelled on that of his namesake in *Borghesia* and which his wife aptly describes as 'floundering about in very deep water' (p. 205). The novel ends with another letter from Lucrezia to Giuseppe in which she relates a visit from Fegiz and Ippolita, who need her help to negotiate the purchase of Giuseppe's old apartment, where they will live together, a supremely insensitive gesture in keeping with the author's fine sense of irony.

Ginzburg's decision to devote as much space to Lucrezia's tortured emotional meanderings as to Giuseppe's pathetic attempts to give his life some meaning is plainly indicative of her new desire to give both sexes equal standing in a novel which has been described as her 'most despairing creation to date',[49] and their common failure to achieve their respective aims clearly represents her belief that in this day and age men and women are equally vulnerable, equally unable to take charge of their lives, and thus condemned to dissatisfaction with their lot and indeed with themselves.[50] Thus in her first letter to Giuseppe, Lucrezia's reproaches as she evokes the reasons for their separation include her awareness that her lover's feeble protestations about not being able to act as a father to her children conceal a deep and lasting fear in all his human relationships that 'someone will make you take on the role of a father' (p. 21), something the reader already knows him to be incapable of; when Giuseppe replies he shows equal perception in his claim that all her life Lucrezia has been searching for someone to replace *her* father, who died when she was still a child, and that her emotional ties have all been vitiated by this obsessive need, which he then admits to sharing with her, significantly stating that 'perhaps neither you nor I have ever become adults . . . we are a brood of children' (p. 35). The statement finds ample confirmation in Lucrezia's lengthy account of her mother's progressive neurosis and eventual death, a long and harrowing sequence rendered even more distressing by her daughter's total inability to take any decision, however trivial, without consulting the old lady beforehand; thus we learn that 'At twenty-five I had been married for three years and I already had two children, nevertheless my mother still gave the orders and I obeyed them. I phoned her ten times a day to ask how I should dress and what I should cook' (p. 23); it comes as no surprise to read in the same paragraph that 'When I married Piero I realised that I had done well . . . but I knew . . . I had only obeyed my mother' (p. 24), a telling phrase which gives the full measure of her personality and her morbid desire to attach herself limpet-like to those she believes able to protect her from adult responsibility. Lucrezia's pathological dependence on her sole surviving parent makes it easier to understand, if not to accept, her frequent infidelities *vis-à-vis* her husband, whom she has clearly never loved in the accepted sense of the word, while Piero himself, content to accept his wife's long-standing affair with Giuseppe rather than create trouble (an attitude reminiscent of Vincenzino's in *Voices in the Evening*), is also, like Giuseppe, 'one of those who always loses', aware that both men are 'birds of a feather' (p. 107), and it is doubtless no coincidence that each is subsequently infatuated with a supremely unsuitable girl half his age.[51]

Entirely cut off from any parental influence during childhood Giuseppe's son Alberico, now a young man, appears typical of the undisciplined and disaffected youth of our times, a professional hippy whose contacts with the underworld of drugs and violence ultimately prove his undoing. Like Michael before him Alberico has grown up under an exclusively female influence, and in his case this appears to have determined a totally unambiguous homosexuality, which, while pushing him further beyond the confines of respectable society, in no way prevents him from accomplishing far more than any of his older and supposedly more mature relatives and friends, a paradox which is again typical of Ginzburg's sense of humour. A university drop-out with artistic pretensions Alberico somehow gains access to the world of films, first as an assistant director and walk-on and in due course as a writer commissioned to direct his own screen-play in a film which proves highly successful and promises to be a stepping-stone to bigger and better things. His sporadic contacts with Giuseppe, 'always . . . ill at ease when I find myself face to face with Alberico' (p. 40), merely emphasise the difference between the young man's uninhibited and disorganised existence and his father's conventional middle-class life-style. It is only following Giuseppe's departure for Princeton and his son's return to Rome from working on location in Berlin that they begin to relate effectively to one another in an exchange of letters which oblige them to concentrate on matters of importance at the expense of trivia and without the reciprocal embarrassment of physical presence, a phenomenon already apparent in *Dear Michael* and here extended to cover both participants. Prompted by a desire to express his sympathy for Ferruccio's death Alberico's first letter to his father also contains references to two people he is now living with: Salvatore, a graphic artist he has met while in Berlin, presumably his current lover, and Nadia, a pregnant girl whose rich father had put up money for an earlier film and who has struck up a platonic friendship with Alberico that has kept them together. Alberico's decision to register the child as his own after Nadia has resolved not to have it aborted is both unexpected and – apparently – incompatible with his dissipated life-style, in reality clearly revealing his awareness of the importance of a stable environment during one's formative years, as he makes clear in a letter to Giuseppe by stating quite plainly that 'I want to give her what I never had, a father's protection . . . You weren't much of a father' (p. 88). Giuseppe's reactions to his son's gesture and to the news that he is working on a new screen-play are naturally warm and enthusiastic, and he replies

233

with details of his new life in Princeton, adding that he hopes Alberico will meet his wife and her daughter at some future date. The sudden death of Nadia from a bullet intended for Salvatore during a street brawl whose motivations are never properly clarified, followed in turn by her father's decision to remove the child from Alberico's keeping to a more conventional and more prosperous family environment, inevitably both shock and distress the young man, now able to communicate his feelings to Giuseppe in a letter whose tone, both discreet and touching, reinforces the new intimacy growing between them and which is further strengthened when Giuseppe is similarly deprived of his stepdaughter's baby girl, to whom he has grown very attached and whom Chantal decides to reclaim from her mother.

Alberico's subsequent friendship with Lucrezia, a close if necessarily platonic relationship,[52] appears to herald a new period of peace and tranquillity for him while also being a source of great contentment to Giuseppe, who describes the news as 'an unexpected gift' (p. 209), but their satisfaction is short-lived as a little later Alberico is stabbed during a second mysterious street brawl involving Salvatore and dies in hospital without regaining consciousness. He is remembered by those who knew him as 'courteous and gentle', a generous man who 'lent money to whoever needed it, and . . . never asked for it back again' (p. 212), details which indicate how his essential goodness extended beyond his affection for Nadia's child to a more general love of humanity. We may once again discern Ginzburg's wry sense of humour in casting as 'the most sensible member of this band of muddle-heads'[53] an individual whose personality and life-style make him appear the least reliable; in a wider context he clearly also represents the author's pessimism in relation to the increasingly violent nature of contemporary urban society while also perhaps suggesting, on a more confident note, that the younger generation also includes people whose disquieting image and disordered mores do not necessarily preclude genuine affection, disinterested behaviour, and positive achievement. At the same time it is equally clear that his main function is to pin-point a particularly crucial defect in his father's emotional make-up, a defect which Giuseppe admits is largely his fault – 'I never tried to improve our relationship' (p. 216) – while also suggesting that the barriers which exist between father and son are a natural phenomenon inevitably inhibiting meaningful communication; at the end of the novel Giuseppe has established a close relationship with Chantal's estranged husband Danny, a young man of Alberico's generation towards whom he feels far more open than with his own flesh and blood, something which draws from him the ironic comment that 'If Alberico had not been my son I might have been able to get on well with him . . . The fact that we were father and son spoiled everything. It made us embarrassed, stupid, cold, and often insincere' (ibid.). Ginzburg is plainly still convinced that, as she had already shown in *Dear Michael*, close contact between parents and children is only possible when, paradoxically, they are prevented from meeting face to face and obliged to rely on methods supposedly less intimate but in effect more conducive to genuine communication of emotions and states of mind.

Within this framework the two fixed points of the city and the house are what determine the characters' movements and the type of life they lead. The city is first and foremost Rome, the large anonymous capital where Giuseppe has lived and worked for twenty years and which he then wishes to exchange for Princeton, 'a tiny American town' with 'lots of libraries' (p. 9) where he naively imagines he will lead a more meaningful existence. It is likewise to Rome that Lucrezia moves when she leaves her husband, and to Rome that Alberico returns after finishing his work on location in Berlin. In this rambling anarchic metropolis, where violence flares unchecked and where first Nadia and then Alberico are killed, the house – or, more accurately, the apartment – is a place of refuge, a haven from the harshness of life in the streets, and therefore by extension, as Ginzburg herself has said, 'something at the centre of our lives' which represents 'the longing for a domestic nucleus, or, more accurately, for stability'.[54] Giuseppe's decision to sell his apartment before leaving the country is thus much more than a mere commercial transaction, and indeed little short of what his cousin Roberta calls 'a real piece of lunacy'; as he struggles to adapt to life in the New World he soon realises that her advice to 'Never sell bricks and mortar, never . . . hang on to bricks and mortar for dear life' (p. 8) was all too sound, and that now he lacks a place affording shelter in his old environment there can be no question of his changing his mind and returning to Italy. Later on Alberico begins negotiations with the new owners in order to buy the apartment back and make a present of it to his father, but is killed before he has signed the relevant documents, his estate passing automatically to his legal heir, Nadia's daughter. In the last we see of Giuseppe he is still stuck in Princeton, where he has lost both his brother and his wife, aware that 'If I return . . . I shall have to look for a house' (p. 216) and still too traumatised to come to any decision about his future. Equally central to Lucrezia's life is her country villa Le Margherite, a meeting-place for her many friends and a symbol of human fellowship and warmth which is then sold, following the breakdown of her marriage, becoming an anonymous hotel inhabited by strangers and totally lacking in atmosphere; and if her access to people and places ensures that in due course she succeeds in obtaining a mortgage and buying an apartment she is none the less, like Giuseppe, 'alone a great deal . . . she almost never sees anyone' in contrast to her life when married, 'surrounded by people . . . Le Margherite was like a sea-port' (p. 187), eventually suffering the humiliation of being approached by Fegiz and Ippolita in connection with the purchase of Giuseppe's old apartment.

Alongside these people, whose experiences form the backbone of the novel, Ginzburg has placed a variety of minor characters, all 'beautifully and economically realised', as Dick Davis has accurately stated,[55] and all contributing in their various ways to the author's intensely credible picture of human relationships in the 1980s. Thus Albina, a sensitive graduate who is still single at thirty-three, decides to marry a widower with a nine-year-old son who lives next door, and this despite having no particular feelings for him, because 'life is very wearisome . . . and I think . . . it'll be easier when I'm married' (p. 139), inevitably becoming 'dry inside . . . serious and hard' (p. 171) as a result; her youthful independence in a Roman bed-sitter is now displaced by a ceaseless round of domestic duties as she cooks and irons for her father, her brother, and, in due course, her husband. Serena, a younger girl, is an ex-nanny turned feminist who opens a squalid and unsuccessful Women's Centre in a small rural town where she indulges in third-rate amateur dramatics, eventually taking over Albina's bed-sitter in Rome and gaining access to 'a small inconvenient theatre' (p. 169) where her production of an eighteenth-century classic is torn to pieces by the critics. Originally a timorous and tearful girl constantly needing reassurance from Lucrezia she too gradually changes, becoming self-centred and insensitive, chiding her mentor while they are on holiday together for her foolishness in leaving her husband and thus adding to her troubles, oblivious in her new-found assertiveness to the fact that she has no talent and thus no chance of achieving success as an actress. Giuseppe's cousin Roberta, in contrast, is 'a cheerful, interfering busybody' (p. 17) fully in control of her life and always ready to help and advise others; she it is who sorts out the bureaucratic complications resulting from Alberico having died before completing the purchase of his father's old apartment. Egisto,

236

the family friend who first introduces Lucrezia to Ignazio Fegiz, is a solitary journalist basically content with his lot and enjoying good relationships with the other characters, in due course repairing the harm he has unwittingly done by fostering the friendship between Lucrezia and Alberico when she is at her lowest ebb emotionally. Other characters make more sporadic appearances, touching on individual lives and providing small but significant contributions to the whole, in every case skilfully rendered with 'the force of truth' so that 'we recognise them and feel irritation and sympathy for them',[56] while occasionally adding to the many humorous moments in this novel. Indeed it seems clear from Ginzburg's decision to end the book on a note which is both elegiac and comical that the pessimism and deep compassion she has always shown for her characters, now extending to all sorts and conditions of humanity, is once more fully integrated with a lively awareness that although life is an eminently serious business in which sorrow tends to predominate over joy and pain over pleasure, with old age and death as the ultimate truths of existence, life also provides endless examples of the absurdity and illogicality of human behaviour which temper and relieve an experience we might otherwise find too stressful and at times even unbearable. In this context Lucrezia's final affectionate evocation of Giuseppe, a weak man whose suffering has given him a certain dignity while also ensuring the sympathy of the reader, recalls Ginzburg's statement thirty-five years previously that human beings are 'funny and at the same time sad':[57]

> Your long thinning hair. Your glasses. Your long nose. Your long, bony legs. Your big hands. They were always cold, even when the weather was hot. That's how I remember you. (p. 219)

This early criterion, consciously realised by the author on completion of her 'first real story'[58] as long ago as 1933 and now once more fully confirmed, is a clear indication that Natalia Ginzburg has re-established an essentially positive relationship with life and art which is unlikely to be dissipated in the years to come. If, on the one hand, the range of new social and emotional problems that have come to the fore in Western society in recent years seems to have created within her a strong sense of nostalgia for the unthinking naivety of past generations, it is equally clear that her acknowledgement of the need for individualism also makes her an admirable representative of attitudes and life-styles typical of contemporary European youth; in addition her attention to the minutiae of day-to-day existence demonstrates how the simple things of life are often indicative of deeper and more disturbing realities which determine the behaviour, and so, ultimately, the destiny of those same individuals to whose needs she responds.[59] In this context Ginzburg's interest in the family as a fundamental influence on individual character is typical of both Latin and Jewish sensibilities, while at the same time her realisation that it can often do incalculable harm to those whom it most wishes to nurture reveals a strikingly original approach to one of life's most basic relationships, an approach which sets her apart from other Italian writers of her generation and which is further sharpened by a uniquely personal sense of humour that frequently softens the disturbing implications of her awareness that our chances of happiness and fulfilment as human beings are conditioned by our relationships with our fellows.[60] Ginzburg's election to the Italian Parliament, something which shows a remarkable energy and drive in a woman of her age, is further indicative of a lasting interest in human problems which one hopes she will continue to examine in an artistic medium for the foreseeable future. Though not everyone may agree with Ian Thomson that she is 'the most interesting of Italian female writers alive today'[61] there can be no doubt that her ability to create what Elaine Feinstein has elsewhere called 'human content that has . . . some kind of irrefutable rightness'[62] ensures that she occupies a leading position in contemporary European literature.[63]

Notes

1. *Human Relationships* in *The Little Virtues*, p. 81.
2. There are strong hints of latent homosexuality in his subsequent awareness that 'he could not recall ever having felt any strong desire for a woman' (p. 373), and his recollecting that at fifteen years old he was still wearing pinafores and 'didn't find girls attractive' (p. 374).
3. Delia describes her as 'so ugly and old' (p. 67).
4. Clotilde Soave Bowe comments in 'The Narrative Strategy of NG', p. 790: 'In fact his death amounts to a suicide'.
5. However see the first paragraph of *Mio marito*, where the static quality of the narrator's life before her marriage is skilfully rendered by her informing us that together with her sister and an elderly aunt she spent her days doing the housework and 'embroidering large tablecloths for which we had no real use . . . At times we would be visited by some married ladies and we would all discuss these tablecloths at great length' (p. 383).

6. See the narrator's statement on p. 83; 'Once Alberto told me he had never done anything in earnest. He knew how to draw, but he was not a painter; he played the piano without playing it well; he was a lawyer but he did not have to work for a living . . . he stayed in bed all morning, reading.'

7. See the narrator's comments on p. 143; 'There are other things in life, I told myself, than making love or having children. There are a thousand things to do, and one of them is writing a book on the origins of Christianity.'

8. His sister reflects ironically that 'he . . . has never neglected for one day to pamper his curls in front of the mirror and smile at his reflection' (p. 49), doubtless even on the day of Kit's death.

9. Avril Bardoni translates differently, p. 41.

10. His duplicity is further evidenced by his stating that 'he had not even touched this woman' (p. 227), later admitting that 'he had perhaps given her a few half-kisses' and finally that 'in thought he had always remained faithful to [his wife]' (p. 229), clearly implying that in more obvious ways he had been the opposite. His final comment that 'It was not his fault if he liked girls' (p. 230) is particularly wretched.

11. Angus Davidson translates *canaglia* as 'brute', p. 28.

12. See his comment on p. 56: 'He was not in the least interested in soap and would like to bash in the face of anyone who dared to show him even the tiniest little bit of it.'

13. Angus Davidson translates *sporchissima* as 'utterly filthy', p. 299.

14. His wife Anna accuses him of having water in his veins rather than blood; see p. 373.

15. F. Riva, 'La Ginzburg e i nostri ieri', *Corriere del giorno*, 1 Feb. 1953, p. 3.

16. Angus Davidson ignores this by translating *sposarsi* as 'mated', p. 25.

17. See for instance the description of her lodgings, a boarding-house where 'a colonel's widow knocked on the wall with a hairbrush every time I opened the window or moved a chair' and 'the landlady's hysterical daughter screeched like a peacock while they gave her a warm shower which was supposed to calm her down' (p. 74).

18. In this novel the only male to realise his potential is Nebbia, a simple soul aptly described by Paolo Milano in 'NG: La vita come attrito' as 'an impressive skier and mountain-climber who is also a Communist . . . he reminds us of some of Pavese's characters', and it is ironic that he should occupy a minor role in the narrative, being executed by the Fascists during the war.

19. T.G. Bergin comments in 'La Vita Evaded Them All', *Saturday Review*, 21 Sept. 1963, p. 36: 'The long attrition of too many blasted hopes, the reaction after the war, the general drabness of provincial life – these seem to have sapped Tommasino's *élan vital*.'

20. D. M. Low translates *merda* as 'dung', p. 23.

21. The direct comparison between messy eating and modern art, clearly expressed in the Italian original, is lacking in the English translation.

22. D. M. Low translates differently on p. 172.

23. In his querulousness he is clearly also recognisable in Anna's father in *All Our Yesterdays*.

24. See his admission to Elena in Act Two that 'In this world there are the amateurs and the professionals. I'm only an amateur, unfortunately' (p. 28).

25. Flaminia accurately describes him as 'A nonentity; cold, cynical, blinkered, probably very stupid' (p. 153), and earlier informs Barbara that 'He never thinks of other people; he thinks of himself' (p. 140).

26. He is clearly an extension of Nini in *The Road to the City*.

27. After a particularly frustrating exchange in Act Two Sofia angrily informs him that 'talking to you is like talking to the wall' (p. 183).

28. In Act Three Titina comments that 'Horses are the only thing that interests him. We could die of thirst here and he wouldn't turn a hair. He only puts himself out for horses' (p. 202).

29. See his reply to her eminently sensible question 'What shall we do if Alvise doesn't offer you this job?': 'I don't know ... I don't want to think about it now. I'm tired' (pp. 62–3).

30. At the beginning of Act Three he mentions during one of his mother-in-law's interminable phone calls that 'I've got today's papers but I haven't looked at the property section yet' (p. 161).

31. Raniero, the stranger picked up by Giorgio the previous evening, appears as the only sane person in the company, a quiet fellow with no emotional ties who perhaps represents normality, speaking little and then usually to make an obvious point no-one appears to have noticed. A marginal character, he none the less appears to enjoy a contented if somewhat humdrum existence, and as the most level-headed among them is an obvious example of the thinly populated third category of male figures, those in control of their lives.

32. He tells Mara that when living with his wife '"I felt as if I was next to a boiling cauldron"' (p. 18) and that '"She wanted me to write books ... I think that I would have written them if she had not expected it. But ... it was killing me"' (pp. 18–19).

33. *The Little Virtues*, p. 8.

34. *Human Relationships* in *The Little Virtues*, p. 81.

35. Maurizio in *Un'assenza*, Manolo in *Ti ho sposato per allegria*, and Valentino are all in their separate ways inadequate males whose sexuality contributes to their unhappy or destructive natures.

36. The most striking is, of course, Cenzo Rena in *All Our Yesterdays*, who is shot by the occupying Germans, while Pietro's eccentricity and independence in *Ti ho sposato per allegria* are seen in the context of his marriage. Mario's self-affirmation in *Voices in the Evening* likewise finds expression in conjugal bliss and is also short-lived, while Chaim Wesser in *Sagittarius*, though worthy and deserving of esteem, is a penniless refugee who achieves self-sufficiency through a dubious marriage. There is some resemblance to Augusto in *The Dry Heart* and Raniero in *La porta sbagliata* (whose sexual proclivities are questioned by Angelica, interestingly) but both are minor characters.

37. In this he recalls Philip's expression of 'false determination and authority' in *Dear Michael*, p. 49.

38. R. Signorelli Pappas, book review, *World Literature Today*, vol. 60, no. 1 (1986), p. 89.

39. Carrano, 'Lei ha vinto', p. 38; the same point is made in Cesari, 'NG

parla del suo nuovo libro'.

40. Del Pozzo, 'Letteratura/Il caso Ginzburg', p. 133; here too Ginzburg repeats her claim that men have become weaker than women, adding that her decision seven years previously to write *Family* had been motivated by a desire 'to examine a male character from the inside', aware that 'men had also now become victims' (ibid.).

41. *La città e la casa*, p. 4; this concluding sentence is omitted from Dick Davis' English translation of Giuseppe's first letter on p. 6.

42. Cesari, 'NG parla del suo nuovo libro'.

43. Ibid.

44. V. Spinazzola, 'E' sempre teatro per Natalia', *Panorama*, 24 Dec. 1984, p. 131.

45. Del Pozzo, 'Letteratura/Il caso Ginzburg', p. 133.

46. Amendola, 'NG parla di se', p. 57.

47. Cesari, 'NG parla del suo nuovo libro'.

48. This comment is clearly a deceptively milder version of Flaminia's anguished description of her marriage to Cesare in *Fragola e panna*, implying that both are conscious of having wasted their lives.

49. Thomson, 'Finely-spun despair'.

50. Lucrezia's bitterness at her own stupidity, already mentioned, is paralleled by Giuseppe's comment in a letter to her husband that 'when I get up in the morning I find in myself a deep disgust for what I am . . . As the day goes on this disgust becomes gradually more and more stifling' (p. 108).

51. The same is true of Ignazio Fegiz, who, after breaking with Lucrezia, falls in love with 'a very beautiful eighteen-year-old girl' and 'wanted to marry her' (p. 202), a relationship which is inevitably short-lived and confirms he is no more able than the others to control his emotions.

52. Lucrezia later informs Giuseppe that 'I could have fallen in love with him if he hadn't been a homosexual' (p. 217).

53. L. Mondo, 'Colore Ginzburg', *La Stampa*, 4 Jan. 1985, p. 3.

54. See the interview with Nico Orengo published in *Tuttolibri*, X, no. 432, 8 Dec. 1984, p. 1, entitled 'Ginzburg: la casa è il rifugio di vite stracciate'.

55. Davis, 'At the breaking-point'.

56. Ibid.

57. *My Vocation* in *The Little Virtues*, p. 58.

58. Preface to *Cinque romanzi brevi*, p. 5.

59. This recalls Italo Calvino's claim that the writer Ginzburg most resembles is Jane Austen; see 'NG o le possibilità del romanzo borghese', p. 181.

60. The point is confirmed in Ginzburg's most recent offering: a play in two acts entitled *La poltrona*, presented at the Spoleto Festival Dei Due Mondi in 1985 but only published in its entirety in the second volume of her complete works (Mondadori, Milan, 1987, pp. 1337–59). Described by the author herself as 'a simple portrait of human beings and what unites and separates them' ('Nella mia "poltrona" c'è qualche fiocco di neve', *La Stampa*, 18 June 1985, p. 23) it has three characters: a husband, Matteo, his wife Ada, and their new neighbour

Ginevra, with whom Matteo has a brief affair that confirms the failure of his marriage while also establishing beyond doubt that he is incapable of forming satisfactory relationships and is happier to live alone, at the same time experiencing strong feelings of nostalgia for married life. An intensely melancholic playlet, it is characteristically enlivened by repartee and many comic exchanges which exemplify the absurdity of these three characters' lives.

61. Thomson, 'Finely-spun despair'.
62. E. Feinstein, book review, *The Times*, 30 Oct. 1980, p. 15.
63. Antonio Russi describes her as 'one of the most important examples of post-war Italian literature'; see 'NG' in G. Mariani and M. Petrucciani (eds), *Letteratura italiana contemporanea* (Lucarini, Rome, 1983), p. 432.

Chronology

1916   Birth of Natalia Levi, the last of five children, to Giuseppe Levi, Professor of Anatomy at the University of Palermo, and Lidia Tanzi, housewife.

1919   The family moves to Turin, following her father's appointment to a University Chair in that city.

1921   Formation of the Partito Nazionale Fascista (PNF).

1922   Mussolini assumes power at the head of the PNF.

1924   Assassination of Giacomo Matteotti, Socialist Deputy, followed by withdrawal of all opposition members from the Chamber.

1925   Filippo Turati, a Socialist activist, is hidden by the Levis while arrangements are made for him to leave the country in disguise.

1927   Natalia attends secondary school for the first time, following several years of private study at home.

1933   She fails her school-leaving examination and composes her 'first real story', *Un'assenza*, published four years later.

1934   While returning from Switzerland her brother Mario is arrested for possession of anti-Fascist leaflets, but escapes. The house is searched by police and her father imprisoned for two or three weeks.

1935   She passes her school-leaving examination and registers at the local University. Italy declares war on Abyssinia.

1936   Capture of Addis Ababa and defeat of Abyssinia; King Victor Emmanuel III proclaimed Emperor of Ethiopia.

1937   Italy resigns from the Council of Nations.

1938   Promulgation of Racial Laws actively discriminating against Jews and prohibiting marriage between Jews and Gentiles. Natalia marries Leone Ginzburg, a Russian Slavist previously dismissed from the University for refusing to swear allegiance to the Fascist government and subsequently imprisoned for anti-government activities.

1939   Italy and Germany sign the Rome–Berlin Axis Pact. Great Britain and France declare war on Germany.

243

1940	Italy declares war on Great Britain and France. Ginzburg is deported to Pizzoli in the depressed south, later to be joined by his wife and their children.
1941	Following the Japanese bombing of Pearl Harbour the United States declares war on Japan and the Axis Powers.
1942	Natalia Ginzburg publishes her first novel, *La strada che va in città*, which, because of the Racial Laws, appears under the pseudonym of Alessandra Tornimparte.
1943	On 25 July King Victor Emmanuel III deposes Mussolini following a vote of no confidence in the Grand Fascist Council, and the PNF loses control of the government. The following day Leone Ginzburg travels to Rome to recommence political activity. On 8 September Italy announces the signing of an armistice with the Allies, and the King, together with government representatives, leaves Rome for Brindisi, already in Allied hands; three days later Marshal Kesselring declares Italy a war zone and the country is rapidly occupied by German forces. Mussolini, previously confined by the Italians, is released, and reassumes direction of the Fascist Party. On 1 November Natalia and the children rejoin her husband in Rome, where he is arrested three weeks later by the police and handed over to the Germans in Regina Coeli Prison.
1944	Death of Leone Ginzburg in the prison hospital, following repeated torture. Natalia and the children go into hiding, eventually reaching safety in Florence, where they are taken in by relatives. Following the Allied liberation of Rome in June she returns there in order to work for Einaudi.
1945	The Allied advance continues. Mussolini is captured by partisans and executed. The German High Command signs the act of unconditional surrender in Caserta. Natalia Ginzburg returns to Turin, where she works at the head office of Einaudi.
1947	She publishes *E' stato così*, written while 'totally defenceless and miserable', which wins the Tempo literary prize.
1950	She marries Gabriele Baldini, Professor of English at the University of Trieste, where he continues to live and work while she remains in Turin.
1952	Baldini is appointed to the Chair of English at the University of Rome, where they both take up residence. Ginzburg, who has maintained her first married name, publishes *Tutti i nostri ieri*, the only one of her novels to deal directly with Italy at war, which wins the Veillon literary prize.
1957	She publishes an anthology containing *Valentino*, *La madre*, and

Sagittario, which wins the Viareggio literary prize.

1959   Baldini is appointed Director of the Italian Cultural Institute in London, where he and his wife remain for two years. Feelings of homesickness, coupled with the discovery of the writings of Ivy Compton-Burnett, enable her to overcome a prolonged period during which she has been suffering from writer's block.

1961   She completes *Le voci della sera*, possibly her most successful novel, and returns to Rome with her husband.

1962   She publishes *Le piccole virtù*, an anthology of essays already printed in various periodicals and literary reviews, together with *Lui e io*, a new composition on her relationship with Baldini.

1963   She publishes the autobiographical novel *Lessico famigliare*, which wins the Strega literary prize.

1965   She completes her first play, *Ti ho sposato per allegria*, subsequently filmed by Luciano Salce, followed by *L'inserzione*, which wins the Marzotto literary prize.

1969   Death from hepatitis of Gabriele Baldini.

1970   Ginzburg publishes the second collection of essays old and new, entitled *Mai devi domandarmi*.

1973   She publishes *Caro Michele*, a semi-epistolary novel, subsequently filmed by Mario Monicelli.

1974   She publishes her third anthology of previously printed essays, together with a new composition, *Vita immaginaria*, which provides the title for the collection.

1983   She publishes *La famiglia Manzoni*, which wins the Bagutta literary prize, and is elected to Parliament as an independent left-winger.

1984   She publishes *La città e la casa*, a novel in the epistolary tradition set in the present day.

1986   Publication of the first volume of her complete works by Mondadori of Milan.

Bibliography

1 Primary sources

These include all Ginzburg's fiction and the three collections of her essays, with details of existing translations, together with any other work quoted. Where I have used editions other than the first printings this is indicated accordingly. All Italian volumes are published by Einaudi (Turin), unless otherwise stated.

Un'assenza, 1933, in *Letteratura*, I, no. 2 (1937), pp. 73–7, under maiden name; reprinted in *Cinque romanzi brevi*, 1964, pp. 369–74

I bambini, in *Solaria*, IX, no. 1 (1934), pp. 66–72, under maiden name

Giulietta, in ibid., IX, nos 5–6 (1934), pp. 54–7, under maiden name

Casa al mare, 1937, in *Lettere d'oggi*, III, s. III, nos 9–10 (1941), pp. 27–32, under pseudonym Alessandra Tornimparte; reprinted in *Cinque romanzi brevi*, 1964, pp. 375–81

Mio marito, 1941 (first printing untraced) in *Cinque romanzi brevi*, 1964, pp. 383–95

La strada che va in città, 1941, published 1942 under pseudonym Alessandra Tornimparte; *The Road to the City*, trans. F. Frenaye, in *The Road to the City, Two Novelettes* (Hogarth Press, London, 1952), pp. 8–67

Passaggio di tedeschi a Erra, in *Mercurio*, II, no. 9 (1945), pp. 35–41

E' stato così, 1947; *The Dry Heart*, trans. F. Frenaye, in *The Road to the City, Two Novelettes* (Hogarth Press, London, 1952), pp. 69–149

La madre, 1948, published in *Valentino*, 1957, pp. 73–93; reprinted in *Cinque romanzi brevi*, 1964, pp. 397–407

Valentino, in *Botteghe oscure*, vol. VIII (1951), pp. 442–81 (reprinted in book form in *Valentino*, 1957, pp. 7–72); *Valentino*, trans. A. Bardoni, in *Two Novellas, Valentino & Sagittarius* (Carcanet, Manchester, 1987), pp. 7–49

Tutti i nostri ieri, 1952; *Dead Yesterdays*, trans. A. Davidson (Secker & Warburg, 1956); reprinted as *All Our Yesterdays* (Carcanet, Manchester, 1985)

Sagittario, 1957, in *Valentino*, pp. 95–228; *Sagittarius*, trans. A. Bardoni, in *Two Novellas, Valentino & Sagittarius* (Carcanet, Manchester, 1987), pp. 51–134

Le voci della sera, 1961; *Voices in the Evening*, trans. D. M. Low (Hogarth Press, London, 1963)

Le piccole virtù, 1962; *The Little Virtues*, trans. D. Davis (Carcanet, Manchester, 1985)

Lessico famigliare, 1963; *Family Sayings*, trans. D. M. Low (Hogarth Press, London, 1967); revised and reprinted by Carcanet, Manchester, 1984

Cinque romanzi brevi, 1964, a reprint of earlier work with introductory Preface, pp. 5–18

Il maresciallo, in *Racconti italiani 1965* (Selezione dal Reader's Digest, Milan, 1964), pp. 25–32

Ti ho sposato per allegria, 1965, in P. Grassi and G. Guerrieri (eds), *Collezione di teatro*, vol. 93, 1966, preceded by Author's Preface, pp. 5–8; reprinted in *Ti ho sposato per allegria e altre commedie*, 1968, pp. 9–74

L'inserzione, 1965, in *Ti ho sposato per allegria e altre commedie*, pp. 75–124; *The Advertisement*, trans. H. Reed, in *The New Theatre of Europe*, vol. 4 (Delta, New York, 1970), pp. 1–46

Fragola e panna, 1966, in *Ti ho sposato per allegria e altre commedie*, pp. 125–58

La segretaria, 1967, in ibid., pp. 159–214

'Filo diretto Dessì–Ginzburg', in *Corriere della sera*, 10 Dec. 1967, p. 7

Paese di mare, 1968, in *Paese di mare e altre commedie* (Garzanti, Milan, 1973), pp. 51–102

La porta sbagliata, 1968, in ibid., pp. 103–73

Dialogo, 1970, in ibid., pp. 5–50

Mai devi domandarmi (Garzanti, Milan, 1970); *Never Must You Ask Me*, trans. I. Quigly (Michael Joseph, London, 1973)

La parrucca, 1971, in *Paese di mare e altre commedie*, pp. 175–85

Caro Michele (Mondadori, Milan, 1973); *Dear Michael*, trans. S. Cudahy (Peter Owen, London, 1975)

Vita immaginaria (Mondadori, Milan, 1974)

'Elzeviri', in *Corriere della sera*, 30 June 1974, p. 3

'Chiarezza e oscurità', ibid., 22 Sep. 1974, p. 3

'L'intelligenza', ibid., 20 Oct. 1974, p. 3

'L'autore si confessa', in *Epoca*, XXV, no. 1260, 30 Nov. 1974, p. 86

'Ricordo di Carlo Levi', in *Corriere della sera*, 8 Jan. 1975, p. 3

'Raccontare i fatti propri', ibid., 10 May 1975, p. 3

'Fra guerra e razzismo', ibid., 25 May 1975, p. 3

'Dialogando con Landolfi', ibid., 21 June 1975, p. 3

'"I temi che avrei scelto"', ibid., 3 July 1975, p. 1

'Lo stile d'acqua', ibid., 20 July 1975, p. 3

Lessico famigliare no. 2: La luna pallidassi, ibid., 10 Aug. 1975, p. 8

Lessico famigliare no. 2: Il cocchio d'oro, ibid., 17 Aug. 1975, p. 8

'Un corteo di dinosauri', ibid., 6 July 1976, p. 3

Borghesia, ibid., Aug.–Sep. 1977 (reprinted in book form in *Famiglia*, 1977, pp. 7–115); *Borghesia*, trans. B. Stockman, in *Family* (Carcanet, Manchester, 1988), pp. 69–111

Famiglia, in *Famiglia*, 1977, pp. 3–69; *Family*, trans. B. Stockman, in *Family* (Carcanet, Manchester, 1988), pp. 5–68

Parole povere, in *Tuttolibri*, VI, no. 12, 29 March 1980, p. 7

La famiglia Manzoni, 1983; *The Manzoni Family*, trans. M. Evans (Carcanet, Manchester, 1987)

Dell'acqua e del pane, in *Belfagor*, XXXIX, no. 3 (1984), pp. 327–34

La città e la casa, 1984; *The City and the House*, trans. D. Davis (Carcanet, Manchester, 1986)

'Nella mia "poltrona" c'è qualche fiocco di neve', in *La Stampa*, 18 June 1985, p. 23

La poltrona, in *Opere raccolte e ordinate dall'Autore* vol. 2 (Mondadori, Milan, 1987), pp. 1337–59

There exist two working editions of *Le voci della sera*: (1) ed. S. Pacifici (Random House, New York, 1971), with introduction and vocabulary; (2) ed. A. Bullock (Manchester University Press, Manchester, 1982), with introduction, vocabulary, and notes. English translations of *Ti ho sposato per allegria* (*I Married You For Fun*), *Fragola e panna* (*The Strawberry Ice*), and *La parrucca* (*The Wig*) by Henry Reed have been broadcast on BBC Radios 3 and 4, but do not appear to have been published.

Ginzburg's complete works, edited by Cesare Garboli, are being published as *Opere raccolte e ordinate dall'Autore*. At the time of writing two volumes have appeared (Mondadori, Milan, 1986 and 1987).

2 Secondary Sources

Amadori, M. G., 'NG ultima crepuscolare', *La fiera letteraria*, XVII, no. 4, 28 Jan. 1962, p. 4

Amendola, A., 'NG parla di se e del suo ultimo best seller: "Vi scrivo da un mondo di gente randagia"', *Domenica del corriere*, 16 Feb. 1985, pp. 56–8

Antonicelli, F., Review of *Le voci della sera* in *Radiocorriere-TV*, 15–21 Oct. 1961, p. 25

Baldini, R., 'Questo mondo non mi piace; Intervista con NG',

Panorama, 3 May 1973, pp. 129, 131–2, 134–5

Bergin, T. G., 'Italy Only Yesterday', *Saturday Review*, 5 Jan. 1957, p. 14

——, 'La Vita Evaded Them All', *Saturday Review*, 21 Sep. 1963, p. 36

Biagi, E., 'Incontro con le protagoniste italiane: la Ginzburg. Natalia, che cos'è il femminismo?', *Corriere della sera*, 16 March 1975, p. 3

Blandi, A., '"L'inserzione" . . . ritratto di una donna sbagliata', *La Stampa*, 22 Feb. 1969, p. 3

Blyth, A., 'New Cast of Lovers', *The Times*, 20 Nov. 1968, p. 9

Bo, C., 'La cenere nelle vene', in *Interventi nella narrativa contemporanea 1973–5* (Matteo, Treviso, 1976), pp. 16–18

Bocelli, A., 'Racconti della Ginzburg', *Il Mondo*, 8 Oct. 1957, p. 8

Bonsanti, S., 'La Ginzburg parla del suo romanzo "Caro Michele" ora portato sullo schermo con Mariangela Melato: "C'era una volta la famiglia"', *Epoca*, XXVI, no. 1313, 10 Dec. 1975, pp. 83–6

Brata, S., Review of *Dear Michael* in *The Times*, 30 Jan. 1975, p. 9

Brooke, J., Review of *Voices in the Evening* in the *Listener*, 15 Aug. 1963, p. 249

Brophy, B., 'Onto the Cart', *New Statesman*, 2 Aug. 1963, p. 147

Calvino, I., 'NG o le possibilità del romanzo borghese', in *Almanacco della terza pagina* (Carusi, Rome, 1963), pp. 178–84

Capasso, A., 'Romanzi della fatalità quotidiana', *La Nazione*, 25 Dec. 1947, p. 3

Capriolo, E., 'La delicata storia di una moglie mitomane', *Vie nuove*, no. 21, 26 May 1966, p. 58

Carrano, P., 'Lei ha vinto', *Amica*, 12 March 1985, p. 38

Cavalli, E., 'Intervista con NG: "Capisco solo la poesia"', *La fiera letteraria*, 30 March 1975, pp. 10–11

Cesari, S., 'NG parla del suo nuovo libro: Ultime lettere di gente comune', *Il Manifesto*, 18 Dec. 1984, p. 7

Citati, P., Review of *Tutti i nostri ieri* in *Belfagor*, vol. VIII (1953), p. 363

——, 'Il mondo di NG', *Il Punto*, no. 34, 24 Aug. 1957, p. 14

Clementelli, E., *Invito alla lettura di NG* (Mursia, Milan, 1972)

Cunningham, V., 'Griding Mistress', *New Statesman*, 28 Feb. 1975, p. 284

Davis, D. 'At the breaking-point', *Times Literary Supplement*, 4 Oct. 1985, p. 1115

Del Giudice, D., 'Commedie di NG: Le chiacchiere quotidiane',

Paese sera, 5 Jan. 1973, p. 4

Del Pozzo, S., 'Letteratura/Il caso Ginzburg: "Cari amici vi scrivo"', *Panorama*, 24 Dec. 1984, pp. 129–33

Dotti, U., 'Nuove lettere da Natalia', *L'Unità*, 15 Dec. 1984, p. 13

Esslin, M., 'Approaches to Reality', in *The New Theatre of Europe*, vol. 4 (Delta, New York, 1970), pp. vi–xiii

Fallaci, O., 'L'Europeo interroga NG: Parole in famiglia', *L'Europeo*, 14 July 1963, pp. 34, 36, 38–41

Feinstein, E., Book Review, *The Times*, 30 Oct. 1980, p. 15

Firth, F., Introduction to L. Pirandello, *Three Plays* (Manchester University Press, Manchester 1969), pp. ix–xxxiv

Frattarolo, R., Review of *E' stato così* in *L'Italia che scrive*, Oct. 1947, p. 205

Freeman, G., 'Fan Fare', *Spectator*, 2 Aug. 1963, p. 155

Garzonio, M., 'Ginzburg e Moravia, dalla letteratura al teatro', *Vita e pensiero*, no. 49 (1966), pp. 1016–18

Gasparini, A., 'Incontro con NG: Ai concerti si addormenta', *La fiera letteraria*, 1 Oct. 1972, p. 9

Giuffré, M. T., 'Sotto la parola cova la desolazione della vita', *Gazzetta del sud*, 29 Jan. 1985, p. 10

Heiney, D., 'The Fabric of Voices', *Iowa Review*, Fall 1970, pp. 87–93

Hill, D., 'Bitter-sweet sensuality', *The Times*, 9 Feb. 1989, p. 20

Hobson, H., 'Flower-powerhouse', *Sunday Times*, 29 Sep. 1968, p. 59

Hughes, H. S., *Prisoners of Hope. The Silver Age of the Italian Jews 1924–1974* (Harvard University Press, Cambridge, Mass. and London, 1983)

Ingrao, L., Review of *E' stato così* in *Rinascita*, IV, nos 11–12 (1947), p. 352

Innamorati, M. C., 'Tutti i nostri ieri', *Il mattino dell'Italia centrale*, 8 April 1953, p. 3

Jacqmain, M. 'Montherlant e NG: identità di vedute pedagogiche', *Rivista di letterature moderne e comparate*, vol. 24 (1971), pp. 59–65

Lennie, D., 'Una scrittrice: NG', in *Posso presentarle?* (Longman, London, 1971), pp. 66–77

Levin, B., 'Domestic suffocation', *Sunday Times*, 9 Aug. 1987, p. 43

Lombardi, O., 'NG' in G. Grana (ed.), *Novecento: I contemporanei. Gli scrittori e la cultura letteraria nella società italiana* (10 vols, Marzorati, Milan, 1979), vol. 8, pp. 7606–27

Lucchesini, P., 'Gli ottimisti di Natalia', *Carlino-Sera*, 5 July 1966, p. 3

Lugli, V., 'Cronaca domestica', *Il Resto del Carlino*, 18 June 1963, p. 3

Manacorda, G., *Storia della letteratura italiana contemporanea 1940–1965* (Editori Riuniti, Rome, 1967)

Marabini, C., 'Due gemme di Natalia', *Il Resto del Carlino*, 29 Dec. 1977, p. 7

Maraini, D., 'NG' in *E tu chi eri?* (Bompiani, Milan, 1973), pp. 119–26

Marcabru, P., 'Mariage réussi', *Le Point*, 6 Oct. 1986, p. 27

Marchionne Picchione, L., 'NG', *Il Castoro*, no. 137 (1978)

Mauro, W., 'Un romanzo di NG: *Le voci della sera*', *Il Paese*, 21 July 1961, p. 3

Milano, P., 'NG: La vita come attrito', *L'Espresso*, 2 July 1961, p. 17

Mondo, L., 'Colore Ginzburg', *La Stampa*, 4 Jan. 1985, p. 3

Nascimbeni, G., 'A colloquio con la scrittrice in occasione dell'uscita del suo nuovo libro: Ginzburg: "Il mio Manzoni giù dal piedistallo"', *Corriere della sera*, 5 Feb. 1983, p. 3

O'Healy, A., *A Woman Writer in Contemporary Italy: NG*, typescript of Ph.D. thesis for the University of Wisconsin–Madison, 1976

Orengo, N., 'Ginzburg: la casa è il rifugio di vite stracciate', *Tuttolibri*, X, no. 432, 8 Dec. 1984, p. 1

Pacifici, S., Review of *Le voci della sera*, in *Books Abroad*, vol. 36 (1962), p. 193

Pampaloni, G., Review of *Tutti i nostri ieri*, in *L'approdo letterario*, Oct.–Dec. 1952, p. 90

——, 'I romanzi di Pomilio e della Ginzburg: Manzoni e dintorni', *Il Giornale*, 30 April 1983, p. 3

Panofsky, G. S., 'Il teatro di NG come testo di lingua straniera', *Italica*, vol. 47, no. 4 (1970), pp. 445–52

Piclardi, R. D., 'Forms and Figures in the Novels of NG', *World Literature Today*, vol. 53, pt. 4 (1979), pp. 585–9

Portier, L., Review of *La famiglia Manzoni* in *Revue des Études Italiennes*, XXXII, nos 1–4 (1986), pp. 173–5

Porzio, D., Review of *Vita immaginaria* in *Panorama*, no. 450, 5 Dec. 1974, p. 19

——, 'NG' in *Primi piani* (Mondadori, Milan, 1976), pp. 76–9

Pullini, G., *Volti e risvolti del romanzo italiano contemporaneo* (Mursia, Milan, 1974)

Pym, B., 'Finding a Voice' in *Civil to Strangers and other writings* (Macmillan, London, 1987), pp. 381–8

Quigly, I., 'The Low in Spirit', *Times Literary Supplement*, 2 June 1978, p. 607

Radice, R., Review of *Ti ho sposato per allegria e altre commedie* in *Corriere della sera*, 2 June 1968, p. 11

Rago, M., 'Le "virtù" di NG', *L'Unità*, 19 Dec. 1962, p. 6

Ricapito, J. V., Review of *Paese di mare e altre commedie* in *Books Abroad*, vol. 48, no. 2 (1974), p. 351

Riva, F., 'La Ginzburg e i nostri ieri', *Corriere del giorno*, 1 Feb. 1953, p. 3

Romagnoli, S., 'Il lessico famigliare e i silenzi di casa Manzoni', *Rinascita*, no. 21, 27 May 1983, pp. 32–3

Russi, A., 'NG' in G. Mariani and M. Petrucciani (eds), *Letteratura italiana contemporanea* (Lucarini, Rome, 1983), pp. 429–41

Sapegno, N., *Compendio di storia della letteratura italiana*, 12th edn (3 vols, La Nuova Italia, Florence, 1959–60), vol. 3

Sergi, P., Review of *Valentino* in *Il Ponte*, Dec. 1957, p. 1884

Seroni, A., 'Racconti di NG', *Esperimenti critici sul novecento letterario* (Mursia, Milan, 1967), pp. 82–5

Siciliano, E., 'NG: il caso, la poesia', *Paragone*, XXII, no. 252 (1971), pp. 124–8

Signorelli Pappas, R., Review of *Mai devi domandarmi* in *Forum Italicum*, V, no. 3 (1970), pp. 474–5

——, Review of E. Clementelli, *Invito alla lettura di NG*, ibid., IX, nos 2–3 (1975), pp. 327–9

——, Review of *La città e la casa* in *World Literature Today*, vol. 60, no. 1 (1986), p. 89

Simonelli, L., 'Intervista-confessione con la più polemica scrittrice italiana: "Oggi i bambini vivono soffocati dalle troppe paure dei genitori"', *Domenica del corriere*, 30 Jan. 1975, pp. 49–51

Soave Bowe, C., 'The Narrative Strategy of NG', *Modern Language Review*, vol. 68, no. 4, pp. 788–95

Sovente, M., *La donna nella letteratura oggi* (Esperienze, Fossano, 1979)

'Spartans and Sufferers', *Times Literary Supplement*, 14 June 1963, p. 419

Spinazzola, V., 'E' sempre teatro per Natalia', *Panorama*, 24 Dec. 1984, p. 131

Stallings, S., 'A Novel of Italians in a World at War', *Herald Tribune Book Review*, 13 Jan. 1957, p. 4

Stampa, C., 'A colloquio con NG, autrice de "La famiglia Manzoni": "Confesso, la prima volta che lo lessi Manzoni mi annoiò"', *Epoca*, no. 1694, 25 March 1983, pp. 102–3

Thomson, I., 'Finely-spun despair', *Sunday Times*, 19 Oct. 1986, p. 54

——, 'Spinsters in Italy', *Independent*, 21 Dec. 1987, p. 14

Tian, R., 'Cronache letterarie', *Il Messaggero*, 3 April 1953, p. 3

Tornabuoni, L., 'I suoi elzeviri: Omaggio a Natalia', *La Stampa*,

5 Dec. 1970, p. 3

——, 'Intervista alla scrittrice NG: "Mi sento il Bartali dell'editoria"', *Tuttolibri*, n.s., VII, no. 269, 9 May 1981, p. 1

——, 'NG accusa in un libro l'autore dei "Promessi Sposi": Manzoni, il mostro di famiglia', *La Stampa*, 23 Jan. 1983, p. 3

Toscani, C., 'Incontro con NG', *Il raguaglio librario*, XXXIX, no. 6 (1972), pp. 210–11

Trevor, W., 'Remembering Well', *Listener*, 2 March 1967, p. 298

'Un-Italian Activities', *Times Literary Supplement*, 23 Feb. 1967, p. 149

Varese, C., 'Due scrittrici nell'ultima rosa', *Il Punto*, 24 June 1961, pp. 8–9

Vergani, L., 'Bagutta-Ginzburg: l'amore per Milano', *Corriere della sera*, 27 Nov. 1983, p. 3

Vigorelli, G., Review of *Le voci della sera* in *Tempo*, 22 July 1961, p. 62

Virdia, F., 'Tre romanzi brevi di NG', *La fiera letteraria*, 4 Aug. 1957, pp. 1, 6

Visintin, L., '"La famiglia Manzoni" della Ginzburg vince il Bagutta', *Corriere della sera*, 26 Nov. 1983, p. 4

Wade, D., 'Grotesque Events', *The Times*, 27 Jan. 1973, p. 10

Wardle, I., 'Unhappy Opening Night for new season', *The Times*, 25 Sept. 1968, p. 9

Index

This index contains proper names of people, places, etc., together with the titles of novels, plays, essays, and works furnishing extended quotations by Natalia Ginzburg. Information contained in the notes is included only if it adds significantly to that already provided or clarifies individual references. Characters in Ginzburg's novels and plays are listed alphabetically under the title of the relevant work, with their names in brackets if they are not so identified in the text.

Aurora, 162–5, 225
Aurora's partner, 163
Domitilla, 163, 165, 224–5
Domitilla's parents, 225
Ilaria Boschivo, 47, 162–5, 167,
    224–5
Ilaria's husband, 162
Ilaria's son, 162
Ombretta, 165
Pietro, 162–5, 224–5, 231
Rirì, 163
Brata, Sasthi, 149, 172n42
Brooke, Jocelyn, 26
Brophy, Brigid, 26
Brussels, 220

Canada, 205
Capasso, Aldo, 72
Capriolo, Ettore, 37
Casa al mare, 15–16, 19, 70, 165,
    177–8, 180
Narrator, 177–8,
Vilma, 70, 177–8
Vrasti, 177–8
Walter, 70, 165, 177–8
Walter's child, 70, 178
Casorati, Felice, 113
Catania, 158
Cavalli, Ennio, 29, 58n110
Cesari, Severino, 44–5
Chekov, Anton, 9, 26
Childhood, 66–7, 116
Cinecittà, 127
Cinque romanzi brevi, 14, 18, 55n54
Citati, Pietro, 89, 92, 117n1
City and the House, The, 44–5, 48, 169,
    228–37
Alberico, 228–9, 233–7
Alberico's aunt (Bice), 228
Albina, 236
Albina's brother, 236
Albina's father, 236
Albina's husband (Nino Mazzetta),
    236
Albina's husband's son, 236
Anne-Marie, 230–1, 234–5
Chantal, 231–2, 234
Chantal's child (Maggie), 234
Danny, 234–5
Egisto, 231, 236–7
Ferruccio, 228, 230–1, 233, 235
Giuseppe, 48, 169, 228–37
Giuseppe's child by Lucrezia
    (Graziano), 229
Giuseppe's wife, 228, 231

Ignazio Fegiz, 231, 236–7
Ignazio Fegiz's child, 231
Ippolita, 231, 236
Lucrezia, 48, 229, 231–2, 234–7
Lucrezia's children, 229, 232
Lucrezia's father, 232
Lucrezia's mother, 232
Nadia (Alba Desiderata Astarita),
    233–5
Nadia's child, 233–5
Piero, 229, 231–2, 235–6
Piero's mistress, 231–2
Roberta, 235–6
Salvatore, 233–4
Serena, 236
Clementelli, Elena, 36
Collective Life, 150, 153
Communist Party, 5, 6n4, 107
Compton-Burnett, Ivy, 24–5, 30, 101
Corazzini, Sergio, 9
'Cuore', 149

D'Annunzio, Gabriele see Annunzio
    (D'), Gabriele
Davis, Dick, 44, 62n160, 45–6, 236–7,
    241n56
Dead Yesterdays see All Our Yesterdays
Dear Michael, 43–6, 149–60, 162,
    164–5, 220–5, 233, 235
Ada, 157–8, 221
Adriana, 46, 150–7, 160, 162, 164,
    220–2
Adriana's husband, 150–4, 222
Adriana's teenage daughters, 150
Angelica, 150, 153, 159–60, 162, 221
Angelica's husband (Oreste), 151
Cloti, 153
Cloti's previous employer, 153
Cloti's previous employer's sisters,
    153
Fabio Colarosa, 157–9, 223
Lillia (Savio Lavia), 158, 221
Lillia's child, 158
Lillia's brother-in-law (Peppino), 158
Lillia's husband, 158
Mara Castorelli, 156–60, 164, 221,
    223
Mara's child, 156–9, 221
Mara's relatives, 158
Matilde, 150
Michael, 43, 46–7, 150–60, 164,
    221–4, 233
Michael's girl-friend, 154, 223
Michael's wife (Eileen), 154–6, 223
Michael's wife's children, 154, 223

258

259

Marco, 142–3, 216–17
Paese di mare e altre commedie, 37, 141
Palermo, 1
Pampaloni, Geno, 33
Paris, 143, 195
Parise, Goffredo, 161
Pascal, Blaise, 151
Pascoli, Giovanni, 9
Passaggio di tedeschi a Erra, 181, 183, 203
  Antonino Trabanda, 181, 183
Pirandello, Luigi, 5, 21, 33
Pizzoli, 2–3, 16–17, 20, 23, 49, 73
Poland, 190, 198
Popular Front, 211
Portier, Lucienne, 33
Portrait of a Writer, 40, 61n152
Porzio, Domenico, 12, 51–2
Potter, Beatrix, 26
Princeton, 228, 233–5
Proust, Marcel, 6, 26, 113
Pullini, Giorgio, 25
Pym, Barbara, 54n39, 56n76

Quigly, Isabel, 47–8

Racial Laws, 2, 6n2, 210
Racine, Jean, 92
Radice, Raul, 37
Rago, Michele, 19
Republican Party, 219
Ricapito, Joseph, 37
Riva, Franco, 197
Road to the City, The, 12, 17–19, 21, 27, 72–5, 97, 108, 122, 179–81, 183, 225
  Antonietta, 179
  Delia, 72–6, 78, 97, 108, 122, 124, 179–81
  Delia's aunt (Elide), 73, 180–1
  Delia's brothers (Giovanni, Gabriele, and Vittorio), 72–3
  Delia's child, 180
  Delia's father (Attilio), 72–3, 179
  Delia's maid, 74
  Delia's mother, 72–3, 97, 179
  Delia's sister (Azalea), 72–3, 179
  Delia's sister's husband, 179
  Giovanni, 179
  Giulio, 73–4, 180
  Giulio's father, 73
  Giulio's mother, 73–4, 180
  Nini, 74, 179–81, 183
  Santa, 73, 181
  Santa's fiancé (Vincenzo), 73
Romagnoli, Sergio, 33
Rome, 2–4, 21–4, 30, 52, 79, 111, 130,

132, 137, 142, 147, 154, 156, 166, 196, 206, 228, 231, 233, 235–6
Russia, 200

Sagittarius, 22–3, 25, 97–101, 110, 115, 204
  Barbara (Fontana), 100
  Barbara's husband (Pinuccio Scardillo), 100
  Chaim Wesser, 99–100, 204
  Estate agent, 100
  Giulia, 98–100, 115
  Giulia's child, 101
  Narrator, 98–9
  Narrator's flat-mate, 98
  Narrator's mother, 97–101, 110, 115, 204
  Narrator's mother's sisters, 99
  Police inspector, 100
  Scilla (Fontana), 99–100
  Scilla's friend (Valeria Lubrani), 100
San Costanzo, 88, 191, 193, 195–6, 200–1, 203
San Remo, 78, 176
Sapegno, Natalino, 26, 56–7n88
Saragat, Giuseppe, 115
Schlesinger, John, 52
Sergi, Pina, 98, 117n10
Seroni, Adriano, 64, 89n1
Siciliano, Enzo, 1
Sicily, 158
Signorelli Pappas, Rita, 12, 121, 228
Silence, 84
Simonelli, Luciano, 120, 170n1
Smart, Elizabeth, 52
Soave Bowe, Clotilde, 64–5
Soldati, Mario, 52
Son of Man, The, 49, 80
Spinazzola, Vittorino, 230
Spock, Benjamin, 121
Stalin, Josef, 115
Stallings, Sylvia, 84, 91n41
Stresa, 87, 193, 195
Sussex, 153–4, 223
Svevo, Italo, 26
Switzerland, 86, 106, 192, 194, 207–8

Tanzi Levi, Lidia, 1–2, 65–8, 110, 113–14, 116, 127
  timorous submissive person, 1
  takes in Natalia after flight to Florence, 2
  insensitive to daughter's problems, 66
  is snubbed by her accordingly, 67

261